# Bapaji
### AND **Me**

# Bapaji AND Me

## A MEMOIR OF INDIA AND BEYOND

SADHNA BHATIA, M.D.

For information about this title or to order other books and/or electronic media, contact the publisher:

Bapaji Press
Weston, Massachusetts
United States
sadhna@msn.com

ISBNs:
978-1-7356522-0-7 (softcover)
978-1-7356522-1-4 (eBook)

Printed in the United States of America

Cover and Interior design: 1106 Design

Editorial Support: Book Architecture

# DEDICATION

*to Bapaji, my grandfather,*
*for giving me the mantra of willpower*

*to Raj, my dearest late husband of over 56 years,*
*eternal love, and greatest gift from God, for his*
*unconditional support during challenging times and*
*for our supreme happiness together—we remember*
*you with fondness and miss you greatly*

*to our son, Mohit, and daughter-in-law, Payal,*
*for giving us the gift of our adorable grandson AVI,*
*the love of our life*

Bapaji, my grandfather

# Contents

# Chapter One

*In 1892, my grandfather,* nicknamed "Bapaji," was born in a town called Dera Ismail Khan, or D. I. Khan, in India's northwest frontier province of Khyber. *Dera* means "encampment." In 1947, Khyber became part of Pakistan. The people are called "Derawal," and they speak Derawali, a language close to Punjabi.

D. I. Khan sits on the west bank of the Indus River. The Indus runs north to south, and even back then, it was packed with water traffic, mostly small ships transporting people and cargo, as well as boats in the summer. There were a couple of small bridges spanning the river, used mostly by *tongas*, two-wheeled horse-drawn carriages, to carry people and produce a mile away to Dera Khan, and from there to the train station and Lahore, the big city two hundred miles to the east.

The town center of D. I. Khan is Chowgalla, and it has five bazaars, each with its own characteristics. There is the Muslim Bazaar and the small Chhota Bazaar, among others, but the most important bazaar to me is the Bhatia Bazaar, which was so called until 2010.

Back in 1900, there were no cars or motorcycles, only bicycles, rickshaws, and the horse-drawn tongas. The rich had two-horse carriages, called *fitten*. Imagine a town of thirty thousand people and no cars. There were eighteen thousand Muslims, eleven thousand Hindus, and one thousand four hundred Sikhs.

For worship, there were many mosques, some Hindu temples, and a Sikh *gurdwara*. For education, there were two or three schools, gender separate until high school, which taught English, Hindi, and Urdu. A handful of doctors ran the town's one hospital, and there were some well-respected *hakims* (Arabic for "doctors"), who offered alternative traditional medicine.

Housing in D. I. Khan ranged from modest dwellings, all in a row with no lawns or gardens, to the lavish, which had their own sheds of two to three cows for fresh milk. The average Indian home had three generations living under one roof. The house itself typically had a courtyard-entry leading to an open kitchen. In the courtyard was a *palang*, similar to a full-sized bedstead with a mattress, which was used both to sit on as a sofa and to sleep on for afternoon naps. The kitchen had a hand pump for water, a wood-burning stove, a mud-encased burner with coals for stovetop cooking called a *chula*, and an oven called *tandoor* for baking whole-wheat *roti* (flatbread) twice a day. Even now most Indian restaurants throughout the world have tandoors. There are different ways to construct a tandoor. In this region and the neighboring Punjab, for example, the tandoor was bell-shaped and made with clay, but in Persia, it was made with brick.

Back in the 1900s, there was no heat or air conditioning. The long, hot summer ran about nine months, and only fans and open windows provided relief. The winter lasted only three months with temperatures dipping into the low fifties. To keep warm, there was a fireplace and *razai*, a comforter stuffed with seven to eight pounds of cotton wool and covered in a fabric of cotton, silk, or velvet.

The staple foods were whole-wheat roti, vegetables, lentils (many different kinds), fruits, and yogurt. The typical beverage was a yogurt- or buttermilk-based drink called *lassi*. Occasionally there were sweets, especially during festivals. There was no meat in the Hindu household. Muslims lived in their own neighborhood and would eat chicken and lamb cooked in their tandoors. Back then, the Hindus and Muslims respected each other and lived in harmony.

Most Hindus at that time were business people as well as landlords and farm owners. A typical farm had one or more wells, and grew wheat, rice, sugarcane, and fruits and vegetables. D. I. Khan was famous for its dates and its Langra variety of mangoes. Farms were the meeting place for the men to picnic and have get-togethers on Sundays (women did not participate).

Many of the businesses owned by the Hindus were in the Bhatia Bazaar. The Bhatia was a very important clan, which branched into many other clans. The cloth business was popular, and so was selling dry fruits, spices, and other staples. The Hindus would trade with the Pathans, who lived in neighboring Afghanistan. The Pathan men would travel to D. I. Khan with their goods, such as walnuts, almonds, pine nuts, dried fruits, saffron, and exotic spices like black cumin seeds. There was a barter system in place between the sellers: the Pathans would exchange their products for staples like cotton and fruit. There were never any cash transactions, as a rule.

The dress code of the Hindus versus the Muslims had some variances. Hindu men, for example, wore a shirt and a loincloth called a *dhoti*, which was tied in a particular way. Muslims never wore a dhoti. None of the men wore shorts, only boys until the age of about ten. Both Hindus and Muslims wore a long shirt (*kameez*), drawstring pants (*salwar*), and a vest (*waskat*, derived from "waistcoat")—D. I. Khan is famous even today for exporting *waskats*.

Muslim women wore a *salwar kameez* and a long scarf called a *chunni*. Hindu women wore either a salwar kameez or a *saree* with a blouse. Little girls wore dresses until age seven or eight. Married women covered their heads in the presence of male in-laws. Typically the father-in-law would alert the women of his arrival with a small cough. Married women always had a small dot on their forehead called a *bindi*, and they would wear bangles, also known as wedding bands. Widows, though, would not have a bindi or wear bangles. Muslim women did not wear a bindi, either. Women used henna to color their hair and mustard oil to moisturize their skin. They also wore *surma*, a kohl eyeliner, which even the children and men used for medicinal purposes. The surma bottle, called *surmedani*, was two inches by one inch, and it had a pencil for dipping into the powder and smudging inside the eyelid. A surmedani could come in a variety of shapes and was made of sterling silver; it was considered an important wedding gift to a bride. I myself have two: one was my mother's, and the other I received at my wedding, which I have never opened.

Women delivered their children at home with the aid of a midwife. The obesity percentage back then was very low.

Returning now to my grandfather, Bapaji, whose given name was Chhabildas. He was a middle child amongst four brothers and three sisters. His family was not extremely rich, like the business people, but they lived comfortably. Bapaji's father was the highest-ranking police officer in their town, a very prestigious and honored position. His father looked dignified, even royal, in his uniform.

In 1907, after completing ninth grade, Bapaji was admitted to the engineering school in Lahore. He was excited to learn at such a distinguished school and eagerly started his studies. While in school, he worked part-time in a cloth shop. It was a good job for him because he had never been afraid to stand his ground. Even as a young teenager, if customers tried to haggle with him, he would simply tell them to take it or leave it and proceed to the next shop.

During this time, Bapaji's family had an unexpected tragedy. His father, who was in his early thirties and looked like Superman with a well-groomed beard, got a finger infection. It didn't appear to be anything of concern, so his father performed minor surgery on his own finger. He soon, however, became very ill with tetanus and died. The family was devastated, and Bapaji, who had completed two years of his studies, had to face an abrupt and sweeping change in his life.

With his family's new financial instability, Bapaji could not continue studying engineering, so he began to look for work beyond D. I. Khan. Many businessmen at that time had expanded their reach east to Lahore and Amritsar as well as to the south in Delhi. Usually the men would go on these business trips while their families stayed in D. I. Khan.

# Chapter Two

*B apaji decided to gather* some references and embark on a long journey to Delhi. This was the first time he had ever left his family to such a faraway big city, and he did it with great courage. He had to take a boat across the Indus River to Dera, take a train to Lahore, two hundred miles away, and then change trains to travel the remaining three hundred miles to Delhi.

He ended up in a commercial market called Phatak Habash Khan, later known as the Tilak Bazaar. He landed a job at a shop that sold wholesale cloth as well as imported/exported dried fruits and saffron.

The Tilak Bazaar is within a half mile of the Khari Baoli, the largest spice market in Asia, and they are connected to each other through narrow, weaving alleys. Both the Khari Baoli and the Tilak Bazaar have been around since the seventeenth century—even today, they still look very similar. Many of their shops go back nine or ten generations, although only a few of them still use their original name.

The Tilak Bazaar is busy and congested, and has the vibe of New Orleans, with shops selling wholesale cloth, dried fruits, and chemical supplies, all interspersed among each other. The shops can be as small as four feet by six feet or as large as two thousand square feet. Even the smallest shops transact hundreds of trades every day. It's mesmerizing to watch the workers carrying huge burlap sacks overflowing with goods to and from the shops' *godowns*, warehouses. To an outsider, it probably looks like a chaotic mess, but the bazaar is actually very well-organized.

Walking around the bazaar can be a challenge. The place feels like a maze and has narrow lanes only six feet wide, which shoppers must share with the many workers and rickshaws carrying heavy loads. There are dogs, cows, and cats in the maze sharing the space with you, often rubbing up against the human beings there.

Of course, a bazaar would not be a bazaar without good food. There are street-food hawkers, some of them with their own permanent cubbies one foot by two feet squeezed in between the shops, cooking over an open fire and offering the same specialty every day for their regular patrons.

The Tilak Bazaar has everything you could possibly need or imagine. There are barbers (*nayee*) sitting on the side of the walkways, giving haircuts and shaving beards. A few yards away are cobblers repairing shoes and polishing boots. A shop down the way offers dental services—walk in, sit on the floor, and get your tooth extracted. Next door, you can buy a snack from the food vendor and then stop at a scale and pay a few pennies to weigh yourself. All the while you are surrounded by hundreds of carts selling utensils, brushes, brooms—everything and anything. Needless to say, many tourists are overwhelmed by the

Tilak Bazaar and all of its accompanying dust and pollution. (And fair warning, I doubt the bazaar has any public restrooms.)

Above the shops are homes. The houses range from detached to semi-detached to clustered, and they can be as high as three stories. Most of them are owned by rich shop owners, who go upstairs to eat a hot lunch prepared by their family or their help and then take a siesta before returning to work.

Bapaji's first job was at 182 Tilak Bazaar, which was coincidentally owned by my husband's grandfather. Up until the shop was sold in 2010, it had a big sign above it that read "Asanand Radheyshiam Bhatia," the name of my father-in-law.

In the early 1900s, my grandfather-in-law expanded his business seven hundred miles southwest of Delhi to Bombay, and he sent Bapaji there to run the new shop.

Bapaji lived in Bombay for about two years, maturing day by day and learning the cloth business. He had grown into a confident, sober young man of medium build who was not necessarily handsome but striking with a larger-than-life, magnetic personality.

During his time in Bombay, Bapaji went back at least once every year to visit his family in D. I. Khan, and during one of these visits, he met my grandmother, Baji, whose given name was Hakam Devi. She was very beautiful: slender, with marble-white, smooth skin, high cheekbones, and sharp, regal features. They eventually married, although my grandmother stayed in D. I. Khan while Bapaji continued living and working in Bombay.

In 1914, Bapaji was offered a big promotion. My grandfather-in-law's partner had again expanded his business by opening another shop, this time in the city of Ahmedabad, four hundred miles northwest of Bombay and seven hundred miles southwest of Delhi. It is the largest city in the state of Gujarat and the fifth-largest city in India. My grandfather-in-law wanted Bapaji to head up the new location. Bapaji accepted, but on the condition that his wife and the rest of his immediate family, who were still in D. I. Khan, could move with him. His partner agreed.

Now living in Ahmedabad, Bapaji, at the young age of twenty-two, was already well-traveled. It did take some time, though, for both him and his family to get comfortable with Ahmedabad's new culture, since the north and south back then were more different than even the U.S.'s north and south.

Most of the people living in Ahmedabad were and still are of the Gujarati ethnicity, which means the cuisine is very different, and the dominant language is Gujarati (Bapaji's childhood language was Urdu). Bapaji worked hard to adapt to all these changes and to learn as much as he could. By the end of his life, he spoke and wrote in many languages: Urdu, Hindi, English, Gujarati, Pushto (the language of the business world in the northwest province), and limited Farsi.

Even though Bapaji was able to successfully assimilate into Ahmedabad's culture, he never forgot his roots. When my father became school-age, Bapaji sent him to a Muslim school in Ahmedabad to learn Urdu, the medium of instruction familiar to those from the northwest province.

For some background on Bapaji's new home, Ahmedabad was named after Ahmed Shah, a Muslim ruler from the north who conquered the area in 1411, when he was only fourteen years old.

Ahmedabad is called the "city of gates," because, back then, it had twelve main gates and four (or more) small gates and a four-mile-long wall connecting them. The gates (*darwaja*) were all different, built by different rulers, most of whom were Muslim. Many of the gates had Islamic inscriptions or words of wisdom. One of those inscriptions in particular stands out to me.

The inscription is on the second of the three arches of Teen Darwaza—which means "door" or "gate"—which still stands today. Teen Darwaza is a twenty-five-foot gateway completed in 1415 when Ahmed Shah ruled. In 1812, the Maratha governor Chimnaji Raghunath decreed and inscribed on the middle arch that a daughter has equal rights to her father's property as his sons.

Today, the wall connecting the gates is gone as well as the smaller gates themselves, but the twelve main gates still stand and always have large, noisy crowds surrounding them.

Once inside the gates of Ahmedabad, the city is full of Muslim architecture, including many forts and mosques. I especially love the Sidi Saiyyed Mosque. It took forty-five artists six years to build; it was completed, more or less, in 1573. The mosque has windows with intricately carved stone latticework called *jalis*. The mosque has ten jalis in all, but the most famous one is a beautiful tree design, set in a sixteen-foot semicircle twenty feet off the ground. The tree's branches spiral and intertwine with hundreds of tiny leaves and flowers, symbolizing love and friendship.

Replicas of this jali are sold in shops; some are made of silver or other metal, while some are of wood. I have one such replica, twelve inches by eight inches, made of silver and set in a wooden frame in my living room.

By far the most popular religion in Ahmedabad is Hinduism, but the city still offers many different places to worship, including Jain temples, Sikh gurdwaras, Parsi *agiaries* (fire temples), Christian churches, and even one Jewish synagogue, the Magen Abraham Synagogue, built in 1934 (although its membership has shrunk over the years to only one hundred thirty-nine members as of 2015).

There are lakes in Ahmedabad, including Kankaria Lake, the second biggest lake in the city, with a circumference of nearly two miles. It was originally called Qutb Hauz and was built in the fifteenth century for the royals to bathe in. There is a garden in the middle of the lake called Nagina Wadi, with a walkway on one side of the shore leading out to it. Around the lakefront are many fun activities, including a zoo, an amusement park, and rowboats for rent.

In 1918, Bapaji left my grandfather-in-law's partner's business to be his own boss, opening his own shop in Ahmedabad in the cloth trade as a commission agent. He named it "Chhabildas Harigopal," as it was customary for businesses in the north during that time to have the father's name precede the son's.

All of Ahmedabad's businesses back then were located within the old city. In 1940, the population of the business center was a half million; it has grown to more than seven million today. In the early 1920s, there were thirty-three cotton mills, which grew to sixty-five cotton mills, and they exported their goods to places as far away as Europe. In fact, Ahmedabad's business center became the biggest textile market in Asia and was nicknamed "The Manchester of India."

Bapaji opened his business on the third floor of a building in the Motilal Hirabhai Market. His shop was fairly large at seven hundred square feet, and his living quarters were connected to it. From 1918 until 1943, this place was home to everyone in Bapaji's family, including me.

The first year that Bapaji was open for business, 1918, the entire world was hit by influenza. It was the most devastating epidemic in recorded history, killing anywhere from twenty to forty million people, one-third of the planet's population—more than were lost in World War I or the Bubonic Plague.

Bapaji had a very calm temperament and never lost his head, even in the most stressful circumstances. So, despite the danger to himself, his wife, and Bauji, their new young son (my father), Bapaji felt strongly that he needed to volunteer and help those sick with the flu. Back then, there were no gloves, no face masks, no sterile hospitals—only handwashing for protection. Bapaji was twenty-six at the time, and the flu was the most deadly for people ages twenty to forty, but Bapaji, his wife, and his son survived.

Bapaji was plenty busy with his thriving business, but he still made time to frequently visit his relatives in D. I. Khan. The journey would take him three days: first he would ride twenty-four hours by train to Delhi; then he would change trains and ride another eight to ten hours to Dera; from Dera he would take a boat to D. I. Khan.

Because of Bapaji's generous nature, he often brought back to Ahmedabad a couple of his teen nephews. He would get them settled in the new city, start their education, and teach them how to run a business. On one such trip to D. I. Khan, he brought back two teenage relatives who were very rowdy. The teens were acting up on the long train ride back to Ahmedabad, and the other passengers in Bapaji's compartment commented that there were enough monkeys in Ahmedabad. It did not need more!

During this time, Bapaji's wife gave birth a couple more times, but none of the babies lived. Finally, in 1930, more than twelve years after my father had been born, my aunt, Bhen, was born in D. I. Khan; she was quickly followed two years later by my uncle, Chachaji.

Outside of family and work, Bapaji also became involved in politics. He was against British rule, and therefore, was a strong supporter of one of Ahmedabad's most famous Hindu politicians and residents: Mahatma Gandhi.

From 1917 until 1930, Gandhi lived in the suburb of Sabarmati Ashram, now commonly known as Gandhi Ashram. Sabarmati

Ashram is four miles from the Ahmedabad town hall, on the banks of the River Sabarmati.

Sabarmati Ashram served as Gandhi's headquarters for his nonviolent fight for independence from Britain. He purposefully chose to live in a place that was between a jail and a cemetery, to symbolize that he and his freedom fighters would end up either in prison or dead. His home, however, was still a calm and serene place, with a museum, garden, and a bookstore housing a vast collection of literature providing deeper insight into the life and philosophies of Gandhi. In his garden, he had the famous statues of three wise monkeys: the first monkey covering his mouth with his hands—"speak no evil"; the second covering his ears—"hear no evil"; the third covering his eyes—"see no evil."

Gandhi's living quarters were modest, with very few personal belongings. One of his most well-known belongings was a spinning wheel, or *charkha*, for spinning cotton into thread to make *khadi*, a homespun cloth he would use for his dhotis (the traditional long loincloth). His wife, Kasturba, also used the charkha.

Following Gandhi's lead, Bapaji also started wearing khadis to support the local cotton industry, and he stopped buying all imported goods. Bapaji supported India's fight for independence in whatever small way he could, such as encouraging the use of a charkha for spinning khadi and insisting that everyone, while at home, speak only Punjabi/modified Derawali to remember their roots.

In 1930, Gandhi left Sabarmati Ashram with seventy-eight of his freedom fighters to walk two hundred forty miles to the coastal village of Dandi, in what is now called the Salt March. The Salt March was a nonviolent protest against Britain's taxation of salt (similar to the U.S.'s Boston Tea Party). Gandhi's protest brought worldwide attention to the Indian independence movement, and Dandi today is still a popular tourist attraction.

Through all these years of sweeping change in India, Bapaji watched Ahmedabad grow and change, too. Bapaji was a very disciplined, healthy man, so every morning he would go for a three-mile walk, crossing the Ellis Bridge over the Sabarmati River and going into the new city. He would always see progress during his walks—new roads, new buildings, new businesses. His own business, in fact, had grown so much that he'd had to hire more staff, and his clients came from all over northern India.

Bapaji's wife, Baji, was also busy with her work at home. She cooked three meals a day, which involved using a hand mixer for churning yogurt called a *madani*. She also made yogurt every night. Part of the yogurt was eaten with the meals as a natural probiotic, and the other part was put in a big, round earthen pot about twelve inches high. Sticking out of the middle of the pot was a twenty-inch-long pole that had a rope with two handles wrapped around it. Baji would pull the handles back and forth, churning the yogurt and turning it into butter and low-fat buttermilk. When she wasn't cooking, Baji spun cotton thread on her charkha to make khadis for the family to wear. In short, Baji's daily life was one workout after another—no wonder she was so slim and beautiful, despite being a mother to many children!

By 1936 Baji's oldest child, Bauji (my father), had graduated from college. He was handsome and brilliant, and he had inherited his father's strong personality. He graduated with both honors and an excellent command of English. Bauji next went to law school.

Bapaji was supportive of his son's higher education, but his business had grown so much that he needed Bauji's help. So, two years into law school, Bauji left to work with his father, mostly traveling to the business's many clients up north, as far as D. I. Khan. It was because of these trips that Bauji ran into Chaeji, whose given name was Shakuntala, a girl he had been distantly acquainted with since childhood. Chaeji was good-looking and had fair skin (a plus among Indians even today). By then it was 1939, Bauji was twenty-two years old, and he was under considerable pressure to marry. He insisted, however, that his bride be educated, which, back then, was not easy to come by. Despite everyone's expectations for him to marry soon, he refused to compromise his values.

As Bauji continued to travel to D. I. Khan for business, he got to know Chaeji. She had graduated from high school and had passed advanced Hindi exams; she could also read, write, and speak English. Chaeji's mother was ahead of her time, too, participating in anti-British rallies and encouraging Chaeji to play the harmonium, similar to an accordion and still popular today in the music of northern India.

Bauji and Chaeji fell in love. But there was a problem: Chaeji was a nice Punjabi Bhatia girl. In D. I. Khan, Bhatia women had no want for suitors, and the Bhatia clan wanted its members to marry only within their own community and stay in the territory. Bauji was not living there and so was not accepted in their eyes. Furthermore, Chaeji's parents were wealthy and had a business in D. I. Khan with branches in Calcutta and Amritsar, and they wanted her to marry someone rich and local. Instead, she had chosen a man who was still finding his way financially and who would take Chaeji far away from them.

Bauji's mother was not happy with her son's choice, either. She wanted him to marry within their social circle. But Bauji and

Chaeji were determined to move forward with their marriage, and eventually both of their families relented.

On December 4, 1939, Bauji and Chaeji were married in a school building in D. I. Khan. They were lucky to have a "love marriage"; 99 percent of Indian marriages back then were arranged, many times with the bride and groom meeting each other for the first time on their wedding day.

Their married life began by traveling back to Ahmedabad. This journey was very familiar to Bauji, but Chaeji was traveling to a foreign land where she had no family and no friends, and didn't speak the language. Even the weather was a big adjustment for her; the summer temperatures in Ahmedabad can break a hundred degrees in the months of June and July.

For a while, Chaeji was quite dependent on Bauji, but she adjusted soon enough and found her way. She got along well with Bauji's brother and sister, Bhen and Chachaji, but she struggled with her mother-in-law, Baji, who was very demanding of her.

Almost ten months after their wedding, on September 15, 1940, I was born in a city hospital, delivered by a doctor (many babies back then were delivered at home by midwives). My grandfather, Bapaji, was thrilled when he heard the news. He said in Gujarati, "Lakshmi Chandlo Karva Avi Che." Lakshmi is the Hindu goddess of wealth, fortune, and prosperity. *Chandlo* is a red powder applied to the forehead for auspicious occasions. Therefore the full translation means: Lakshmi has arrived to bless with the chandlo. What a royal welcome! He reminded me many times throughout the years of his joy at my birth, because in India, boys are preferred over girls, and everyone wants a son to be the firstborn. (Boys support the family, while girls are a big financial responsibility with their dowries, weddings, etc.)

I was lucky that my whole family was excited at the birth of a girl. A *pandit* wrote my *kundali* (birth horoscope) based on the date and time of my birth and the alignment of the planets and the moon. A kundali reveals future important dates in the person's life, and it determines compatibility in matchmaking. Kundalis are taken so seriously, in fact, that potential brides and grooms often read the pandit's review first before proceeding with any arrangements.

My uncle, Chachaji, was eight years old at the time of my birth. He was so overwhelmed with excitement that he went straight from school to the hospital. When he saw me, he thought I looked like a doll, and he pressed into my hand his pocket money, a *chavani* (quarter). I was touched when he recounted this memory to me in 2015, on my seventy-fifth birthday.

My father and mother planned my first trip back to D. I. Khan when I was ten months old. During our layover in Delhi, my parents took me to see the Tilak Bazaar, where my grandfather had worked his first job, and it was then that, at ten months old, I "met" my future husband, Raj. This would also be Chaeji's first time visiting her parents since the wedding. She wanted to stay in D.I. Khan with me for three months, and Bauji would return alone after one month. None of my relatives in Ahmedabad were happy to hear about this plan. I was their pride and joy, and they had not spent a day away from me since my birth. Baji, my grand-mother, was so distressed that she came up with her own plan.

She told Bauji that Chaeji could stay in D. I. Khan for three months if she wanted, but when Bauji came back after a month, he must bring me with him. It was a selfish plan, but Baji was adamant. Her thinking was, where the calf goes, the mother cow will soon follow. (Comparing a woman to a cow is a respectful comparison in the Hindu religion!)

With a heavy heart, Bauji told Chaeji about his mother's idea. Of course, this resulted in a great deal of turmoil. For Chaeji, it was a no-win situation, but she had to heed her mother-in-law's wishes.

The time came for my father and me to leave on the train for D. I. Khan.

The month-long visit in D. I. Khan went by quickly, and before Chaeji knew it, I had to leave with Bauji back to Ahmedabad. With many tears, she and my maternal grandmother prepared for my departure, including cutting bedsheets for diapers on my three-day trip. Until then, Bauji had never changed a diaper in his life, but he was not one to back down from a challenge, and together we began our journey.

He quickly mastered changing my diapers and bottle-feeding me frequently. Other passengers on the train were surprised to see a man traveling alone with an infant. Bauji had no stored breastmilk to give me, or even baby formula—and many of these people were sad, thinking my mother must have died. One of the passengers even gave me some Murano glass toys, which I played with for many years.

Thankfully, the trip went without a hitch, and we made it back to Ahmedabad. My parents often told this story, always thankful that nothing had gone wrong.

## Chapter Three

*With the trip over,* Bauji and Bapaji got back to work, business as usual. Bapaji was one of the first men to settle in Ahmedabad from D. I. Khan, an early Punjabi settler. He was proud of his heritage and remained active in Ahmedabad's Punjabi community. As a supporter of Indian independence, Bapaji was particular about wearing clothing of khadi, the Indian homespun cotton. He never took to Western clothes. Bauji, on the other hand, had fully assimilated with the Gujarati culture and adopted their business dress code: a white shirt, a dhoti (long loincloth), a long white coat such as a *jodhpuri*, and a soft cap called a *topi*. For evenings and special events, he wore a two-piece suit and a tie. He looked very dignified.

In 1942, my sister was born in Ahmedabad. With the new baby, I spent all my time with my grandparents, Bapaji and Baji, as well as with Uncle Chachaji and Aunt Bhen, even though we all lived together with my parents. Aunt Bhen and Grandmother Baji shared watching over me while my mother and father made their usual trips to D. I. Khan. I was spoiled with constant attention.

A year later, 1943, India's anti-British movement was in full swing, and the rest of the world was in the middle of World War II. Bapaji's business, however, was flourishing, and he was looking for a new house. He wanted a place in the suburbs that had more office space.

After some house-hunting, Bapaji was interested in a house located in a development. He made an offer, but the owner refused to sell it to him, stating that my grandfather was Punjabi, and, therefore, not a vegetarian. Bapaji politely explained that his family was indeed vegetarian. The owner, however, still refused and said, *What about the future?* Bapaji's children or grandchildren might eat meat in his house. Bapaji was shocked and responded firmly that the owner had no way of knowing whether his *own* children or grandchildren would always be vegetarian. Bapaji then withdrew his offer and walked away, saying he would not want to live in a neighborhood with such people. Bapaji always had strong principles and high values, but he didn't let his temper get the best of him.

Bapaji resumed his house-hunting. Soon he found a two-story building only a half mile away from the development where the other house had been. This building sat at the entrance of the university campus and bordered the city limit. Due to the current social unrest in India and throughout the world, the building's owner was desperate to sell. Bapaji's offer was accepted, and he immediately renamed the place The Bhatia Building.

The Bhatia Building had a dorm-style layout, with eighteen rooms on each floor, configured in the shape of an L, and an atrium in the middle. The outside had a yard on all sides, with a six-foot brick wall, and the building stood ten feet from the main road. The bathrooms were communal and were not connected to the main building.

Bapaji was very happy with his purchase, but my father did not agree with him. While Bapaji was house-hunting, Bauji had been out of town, visiting clients in the north, which he frequently did for weeks at a time because the business was doing so well. The only way we could communicate with him was by letter. So, when my father saw the building upon his return, he was greatly distressed that it was not an actual *house*. There was nothing he could do, though—the deal was done. We lived in The Bhatia Building for fifteen years, until 1958 (and the building still exists today, although it is in shambles).

The house renovations started as soon as we moved in. First, we built bathrooms, and then we divided the L-shaped atrium into two sections. The front eight rooms were occupied by my parents, while the back eight rooms were for Bapaji and his family as well as for me. Two of the rooms remained empty. (I don't remember having my own room early on, but I later selected one on the front side of the building, close to the formal living and dining area, away from the kitchen, so there would be minimal traffic.) There was also a veranda along the whole building that was eight feet wide, and every room opened onto it.

When we were finally done with the massive renovations, the results were rewarding, and Bauji was able to come to terms with our new home.

We all lived on the second floor, and we rented out the entire first floor. As the rooms started filling up, Baji and Chaeji were relieved to have some additional security on the premises. Most of the tenants were college students or professors and their families, since the wall of our building adjoined the H. L. College of Commerce, and next to it was the L. D. Arts College (beyond them, in the mid-1940s, were only mango orchards).

We hired a foreman to manage our property. We called him Bhaiaji, which means "brother." (*Ji* is a sign of respect for an elder.) Bhaiaji worked for us the entire fifteen years we lived at The Bhatia Building. He was tall and lean, and had a wife, son, and daughter. As usual, Bapaji treated Bhaiaji and his family the same as he would anyone else, and he encouraged Bhaiaji's children to go to school and study hard.

Bhaiaji had only a bike for transport, and we provided him and his family with housing, a mud hut in a corner of our property. (Living in a mud hut might sound unbelievable today, but, back then, it was normal.) Bhaiaji was a jack-of-all-trades, including gardener, handyman, security guard, and even snake-killer. There were many trees around our house, and, once in a while, he would find snakes in them (some of them rather large!). It was a challenge to catch them and kill them, and he would proudly show us his successes.

The highlight of our new home was the terrace. The terrace was about twenty feet wide and five hundred feet long, and our six-foot wall surrounded it. It was a private and safe place—a prized possession. In the summers, we would sleep on the terrace under the open night sky. When morning came, we'd roll our cots away until we needed them again that night.

The terrace also served as our own personal bleachers for watching cricket. Every year Ahmedabad would host a three-day cricket event on the H. L. Commerce College's field, as the city did not have its own permanent cricket stadium. Cricket is the most popular sport in India. It requires only eleven players on each team, who compete on an open field with bats and balls the size of tennis balls. With such inexpensive equipment, it is an approachable game for all people, rich and poor, and it is played everywhere in India—in big cities, tiny villages, anywhere there's an open field.

In the big cities of Bombay, Delhi, and Calcutta, there were big annual five-day cricket matches, in which India would play against many different countries, such as Australia, England, the West Indies, and South Africa. Even though Ahmedabad's cricket match was on a much smaller scale, it was still so much fun, and we had front-row seats on our terrace!

Ahmedabad's cricket match was always held in the winter, when the temperatures were in the seventies and the sky was bright and sunny. So, every year, with our terrace in clear view of the cricket field, we would set up a tent that could hold more than a hundred people, and we would send invitations to all our family and friends. With our incredible view of the field, paired with free drinks and refreshments, no one could resist!

The matches would start at 10 a.m. and go for eight hours. There was always so much excitement in the house during those three days. In fact, it was so much fun that some of our friends would invite *their* friends, and we would even have a few gatecrashers.

Back in 2013, I hosted a fifty-sixth reunion for my college classmates. I was familiar with most of them, but there was one I couldn't quite place. He introduced himself and said he had wonderful memories of watching the cricket matches on our terrace. I replied that I didn't remember knowing his family back then, and I wondered aloud how he'd got an invitation. He smiled and said that his sister and my sister were classmates, and he snuck in to our party by telling my father that he was a friend of my brother's. We both had a good laugh over that.

My clearest memories begin around 1944, when I was four years old and starting school. Bauji decided to enroll me in Mount Carmel Convent's school, an elite English-language private school run by Catholic nuns. (Bauji was always keenly involved in our schooling, staying up to date on our activities, homework, and grades.)

School started for all of us at nine in the morning and finished at five at night. Since it was a Catholic school, the day always began with a morning prayer and ended with an evening prayer. Non-Catholic students had a class on moral science, while the Catholics had one on the catechism. The school also had a chapel, and I visited it before every exam to ask for blessings.

The school uniform was a navy pinafore with a white shirt and a red tie. The only time students were exempted from wearing the uniform was on their birthday.

English was the only language allowed on campus, so I caught on to it quickly; I learned to speak, read, and write it before even Hindi or Gujarati.

On my very first day of school, one of my aunts accompanied me, spending the whole day with me on campus; then she brought me home. It took me a couple of days to get comfortable and adjust to the new environment. For one thing, I had never before seen nuns. They were covered from head to toe in their outfits called *habits*, and all of the students addressed them as "sisters." The principal of the school was Mother Superior.

Although Bapaji did not voice his disapproval, he was not happy about my attending a Catholic school. It was not that he disliked Catholics. In fact, Bapaji was a very open-minded man and did not discriminate against people of other religions or lower-caste Hindus. He would share a plate of goodies with any guest, even though the rules of the caste system called for separate tableware depending on the person's rank. It was simply that Bapaji was concerned my religious preferences would be unduly influenced by attending a Catholic school. Many poverty-stricken Hindus in southern India's Kerala, for example, were converting to Catholicism with the promise of better living conditions.

Early on in my schooling, my uncle, Chachaji, signed me up for piano lessons, which were offered after school and taught by our teachers, the nuns. She ordered a piano-instruction book for me, and it arrived in the mail one week later, all the way from Bombay. I was so excited for my lessons, but after my second one, Bapaji found out why I was staying late after school. He was not happy, and he bluntly told my mother that the nuns might use the one-on-one time with me to persuade me to convert to Catholicism. Bapaji was a very gentle man at heart but still a benign dictator, so that was the beginning and end of my piano lessons. I sadly put my little blue piano book away, treasuring it for many years before finally parting with it.

Despite Bapaji's initial concerns, I had many happy days at Mount Carmel, and one of my happiest was my second day, when I met Ragini. She was a nice girl, and we quickly became best friends. We have an eternal bond—a friendship made in heaven. Even though I eventually moved away and she still lives in Ahmedabad, we have always stayed in contact (thank goodness for modern-day technology). We have shared with each other our happiest and our saddest times. Today our friendship is seventy-one years young.

My life was very predictable as a child. Bapaji and Bauji worked six days a week, leaving at ten in the morning and returning at eight at night. Their office was three miles away, and their commute was one hour by bus, changing buses once. We'd all eat dinner together at 8:30 p.m.

As we children grew older, we were expected to stay current on the news. Every day we were to read the *Times of India* as well as the local English newspaper and the *Illustrated Weekly*, which had world news similar to the U.S.'s *TIME* magazine. Bauji would quiz us every night on our readings. (We would save these newspapers in a storage room, and the same man would regularly stop by to pick them up and sell them to the food hawkers and vegetable shops for wrapping.)

On Sundays (Bapaji's one day off work) we children would accompany him on his morning walk. Every week our route was the same: we'd walk a quarter of a mile past the two university campuses and into the mango orchards, a beautiful place. I loved unripe mangoes, and we would all look on the ground for any that might have fallen off the trees and bring them home to eat. The unripe mangoes were not sweet, and even now I can still taste their sourness in my mouth. Bapaji knew my fondness for mangoes, so during his weekday walks, when I could not accompany him, he would bring some home for me to eat.

I also remember during this time traveling with Baji and Chaeji to D. I. Khan. They went frequently, since most of both their families still lived there. On every trip to D. I. Khan, they packed bags of household goods for Aunt Bhen's dowry. Even though it was too early for her to get married, preparations were still being made because her wedding would definitely be in D. I. Khan rather than Ahmedabad.

I also fondly remember our bedtime stories. Every night Bapaji would read to us from the *Ramayana, Mahabharata*, and the *Bhagavad Gita*—the three books of sacred Hindu mythology. He had the talent of bringing these stories to life for us children, adding examples from our own everyday lives so we would better understand them.

He especially focused on the attributes of willpower and positive thinking. One of his favorite sayings was, "Simple living and high thinking." He also taught us Gandhi's principle of nonviolence, referring often to the statues of the three wise monkeys found in Gandhi's garden at the ashram and the garden at Kankaria Lake.

Bapaji also believed in fairness and respect for all humankind; any honest job, he said, was respectful. One of his other frequent sayings was, "Pay the porter before his sweat dries." Or, in other words, do not wait for the laborer to ask you for his due.

Discipline and time management were two other important qualities to Bapaji. He would say in Hindi, "*Jo kal karna hai vo aaj kaar jo aaj karna hai vo aab kar*," which means, "What you plan to do tomorrow, do today; and what you are planning to do today, do now, as time waits for nobody."

But Bapaji's most valued quality (and one I have many memories of) was generosity. He believed in charity, in helping humanity—not for recognition but simply to make the world a better place. And he practiced what he preached.

In 1943, the Bengal Province was hit by a tidal wave, which resulted in a crippling famine. The price of rice skyrocketed four-fold, and three million people starved to death. The poorest Bengalis, who had no money and no land (or their land had been flooded) were the most at risk. Ration cards were issued across India for a weekly quota of rice and wheat, to be purchased at a government grain shop. (If you were rich, you could buy more on the black market.)

We did not have big eaters in our family, because we had always been taught to eat a balanced diet and not to overindulge our appetite. Even though we had no gyms or health clubs, we were all a healthy weight, and we could live well under our ration quota. So, Bapaji decided that the whole family should sacrifice its share of rice and grain once a week and send it to those truly in need in the Bengal Province. We substituted these meals with lentils, vegetables, and fruit. I remember being so proud that I could help others in such a real and important way. (Of course, Bapaji took his contribution one step further and donated his share of rice and wheat from a meal *every day*, substituting his lunches with yogurt and fruit.)

Bapaji's generous spirit was not limited to extreme circumstances, though; he regularly shared in whatever way he could. On Sundays a handful of eight- to ten-year-olds from the nearby orphanages would knock on our door, asking for donations of wheat, rice, sugar, and lentils. Bapaji would open the door with a smile on his face and tell us to go to the pantry and fill a bowl for each one of their bags.

The distance between the front door and the pantry was about twenty-five feet, and sometimes we would drag our way across it, even though we knew the orphans were anxiously waiting for their food. Bapaji, seeing our laziness, would share with us another one of his favorite sayings, *"Jab tak Deh hai to De; Jab Deh na hogi to kaon kahega de?"* *Deh* and *de* are closely related words with different meanings. *Deh* means "to be alive," while *de* means "to give." Bapaji was telling us, "You can give only when you are alive and around; once you are not around, who will ask you to give?"

Bapaji also founded, with Bauji's aid, the *"Punjabi Samaj"* (the Punjabi Association). With this organization, they helped Punjabi newcomers from northern India settle into Ahmedabad. They would meet on Sundays to socialize and teach the local customs. During this time, Bauji helped open a Hindi-focused school as well, since most of the schools in Ahmedabad were based on the Gujarati language.

A few times every year, we would travel to the Hindu temple Ved Mandir and offer a donation and visit the *Maharaj* (head priest) for sermons and blessings. (Our family was, for the most part, practicing Hindus, although we were not orthodox. At home, we would pray at a one-foot-by-one-foot mantle that had statues of the different gods.)

On our birthdays, Bapaji would encourage us to visit the leper colony or the orphanages and donate food. These visits especially opened my eyes to how fortunate our family was.

Although these sacrifices of Bapaji's might sound small and personal, they added up over a lifetime to a man who was determined, honest, and, most of all, generous.

I was personally very lucky that Bapaji did not believe in gender discrimination. Bapaji's thinking was a hundred years ahead of his time. It was common in those days to give sons preference over daughters, but my younger brother was never allowed to have an unfair advantage simply because he was male.

I was brought up as a princess—not with materialistic possessions but with the strong relationship between Bapaji and me. He was my mentor, believing in me and teaching me when I was as young as four years old to be focused and have goals in my life. He encouraged me to be independent before getting married, and his dream for me was to become a doctor. It was a noble profession, he said, because I would be helping humankind and saving lives. I immediately liked the idea, and, from then on, the only future I could envision for myself was one as a doctor. My destiny was carved in stone, and my determination grew deeper every year.

Despite some rather grown-up goals, I still had a very fun childhood. Our birthdays were treated with great importance: nothing too lavish—good food and a small party—but enough so that each child felt loved and special. One of our gifts was always a small amount of money in *rupees*, most of which would go into our individual savings account at Bapaji and Bauji's office. Throughout the year, Bapaji would periodically give us updates on our balance so that we could both practice our math as well as learn the importance of being financially sound. Bapaji would even keep track of the interest we were earning and would double our savings after seven years. A wonderful lesson for a child!

Diwali was another huge celebration in our household—the "festival of lights," the biggest festival in all of India. According to the lunar calendar, it falls between mid-October and mid-November, and it signifies the prevailing of good over evil, like Christianity's Christmas, and it also celebrates the homecoming of the god Rama after fourteen years of banishment.

During the Diwali season, shops are full of sweets and decorated with lights. The streets look colorful and festive, with the outside of buildings getting a new coat of paint and the insides getting deep-cleaned. Everyone is busy shopping for new clothes and jewelry. Even the poor save their money for Diwali. On the day of Diwali, the entrances in Gujarati are decorated with dry paint drawings called *rangoli*, patterns created on the floor using colored sand, rice, and flour. Firecrackers were also for sale.

In the evening of Diwali, we would celebrate at Bapaji and Bauji's office with all their staff and the staff's children. Bapaji and Bauji's business had continued to expand, and they were now working on commission for many cloth distributors. They had twenty full-time staff, including an in-house chef to prepare the staff's lunch every day. Their main office was fourteen feet by twenty feet and had no desks or chairs, with one main entrance and one side entrance from the veranda. Beyond the main office were the kitchen and the bedrooms. The office was outfitted with mattresses, several of them on their sides with round back cushions and low desks in front of them. Office space was divided by each staff member's rank and job.

Bapaji and Bauji's office faced everyone else's. On their office wall, they had two-feet-by-four-feet portraits of ancestors, and on their bookshelves were *wahis*, business textbooks bound in red cloth with the pages one foot by two feet.

For Diwali, we would come to the office dressed up and excited to celebrate. The ceremony started with the arrival of the Ram pandit—the designated family priest for all our celebrations. He would perform the Diwali *puja* (prayer) called the "Lakshmi Puja" (Lakshmi being the goddess of good fortune and wealth); then the new wahis were all blessed with the inscription of the god Ganesh written on the front page in the yellow-gold of saffron. Ganesh was the god called upon for help in overcoming obstacles. Thus the new business ledgers, and indeed, the whole business, was now ready for the start of the new fiscal year.

After the puja ceremony, the fun would begin for us children. First, Bapaji would call our names individually, starting with the eldest down to the youngest, and he would give each of us an envelope with a gift of money inside. Everyone, including the children of the staff, received the same amount of money; there was no discrimination. Then, Uncle Chachaji would give each of us a gift bag with sparklers and an assortment of other fireworks. We could hardly wait to light them up! But first, we said our goodbyes and went back home to prepare for a festive dinner.

We would decorate on the veranda, surrounded by small oil lamps about double the size of tea lights. After dinner, Bapaji would give us another envelope with money inside. He would wait to give us our bonus until after the office party, as he wanted to treat all the children in attendance the same, no matter if they were staff or family. Then came the moment all us children were waiting for: fireworks.

We were allowed to handle the sparklers, but Uncle Chachaji handled the more advanced fireworks (and, of course, we would save some for more fun in the future). It was always a memorable celebration, and we would go to bed exhausted.

Another big festival was the Uttarayan Kite Flying Festival. Over the years, this festival has become famous across the state, an important tourist attraction for Ahmedabad. It is held annually on January 14, when the weather will, most likely, be sunny and seventy degrees. Preparations for this mega-festival start many weeks before the day, with stores selling every kind of kite you can imagine: balloon-shaped kites; kites with lighted lamps attached; even long strings of kites attached together like a chain.

The strings on the kites are coated with glass powder to cut the other kites out of the sky during the competition. Seeing all these kites up in the sky, swerving and charging at each other, is overwhelming and beautiful. The kite-flying competition is a team event, and, back then, I would hold the reel while Uncle Chachaji would cut the other kites.

As with the cricket matches, our terrace gave us a front-row view to the kite flying. We'd put up a tent and invite as many people as we could fit in. Although, unfortunately, you would learn later about accidents happening in the city due to younger, more excitable players falling off the roof while flying their kites. For those of us who managed to escape serious injury, many still left with Band-Aids on their cut fingers from the glass-coated strings.

Besides festivals, we also had fun by going to the circus when it came to town and visiting the Kankaria gardens and zoo once or twice a year. Honestly, though, we didn't *have* to travel to find entertainment. There was enough going on right outside our veranda to keep us entertained for hours!

Since our house was on the edge of rural territory, the village women would walk by our house every morning with donkeys pulling carts loaded with bricks and mortar, delivering them to construction sites. The women were usually dressed in colorful attire, mostly long skirts and short blouses, showing three inches of midriff decorated with a stole showing lots of mirror work, and they would be covered from head to toe in jewelry—nose rings, ankle bracelets, rows of earrings. They always looked very happy.

There were also bullock carts transporting heavy goods, steered by men, and herds of cows, water buffaloes, and goats with their cute black-and-white kids. In the evening, they would all pass by us again on their way back to their village and mud huts.

In addition to all this commotion, there was the usual traffic of buses, bikes, and many pedestrians (but no motorbikes, scooters, or rickshaws).

Periodically, snake charmers would come to our street. The charmer would play his *bansuri* (flute), and out of his basket would come a big cobra dancing to the music.

The monkey man would also visit, with his little red-faced monkeys performing tricks. These monkeys were professionals, very well-trained. We had many bigger, black-faced monkeys among the trees in our backyard who were more timid; luckily, we had none of those devious red-faced monkeys on our property.

Every few months, the *kalaiwala* would come with his cart of kitchen utensils. All his utensils were made of copper or brass, since these metals are heavy conductors and more versatile than steel. Copper, however, reacts to acidic foods—discoloring it or giving it a bitter taste—so these utensils need to be coated with tin. We would watch the kalaiwala heat up the utensil and then the tin, and quickly rub the melted tin around the utensil to create a silver lining. The lining would last for three months, and then the kalaiwala would come back to re-tin.

Re-tinning is considered not only a business but also an art, passed down from one generation to the next. These days, though, it is a dying art, even in the villages, with the advent of the pressure cooker and stainless-steel utensils.

Among all this commotion was the usual community gossip. As children, we only overheard the gossip, because we were supposed to be seen, not heard. One of the bits of gossip concerned a local businessman in the Punjabi community. He was Bauji's age, the father of many children, and had been caught more than once fondling young girls. His only punishment was a minor reprimand.

Another frequent subject of gossip was Chaeji's friend, who was very fashionable and impressive-looking but suffered from seizures, which some said were actually hysterics. I still liked her.

Baji, who was well-mannered and sophisticated, also had a close friend of her own of whom she did not approve, because the friend was loud and liked to razz everyone around her.

One sad piece of gossip was about a woman who had been forced by her husband to give up her baby girl for adoption to one of his relatives. The woman was traumatized and fell into a deep depression. She later had a stillborn and refused to part with it for some time. Her mental condition deteriorated so badly that she was sent away to a mental hospital near Delhi. As far as I know, no one in her family ever visited her. Many years later, one of my rotations during medical school was at this same hospital. It was heartbreaking to see her; she had been such a beautiful woman once, but now she was nothing more than a living vegetable. I still think of her and wonder how her life could have turned out differently.

There were stories, too, about our neighbors who lived in a house behind us and had a summer home in the very desirable location of Mussoorie, a town at the foothills of the Himalayas. They were rich, proud, beautiful, fashionable, and big snobs. We would occasionally see each other from our terraces, but there were never any exchanges. Bauji said they were corrupt and had no ethics; even Bapaji did not have a single good thing to say about them. One story about this family involved a father of one of my classmates who was in the same business as Bauji. He once told Bauji that our neighbors pulled the wool over his eyes with a fraudulent business deal, and he'd suffered heavy financial losses because of it. The man tried to approach them about it in Mussoorie, but they had guards around their summer home and refused him entry. I felt sorry for my classmate whose family had lost all that money her father had worked so hard to earn. (I remember this neighbor's family were not vegetarians, and they kept chickens in their backyard. I enjoyed watching them from our house, but I think they later migrated to somewhere else.)

Our family continued growing. In September 1945, my sister Varsha was born. The following year my sister Veena was born in a private hospital, and Chaejis's sister got married in D. I. Khan. Unfortunately, it was also a year of great violence, with Indians fighting British rule, and Hindus and Muslims fighting each other.

Bauji, Chaeji, Nirmal, Veena, and my brother Vijay all went to D. I. Khan for the wedding of Chaeji's sister; Varsha and I stayed behind in Ahmedabad. After the wedding, their trip back became very dangerous. Massacres had become an everyday affair, and the trains were being attacked, so my father bore the heavy responsibility of chaperoning eight females by himself. The trip was even more stressful because they were traveling in third class (the reservations having already been made by relatives). Luckily, their train was one of the last to escape massive mutilation and murder. Bauji was incredibly relieved when they finally passed into Indian territory in Amritsar.

Even in Amritsar, though, chaos reigned. Shops were on fire next to Chaeji's parent's house, including a tailor's shop, where a coat was being taken in for me. My sister Nirmal's coat had already been finished and given to her; it was dark red and woolen with an embroidered left lapel. I never got my coat. I did envy her a little when she was wearing hers, but I guess that, in retrospect, a seven-year-old can be forgiven for being blind to the much more serious problems at the time.

On August 15, 1947, India finally won independence after three hundred years of British rule, but our freedom came at a heavy price. Colonial India was divided into two separate states: Pakistan for the Muslim majority, and India for the Hindu majority. This new Pakistan was also built on two halves: East Pakistan in Bengal, and West Pakistan in Punjab and Sindh. The result was the largest mass migration in history—more than ten million people walked away from everything they owned. Most people thought they'd be leaving for only a short time, returning once all the turmoil settled down. The situation, however, was much more permanent and traumatic than anyone could have foreseen.

The trains were packed. People hung out the windows and on to the doors; entire families sat on train roofs, children clinging to their mothers and vice versa. People who could not get on the trains joined foot caravans, some of them walking fifty miles or more in search of safety. As many as one million of these refugees were killed along the way.

The violence was unimaginable. Whole villages were razed to the ground. Trains were set on fire. Women were raped, tortured—their breasts cut off—paraded naked through the streets, sold into prostitution. At least 83,000 of them were abducted. Men were forced to strip; if they were not circumcised, they were killed by the Muslims; if they were circumcised, they were killed by the Hindus.

There were forced conversions and suicides and family homicides to avoid shame. The violence was especially horrendous in the western region of Punjab, because it had been cut in half with the new state borders. The violence went on all day and all through the night.

Thankfully, we lived outside the city and were much less affected. Bauji would go to the office in the city and stay two days at a time. Aunt Bhen and I would check on him by using a neighbor's phone on the way to school every morning. The phone was a two-piece black upright, and I was excited to talk into this strange new contraption (I think we got our first in-house phone in 1949).

Since Bapaji's family was settled in Ahmedabad, they lost their home and some valuables in D.I. Khan, but it was not a severe financial loss. Bapaji's extended family in D. I. Khan, however, were in great danger and lost everything. My cousin once told me that they were all crying as they watched house after house burn down around them. They could do nothing but wait for their turn to die. The emotional trauma from this massacre lasted a lifetime.

Bapaji and Bauji understood the seriousness of the situation and invited all our family in D. I. Khan to come to our house at Bhatia Bhawan. Four or five families made the trip, and although we could offer each family only one room, it was a roof over their heads, and it was safe.

Bapaji trained three of these refugee nephews, who were brothers, and gave them work at the office. Two of them eventually earned their own client-portfolios, and the third became the firm's accountant; they all stayed with the family business until they died.

Later on, some uncles from my mother's side also came to stay with us while they looked for new permanent homes. With so many relatives in the house from both sides of the family, romances sprang up, and weddings were celebrated.

I enjoyed having even more family around, including three cousins who were like uncles and an aunt to me, even though they were only a few years older than me and were going to school. We played many games and had a lot of fun together.

Bapaji and Bauji always had an open-door policy. They believed it was their duty and responsibility to unconditionally help family. Thanks to Bapaji's kind and giving nature, all child relatives who stayed with us were settled in to good businesses with good jobs all over the world—the U.S., the UK, Canada, Australia, and across the Middle East. Probably more than a hundred people received significant help and guidance from Bapaji.

Bapaji also continued to be generous outside the family, especially now with so many Punjabis migrating due to the new state borders. With his Punjabi Association, he helped refugees connect, assimilate, and find work.

Bauji, too, became even more active in his interests, especially in the politics of his business. Despite his high level of education and experience, he was not getting the recognition he deserved in the textile market, because he was a Punjabi in Gujarat. But he was persistent and motivated, and so, after first losing by only a few votes in the Maskati cloth market elections, he eventually was elected to the board, and he went on to become its president.

He also became the trustee of the Hindi school and the bank trustee, among many other social obligations.

At school, my brother had joined us. Even though it was a girls' school, boys were allowed to attend until the third grade, which made it convenient for my parents. Every day we brought with us our tiffin lunch boxes, a portable way of carrying food whicht consisted of nested containers inside each other, as the school did not have a cafeteria for buying food.

We also continued to learn from Bapaji, who was always gently reinforcing his lessons on humility and tenacity. By that time, I was certain I wanted to be a doctor—Bapaji had ingrained in me the importance of independence and a noble profession. One night I told Bapaji, "When I become a doctor, I will give free care to everybody." Bapaji replied, "Yes, you will give free care to the needy, but you will charge the patients who are wealthy and can afford your fees." Here was a crash course in business management for a seven-year-old.

Over and over again, Bapaji taught me to be confident and capable, to stick to my beliefs, but at the same time, to learn every day from everyone around me. Be assertive but not arrogant. All of this he had learned from his own experiences, which had molded him into a wise man at a young age. He had a healthy, balanced approach to business. For example, he sometimes incurred losses because of clients, but he still maintained a civil relationship with them. "Money is not everything," he said, "and relationships are very important."

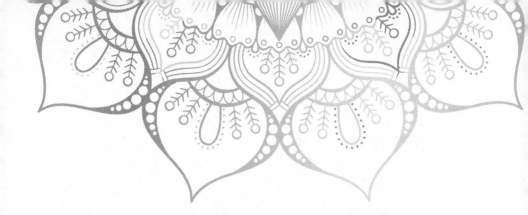

# Chapter Four

*B*y 1947, Bapaji and Bauji had settled all our relatives
who had fled D. I. Khan. They found them employ-
ment and stable homes and helped them adjust to their new
environment. Baji, however, still had not emotionally recovered
from her losses in D. I. Khan, where she had been storing all
the goods and treasures for her only daughter's trousseau. Bauji
comforted her, saying Bhen would still have a very lavish wedding. There was no groom in mind yet, but it was assumed the
marriage would happen soon, and the search for a nice Bhatia
boy was ongoing. (In those days, it had to be a Bhatia match.)
Bhen was now eighteen years old and going to college; she had
always been a very kind person with strong values, and she gave
me a lot of attention.

The following year, Baji traveled to Delhi for a fortnight to
visit a sick cousin, but she returned to Ahmedabad sick herself.
We all initially thought it was post-traumatic stress due to her
heavy losses in D. I. Khan and her shattered dreams for Bhen's
wedding, but she continued to get sicker and sicker. Eventually,

it was discovered that Baji, at fifty-seven years old, had stomach cancer (although I have since suspected that it could have been ovarian cancer). Some in the family believed that the stress Baji was suffering from had brought on the cancer.

Even though I was only eight years old at the time and could not comprehend the true seriousness of the situation, I still felt the emotional upheaval.

It was during this shocking time, while Baji was going through many medical tests, that Bapaji asked Bauji to travel nine hundred miles north of Ahmedabad to Punjab on a business trip and, while there, visit some friends of Bapaji's and approve their son as a match for Bhen. The families had already agreed by word of mouth, exchanging information on the bride and groom's education. No photographs, however, had been exchanged. This was how it was done back then, even by educated, well-to-do families; arranged marriages were the norm, while love marriages, like my mother and father's, was the exception.

Baji was happy and relieved that Bhen's wedding was soon to be, but she was still getting sicker by the day. Her doctors recommended surgery at Tata Memorial Cancer Hospital in Bombay. Baji agreed, on the condition that her family surround her during her stay in Bombay.

Her wish was respected. We all packed our bags and rented a house in Bombay. (It was June, so we children were on summer vacation.) Baji's brothers also came from Ahmedabad and Delhi. Going to Bombay was like going to New York, and we all had mixed emotions about it.

Once we arrived, Bauji made time between his hospital responsibilities to take us sightseeing. We went to Chowpatty Beach, where we saw the vast blue ocean, the beautiful sand, and the many food carts. I also enjoyed my first-ever ride on a double-decker commuter bus, and we rode on a tram (Bauji even bought us a toy tram, which was a very precious gift back then).

Baji underwent her surgery, and all of us waited to hear the good news that she'd been cured. While we sat in the visitors' lobby, Baji's brother cried, and I remember feeling confused, wondering why he was sad when he should be happy. Later we found out that Baji's cancer had spread; there were metastases all over. She was given only a few months left to live. The news was very traumatic for me.

We returned to Ahmedabad within the same month we had left. Baji was already frail and bedridden, and Bhen had left college to take care of her. Bapaji, Bauji, and Chaeji decided to expedite Bhen's wedding so that Baji could see her dream come true. With heavy hearts, everyone began preparing for the wedding; the date was set for the middle of September.

Chaeji, who was only twenty-seven years old at the time, had a great deal on her plate and was expected to multi-task constantly: running the household, raising five kids, watching after both Bhen and sixteen-year-old Chachaji (who was graduating from high school), and, of course, planning a wedding.

An Indian wedding requires mega-preparation. Chaeji was in charge of shopping for Bhen's trousseau, to include silver utensils, china, bedding, many other household items, gifts for the groom's family, lots of gold jewelry, and more than twenty-one sarees. Chaeji also had to throw a lavish wedding shower and prepare the house for the groom's party, who would be staying for two or three days after traveling nine hundred miles by train. Chaeji did an incredible job, and, looking back, I admire her for putting her whole heart into accomplishing all these responsibilities.

Every day the family hoped that Baji would live long enough to see her daughter married. I was very sad to watch her struggle, but I didn't share much of my feelings with anyone.

As we feared, Baji passed away, after much suffering, on August 23. I was devastated; there is never a right time for death. We had all been hoping against hope for one more month with her, but she was living on borrowed time and was in great pain. Bhen's wedding was postponed until March 11, 1949.

Despite our grief for Baji's death, life moved on. At the end of 1948, we bought our first car—a blue British-made Hindustan. Bapaji and Bauji hired a chauffeur at fifty dollars a month to drive them to the office six days a week. We went for joy rides on Sundays. The car was expensive even though it had no "extras": ten thousand rupees (more than two thousand dollars). A similar car sold in the U.S. would cost one thousand dollars or less.

As 1948 turned into 1949, I was consumed with worry over Bhen's wedding. I dreaded losing her—the thought alone made me anxious. We had a strong bond; she was like a big sister/ second mother to me. At the age of nine, I had not spent a day without her, and I was still grieving the loss of Baji. I asked Bhen why she had to get married and leave me. She replied, "I have no choice." I told her we could lock the door from the inside; then she wouldn't be forced to go. I knew I was being childish. I knew, as Bhen did, that she had no choice, but, at the time, I could not accept it.

Bhen's bridal party consisted of forty to fifty men and only one aunt to chaperone her two-day train trip to Punjab. The groom's family was very conservative, so the females did not attend the wedding.

The wedding went smoothly, and I felt reassured when I met her husband, Jijaji (uncle). He seemed like a nice man who would be kind to Bhen and take care of her. Far too soon, Bhen had to leave for Morinda, and I was in tears to see her go. Bapaji and

Bauji never showed emotions in public, but I knew Bauji under-stood my pain. He picked me up and comforted me.

As time went by, I adjusted to Bhen's absence, even though it still made me sad. Bapaji always kept a calm demeanor, but I know he must have felt pain, too—losing a wife and then a daughter. What is so precious at times like these is having the presence and support of family—grandparents, children, grand-children—complementing, strengthening, and encouraging the good in each other. We were all lucky to have one another during this difficult time.

Bhen and I corresponded regularly by letters. She was a very good writer, and her letters were long and had nothing but happy news. It bothered me, though, when she told me that her village had no electricity or running water. She had married into a wealthy family, but there were only hand pumps and no-flush toilets in her home. Early every morning, the villagers would walk to the train tracks in groups—men in one, women in the other—to carry pitchers of water back for washing. To me, this was barbaric and disturbing, and I felt sorry for Bhen. But Bhen was an angel, and she adjusted without complaining, choosing instead to be content and happy.

After a few months of exchanging letters, Bhen came back to Ahmedabad for her first visit since her marriage, and we spent the summer together.

In 1950, Bapaji and Bauji opened a free medical clinic for the poor and needy in honor of Baji. The clinic was in a busy, densely populated part of the city. It was staffed by a general-practice doctor and a compounder (pharmacist), and it had an in-house pharmacy. The hours were 8 a.m. to 1 p.m. and 5 p.m. to 8 p.m. daily. Patients could see the doctor for free, and prescriptions cost only two pennies. Bapaji explained why the medicine had a token charge and was not entirely free: he said it gave patients a feeling of self-respect; also, they would be more likely to value the medicine if they were expected to pay for it. At the age of ten, I was being taught a great deal about the importance of respecting myself and everyone else around me.

Bapaji and Bauji had always been philanthropists, wanting to help in whatever small way they could, as often as they could—because above all, they valued helping human beings rather than helping things (although they did their share of donating to the construction costs of the Hindu temple Ved Mandir, which we visited several times every year).

Bapaji said the free clinic was only the beginning. Once I became a doctor, he wanted to expand the clinic into a private hospital with access to greater care. This was his ultimate dream for me, and we were both united in our desire and drive to make it happen. Looking back, I think Bapaji felt limited in what he could do for Bhen because of the old-fashioned values and time constraints. I was his second chance to dream big, and he kept reinforcing it in subtle ways. He never had any hesitations or second thoughts.

That same year, we bought our first refrigerator. We were excited to always have ice available and to have a place to store goodies like store-bought ice cream. Bapaji had mixed feelings, though. He worried that now the beggars would be deprived of leftover perishables; he always had a kind and generous attitude.

In July 1953, Chachaji got married at the age of twenty-two, after graduating from college and joining the family business. This was an arranged marriage, but the bride and groom had at least met each other after the engagement.

We all went to Delhi as a *baraat* (groom's party), as it was customary for the groom's side to travel if the bride's family lived in a different city. Delhi had officially been named the capital of India on December 12, 1911. It was a very cosmopolitan place, and Chachaji's new wife was modern and classy, too—the more we got to know her, the more we learned from her.

We were all one big, growing happy family with a built-in social life, spending all our vacations together. For our summer vacations, we visited places close by, like Mount Abu, a four-hour drive and 4,500 feet above sea level. It was cooler there, and we spent the days boating, horseback riding, and playing board- and card games. Bapaji would usually play cards with us and do some hiking.

One year, we went to an oceanside resort in Dwarka. Dwarka is a holy place, one of the four sacred Hindu pilgrimage sites. During our visit, we spent most of our time looking for seashells at the beach and reading many books, including Shakespeare. Bauji strongly believed in and encouraged reading, but he was also health conscious, so he would buy books for us rather than having us borrow from our small-town library, where the books had passed through many hands.

In 1954, we took a dream vacation to Kashmir. Bauji was in charge of planning the six-week long trip, and he had to coordinate with many people, including the chef from our office and Bhen and her infant daughter. Our excitement knew no bounds. Visiting Kashmir was like visiting a foreign country: it was nicknamed "the Switzerland of India"; poets called it "heaven on earth"; it was even a favorite location to shoot movies.

First we took a twenty-four-hour train ride to Delhi; then we got on a different train and rode for another twelve hours to Pathankot. We spent the night in Pathankot and rode a bus for sixteen hours to Srinagar. Our route took us through the Banihal Mountain Pass, where we pulled over to grab a little snow leftover in the shade of a tree—my first-ever encounter with snow!

Despite the long journey, we were excited when we reached Srinagar, the capital of Kashmir. It lived up to all our hopes and expectations: sunny, seventy degrees, and breathtaking scenery of mountains, rivers, gardens, and lakes. Even as a teenager, I was in awe of the gardens Nishat, Shalimar, and Chashme Shahi, with their spectacular waterfalls and unsurpassable beauty. The lakes teemed with a variety of boats, some for transportation, others for living in—mobile hotels and homes with full amenities. We went sightseeing on especially small boats called *shikaras*, similar to gondolas, that were oared by men and women dressed up in colorful attire. We stayed in a big house Bauji had rented in the suburbs; it had a beautiful garden full of roses and fruit and nut trees and bushes—cherry, strawberry, apple, almond.

Most of the population in Srinagar was Muslim. All the females, even the children, were covered head to toe, and the men wore traditional clothing as well—no shorts, no Western clothing. They were very beautiful people.

The local economy was mostly tourism, selling everything you could imagine: silk, furniture, intricate woodwork, crewel embroidery, leather goods, and woolens, which, of course, included the famous *pashmina* and *shahtoosh* (the latter made from antelope hair and the former from mountain-goat hair). We did a lot of shopping, and even Bapaji indulged in a shahtoosh shawl.

Our next stop was Pahalgam. Camping was a popular choice in this area, but we rented a cottage on the bank of the beautiful river Lidder. Bapaji was the only one bold enough to bathe every day in the glacier water. We took a daytrip on horseback to Chandanwadi. The road was rustic and narrow—three feet wide—and the horses walked in precise single file for two hours until we reached the mountain peak and its stunning views.

There was not much shopping in Pahalgam, so we mostly took walks around the area. Devi Singh, our chef, was very unhappy and complained of being overworked. When we were in Srinagar, we spent our days out and about, eating as we went, but here all our meals were at home, except for some snacks.

Our next stop was another small town, Gulmarg, a popular skiing destination with beautiful valleys and rolling hills. Here we were joined by Jijaji, Bhen's husband, and his young cousins, who had recently lost their father in a tragic accident. The cousins were our age, and we figured the more, the merrier. Our family valued hospitality and were excellent hosts; we hoped to give Jijaji's cousins some happiness.

We noticed during our trip that both the rich Kashmiris and the poor kept themselves warm by wearing small baskets called *kangris*, which were filled with coal and hung around their necks under their loose tunics. These kangris were useful as personal portable heaters, but most people had chronic burn marks from them. A Kashmiri friend said that every night her mother would go around collecting all the kangris in the family to prevent accidental fires. Kangris are still used today by most Kashmiris.

After an enjoyable trip, we began our journey home, but first, we took a detour planned by Bapaji to the holy city of Haridwar. Haridwar sits at the foothills of the Himalayas on the Ganges, a river which was blessed by all the Hindu gods—Brahma, Vishnu, and Mahesh (Shiva)—and is the most sacred river to Hindus. The Ganges travels across one hundred fifty miles through the Himalayas before entering the Indo-Gangetic Plain, arguably the most important social and economic region of India. Millions of

Hindus visit this river every year to cleanse themselves of sin and attain *moksha*, liberation from the cycle of death and rebirth.

Our detour was to serve two purposes: one, it was for us to see such an important Hindu site (similar to Jerusalem for followers of western faiths); and two, as much as Bapaji was a modern man, he was still a religious man, so it was also for us to bathe in the Ganges and wash away our impurities from eating in Kashmir under unknown conditions.

The bathing *ghats* (platform steps) on the Ganges were filled from sunrise to sunset with people bathing and performing ablutions, even though it was a brisk fifty degrees. Har-ki-Pauri was the most crowded bathing ghat because it reputedly contains the footprints of Lord Krishna embedded in its stone. Most pilgrims take home from Har-ki-Pauri a pitcher of water called *Gangajal*, or holy water from the Ganges, and use it for important religious ceremonies (*pujas*) and cremation.

There is a separate section of the Ganges for cremation according to the Hindu faith. People from all over the world carry their loved ones' ashes in a clay urn to perform their last rites. Relatives of the deceased sit while the priest prays, and then the urn and flowers are floated down the river. This service is performed only in the daytime.

Since Haridwar is so often used for death rites, it has also become known for its genealogical records. For many years, *pandas*, short for Brahmin pandits (priests), have recorded the ancestry of Hindu families to Haridwar—noting deaths, marriages, births. In short, they maintain family trees. Pandas can trace a family's ancestry as far back as seven generations by using their handwritten registers, and special pandas are in charge of designated district registers. Being a panda is a family business handed down over many years.

It was customary while in Haridwar to visit the pandas for a so-called "refresher" on your family history, so we stopped by during our stay. It was fun, almost like going to a palm reader. I was amazed by how detailed and accurate the registers were—and without the help of computers! As far as I know, the pandas are still in Haridwar, but they are probably not able to maintain their registers unless they receive ongoing updates from families.

We also attended the Ganga Aarti. Every evening before dark, thousands gather in front of Har-ki-Pauri for this Hindu ceremony of light. The priests offer prayers to the Hindu gods and goddesses, braving the shivering cold wearing only their dhotis (loincloths). Hymns are sung, bells are rung, and people stand in line to float their flower-adorned lamps down the holy river. The river was very crowded during our Ganga Aarti, but it was well worth it to watch the temples light up and hundreds of lamps float down the Ganges. When the ceremony was done, many handicapped people were brought by their families down to the river for blessings, hoping for a magical cure.

Haridwar is a tourist destination as well, so it has a commercial side; many of its priests make up profitable "rules," which the tourists, not knowing any better, follow.

After three days in Haridwar, we continued our journey home—first a train change in Delhi, and then, finally, Ahmedabad. Although we cherished our memories from this trip, we were ready to be back home (and I'm guessing our chef, Devi Singh, was the happiest of all to be out of the trenches and back on his own turf).

I was in ninth grade in 1953, and I decided early on to pursue a Science major with premed subjects. The rule was, once you chose your schedule, you could not change it, but I was certain of my goals. I got good grades in most of my classes, except I needed to hire a tutor to come to my house for Algebra. Unfortunately, the tutor and I did not get along, and the sessions felt like a punishment. I finally convinced Bauji to let the tutor go. I continued working hard, though, under the watchful, encouraging eye of Bapaji. He was a constant reminder to me of optimism and resilience. He had known his own share of tragedy, yet he had deliberately chosen to be positive and roll with the punches.

House calls were a regular part of our lives. Every morning and evening, our milkman came on his bike, loaded with two drums of milk from his farm. This was the only way to get milk—you could not buy it at a grocery store. Needless to say, our milk was organic; it was not pasteurized or homogenized, either, but we never got sick from it.

Our *dhobi* (laundryman) came once a week. He would count and number our clothes, take them to the river, wash them, and dry them on the river banks. Fortunately, his system worked, and our clothes did not get mixed up with anyone else's.

The barber came once a month to give haircuts to Bapaji, Bauji, and my brother Vijay. We girls all had long hair.

The tailor came once every six months and spent a week. Ready-made clothes and boutiques were nonexistent back then. We would first choose some fabric, and then he would make us custom-made dresses. I was more fussy and stubborn (my nature in general) about what I wore; I insisted on choosing everything myself.

We also had the doctor from our private clinic, Dr. Lehri Shanker, only a phone call away and available 24 hours. He would often stop by while riding his bike to the clinic or on his way back home to check on us. Bapaji was blessed with good health and did not need checkups. He never complained and had an iron will. None of the rest of us had annual checkups, either, although Bauji was very health-conscious and an informed consumer.

Dr. Shanker was a handsome man with a warm, caring personality. He had a nice family—a beautiful wife, two daughters, and one or two sons (one of whom became a doctor himself). We would usually see his family once or twice a year at Diwali. Sadly, one of his daughters, who was eight or nine years old at the time, was crippled and had severe rheumatoid arthritis and rheumatic fever. Even we children felt bad for her; she reminded us of the value of good health. Despite the stress from his daughter's situation, Dr. Shanker and his wife almost always had smiles on their faces. Dr. Shanker retired in the early '90s, at which point Bauji decided to close the clinic and divert the clinic's charity fund to the city hospital.

Life was always changing for us, and Bauji and Bapaji were always open to it, welcoming rather than rigid. By now, they had almost entirely assimilated into the region, adopting its business culture and gaining the respect of the various textile associations. Bauji had even been elected president of the Mill Owners Association—a reward for his resilience as well as a feather in his cap, since he was a Punjabi from the north.

During one of Bapaji's teachings to us children, he told us that, around the ninth century, the first immigrants from Persia, the Parsees, came by boat to the west coast of India to escape Muslim rule. When the Parsees met the locals, they assured them that they were a peaceful people and that they would get along with each other like milk and water—once mixed, they could not be separated. Bapaji and Bauji believed in building bridges, in assimilating without forgetting their roots; because of their hard work, they were respected in their community—many relatives and friends came to them for advice.

Bapaji and Bauji made a good team; they complemented each other. Bapaji was the calming force to Bauji's Type A personality, and they had both thrived in the face of challenges. I don't remember them ever arguing in front of us, or even exchanging a difference of opinion. They both knew their boundaries, and they respected each other.

One of life's changes came to our house in 1953. We hired a new jack-of-all-trades housekeeper/governess/supervisor: a young woman, only about twenty years old but working full-time and raising two daughters. She was very mature for her age, exuding a balance of power and grace. She could tackle the most difficult task with a smile on her face, including learning how to cook, which she was taught by Chaeji and Auntyji (Chachaji's wife). She became an integral part of our family, celebrating with us during weddings and grieving with us during difficult times. Like Dr. Shanker, she retired in the early '90s.

It was around the time when we hired our new housekeeper that Chaeji suggested I should learn how to cook, too. My reply was short and simple: "Chaeji, you know I'm going to be a doctor, and doctors don't cook. The help in the house will do the cooking." She asked what I would do if the help got sick or went on vacation. I told her I could eat yogurt and make easy flatbread (*paratha*). Chaeji, however, wanted me to learn how to make whole-wheat flatbread (*phulka chapati*), which is a dough rolled into a circle and placed over an open fire on a flat pan to puff up. Even today, phulka is made every morning and evening in the households of northern India, but making it is an art that requires willingness, patience, and practice—which I had none of, and wanted none of back then. I had absolutely no interest in learning, and Chaeji did not push the issue too much because we had enough help in the house. (My motto in life has always been to do whatever I am good at; if I'm not good at something, then I quit and focus my efforts elsewhere.)

Years later, when I was in medical school, my younger sister did master the art of making phulka; she practiced in the kitchen whenever the help was away. If the phulka was ever stiff instead of soft, Bauji would jokingly say, "Sadhna, did you make the phulka today?" I did learn eventually, despite becoming a doctor, and I can make a pretty good phulka now. Times have changed, though. I'd say only 10 percent of career-focused Indians today know how to make phulka. When they visit India, some of them bring back stacks of three or four dozen phulkas made by the home-help to tide them over for three to four weeks.

Even though I was not a fan of cooking, I did have my own creative hobbies. I was good at knitting and embroidery. In school, we had needlework classes, which I enjoyed. Chaeji was good at tailoring, but I wasn't interested in that sort of needlework. Of course, now I wish I had learned from her because it would have been useful for minor clothing repairs.

In 1954, life was moving along smoothly. School was going well for me, and my grades were good, except for in Sanskrit. At the beginning of the year, my choice for a language class was either Sanskrit or French. Following the family tradition set by Bhen and Chachaji, I chose the difficult route, Sanskrit, and now, with school in full swing, I could not change my mind. Bauji, always a strong proponent of education, was more than happy to hire a tutor to help me. I was doing well in all my other studies, though, including learning my third language, Gujarati; I got better grades in Gujarati than even my childhood friend and classmate Ragini, which bothered her, since she herself was Gujarati. Before the exams, I would go to the school's chapel to pray. It was a Catholic school, and Grace was my favorite prayer.

Around this time, one of the city gardens next to the law college got a facelift. It had always been a beautiful garden, with nice walking paths, small bridges, pretty flowers and bushes, and all of it well-maintained. It was a popular park and especially crowded in the morning with people going on walks. The facelift included adding shops, set up in open cubicles with no doors and their backs against the garden's seven-foot lattice fence.

The shops are still there today, and they are a big attraction for visitors and locals alike. Seven days a week (as long as it is good weather) the cubicles are set up every evening and the shops are open to customers until midnight. The shopkeepers sell all manner of goods brought from the nearby villages or rural parts of the city: beautiful handmade mirror-work, ready-made women's wear and children's dresses, decorative linens, and detailed, expensive silver jewelry. Even shoppers with great self-control will end up splurging, and, of course, the weak-willed shop like there is no tomorrow. (It's important before shopping in India to get a crash course in bargaining. The shopkeepers here are masters at selling and are very astute judges of each buyer's bargaining skills.)

This area is also well-known as a street-food lover's paradise, with countless places to choose from—food carts, stalls, kiosks, and street hawkers with small bags of local candy. There are no health regulations for street food, and people can get sick from it, but we accept that as part of life, and it doesn't stop us from enjoying the delicious variety of eats.

Sadly, this fun, beautiful place is also flocked with beggars, some sitting on the roadside, others walking along beside you. Some of them are disabled, some are elders, some are mothers carrying infants, some are even children as young as five unaccompanied by an adult. Some of these children are victims of child abuse and human trafficking, mutilated to look more pitiable by their slumlords, who train them on what to say, like *God bless you* or telling women they look like movie stars or wishing men beauty queens for wives. These slumlords then wait in the shadows and take away whatever the children are given. It is very sad, with no policing of the situation. Even as a child, I felt blessed to have such a good family, which was added to, with much excitement, in 1954 with Chachaji and Auntyji's first child being born—a sweet baby girl—followed by the surprising announcement that my mother was pregnant, too!

The next year, 1955, I turned fifteen on September 15. Birthdays were always treated as special in our family, and I had a nice party with my family and about ten classmates. I received my usual gift of money from Bapaji, and he updated me on my savings-account balance. The very next day, September 16, my baby brother was born; everyone said he'd waited for me to enjoy my birthday before making his arrival.

The rest of the year, I spent with my nose in my textbooks, cramming for the prelims, which were in December before Christmas break. I got so nervous and stressed over them that I eventually decided to drop my optional Sanskrit course. I was hesitant at first to let it go because even if I failed one subject out of eight, I would still pass, but Bauji encouraged me to drop Sanskrit so I could concentrate on my other, more important subjects. He was right—I felt much more prepared and focused when it came time for the prelims.

After Christmas break and for the New Year (1956), my entire class of twenty-three students took a trip with the school nuns to Mount Abu. It was a short trip, three or four days, but it was full of excitement—some good, some bad. At breakfast, I tasted Kraft cheese for the first time and liked it. Then, during an outing, one of my classmates fell off a horse. Since I had been to Mount Abu many times with my family, I was able to help by bringing my classmate to one of Bauji's friends, Dr. Khurana. It was very rewarding to be able to offer important and timely assistance.

By 1956, we'd had a phone in our home for about five years, but we were not dependent on it. We saw our friends often. The phone was mainly used to call Bauji's office and communicate the grocery list to the office help.

# Chapter Five

*The year of 1956* was my most important year yet in schooling. I studied constantly and had no time for anything else. Bapaji could see my stress and worry, but he had faith in me—more than I probably had in myself. He was confident that he had imparted his values to me and had opened all doors for me so that I could be independent and pursue my dreams. Perhaps he could see how seriously I was taking my future and how hard I was willing to work to get there.

In March, Bauji left on a business trip for a couple weeks, and Bhen came to visit during his absence. After my exams, it was planned that I would go on vacation to her house, which I had never been to before. Bhen had always been a big support in my life, and I felt safe with her—she was my security blanket.

While Bauji was on his trip, my new baby brother had a check-up with the doctor, so Bapaji accompanied Chaeji. My brother was cute and healthy, but he was also a very colicky baby. Bapaji commented to the doctor how frequently this little boy visited him, and here Bapaji was sixty-four years old, in excellent health, and never had to go to the doctor.

The SSC Board Exams began on March 21 and continued for three and a half days—one exam in the morning and the afternoon—until the process was over. It was very hot every single one of those days—in the hundreds. Luckily, the testing center was at H. L. College of Commerce, which was practically in my backyard. The other students had to bike or bus through the heat; a few privileged ones had cars.

Bapaji, always thinking ahead, told Chaeji to save one glass of milk every morning for a few days so she could make homemade ice cream for all my classmates and serve it after the final exam. We could not simply buy a surplus of milk because everyone at the time got milk from a milkman, whose supply was limited to the production of his cows, which was especially low in such hot weather.

When I heard about the ice-cream plan, I at first wanted to share it only with my friends, but Bapaji convinced me that my entire class deserved a treat; to discriminate or to show partiality would not be kind. So, on March 24, my classmates walked out of their last exam into the broiling afternoon sun to be surprised with some deliciously cold ice cream served by Chaeji and Auntyji.

This ice-cream idea might seem like only a small act of kindness by Bapaji, but if you were to lay down all his small daily acts such as this, they would stretch for miles and miles.

I was so relieved to be done with exams. When Bauji returned from his business trip, he asked me how they had gone, and I told him I felt confident I had done very well in all my subjects.

On March 27, only three days after my exams, tragedy struck our family. Bapaji collapsed while at the office and eating fruit for lunch (his discipline since 1947). We were all shocked; Bapaji had never once called into work sick. He was brought to the Civil Hospital, where we were told he was in a diabetic coma. Unfortunately, his prognosis was grave. Doctors were treating him, but he was showing no improvement. Finally, we decided to bring him home by ambulance.

He was not responding at all—not a single word, not a single movement, not a single expression, not even of pain. He looked like he was in a deep sleep.

In the early morning of March 31, Bapaji passed away peacefully, in his own bed, surrounded by family. With Baji, I had at least been somewhat prepared when she died from cancer. And with Bhen's marriage, I had had time to mentally prepare for her leaving. But with Bapaji, I could not handle it. His death was too sudden, too unexpected. I was heartbroken, inconsolable, constantly crying. I could not accept that I had lost him forever. His daily encouragement, his guidance, his warmth, his unconditional love every minute of every hour of every day, were gone. The only time we had not been together in the last few years of his life was my school trip to Mount Abu; otherwise, every single night, I had been there to listen to his bedtime stories.

According to Hindu rites, Bapaji was cremated the same morning of his death on the banks of the Sabarmati River. A few days after the ceremony, Bauji took Bapaji's ashes to the holy city of Haridwar and performed his last rites on the bank of the Ganges. (He had also brought Baji's ashes there, but this was before we had visited Haridwar as a family.)

Later, Bhen confessed that the plan had never been for me to go back with her to her house. Bapaji had not wanted me to be gone for such a long time—he would have missed me too much—so he had asked Bhen to stay through my exams. I guess even the best men aren't entirely selfless, but to me Bapaji was an angel on Earth. He was forgiving and caring, and he never looked down on those who were less privileged. He was generous; he did not wait for people to come to him; he reached out to them. His own needs were few, but he was always considerate of others' needs. His acts of kindness were unconditional, limitless, and unannounced. He lived a life of gratitude, and he enjoyed every day without complaint.

As I think about Bapaji's gratitude, I want to express my own. I am thankful to my grandparents, parents, and Bhen for the love and support they have given me over the years to make me who I am today. I am also thankful that I could accomplish my dream of becoming independent and a doctor (even though I could not expand our clinic, as it closed when I moved to Delhi after marriage).

Bapaji was not a materialistic man; all of his possessions, mostly clothes, were in a big, wooden blue trunk. A while after his passing, the trunk was emptied and his clothes donated to charity (no western clothes, only khadi dhotis and shirts). In the trunk were also my school report cards over the years. Bapaji had saved them; I was deeply touched.

My grief during this time was overwhelming. First losing Baji, then the long-distance separation from Bhen, and now Bapaji. I had lost the three most important people in my life, and I was only fifteen years old. I did still have the support of Bauji and Chaeji and the rest of my family, but they could not replace what Baji, Bhen, and Bapaji had been to me. They had left a permanent vacuum in my life that time could never fill.

Sometimes, looking back, I wonder if Bapaji had an almost unearthly willpower—something he believed in and taught to us. There is a famous philosopher-poet, Dr. Allama Iqbal, who wrote, *"Khudi Ko kar buland itna ki har taqdeer se pehle, Khuda bande se khud puche bata teri raza kya hai.*" Roughly translated it means, "Resolve to strengthen your will to a level where even God Himself asks for your consent before issuing your destiny." Maybe Bapaji had controlled his own destiny (and it is this destiny which I believe eventually brought me to marry the grandson of Bapaji's first boss; more on that later).

Bapaji died while Bhen was visiting and after Bauji returned from his business trip; my exams were over, and his last act of thoughtfulness was to suggest serving ice cream to all my class-mates. He had finished laying down the foundation of my future: guiding me through my first important step of graduating from high school, preparing me mentally for the road ahead, and elimi-nating the glass ceilings that might prevent my growth. Perhaps he believed his job was done—he had instilled in me an internal compass, and now I needed to move forward on my own. Even today, if I am debating what to do, I still turn to my Catholic school teachings and Bapaji's words of wisdom to guide me.

It is this belief in destiny that has helped me find peace. Bapaji had accomplished his mission toward his family, friends, and community, and so he chose to leave. He was healthy through-out his life, and at sixty-four years old, he had gained so much wisdom and helped so many people. There are thousands of families across the world today whose successes are rooted in Bapaji's generosity. In my humble opinion, he was deserving of a Nobel Peace Prize, not because he was my grandfather, but because he had earned it over and over again.

A quick word on Bhen. We always stayed in touch over the years, and she frequently visited Ahmedabad. She was affection-ate and kind, a result of Baji and Bapaji's wonderful parenting. An example of her sweet nature was her generosity toward her sister-in-law, Jijaji's brother's wife. Bhen had a daughter and two sons, and she felt her family was complete, but her sister-in-law could not have children. Bhen felt deeply sorry for her sister-in-law, so she and Jijaji decided to have another child and gift it to their sister-in-law for adoption.

Like Bapaji, Bhen was also generous on a daily basis with small acts of kindness. She remembered every family member's birthday and anniversary, and she would send us long, loving letters. In this e-mail-deluged world we live in today, I miss her beautiful handwritten letters.

Like Bapaji, Bhen never complained, either. At one point, Bhen and her husband enjoyed great business success and became wealthy, traveling across the world, including to the U.S.; then they suffered severe financial losses, yet Bhen was content, never breathing a word of complaint.

Later in life, Bhen became disabled, but still she did not complain. She died in 2014 with a very small bank balance. Two months before her death, she drew up a will leaving me a token gift of money to express her love. Her generosity even in such difficult times was both touching and heartbreaking; I am saving this money to give to her children on their wedding day.

I could go on and on praising Bhen. I think very few people could be as generous and noble as her; I was lucky to have her in my life.

In May, my SSC results were finally available. The whole family waited eagerly as Chachaji drove to the university to pick them up. He came back beeping his horn with the good news. I had passed in the "first class" category. There were no letter grades. The grades were the following: "distinction" for passing above 70 percent; "first class" for above 60 percent; "second class" for above 50 percent; "pass" for above 35 percent. My guess is "first class" would be similar to an A minus.

I was ranked second in my class, and admission to any college of my choice was guaranteed. The whole family joyously celebrated, but I know we were all also thinking about Bapaji and how proud he would have been to see me moving forward, pursuing my dreams. Even though he is no longer with me in person, he is always in my thoughts, today and for as long as I live.

When it came time for me to choose a college, students at the colleges in Ahmedabad were rioting for Gujarat to separate from Bombay and become its own state. One of their demands was to have Gujarati be the medium of instruction in all subjects, but it would be completely impractical in India to study any science-related subject in any language other than English. Luckily, this particular demand never came to fruition, but Gujarat did become a separate state in 1958, after years of on-and-off turmoil. Because of these riots, I had to look into other possible colleges to attend. Chachaji and Auntyji accompanied me to a college in Baroda, and I liked the campus. My favorite, however, was a new college, St. Xavier's, which already had a well-regarded campus in Bombay. I applied to the new Ahmedabad campus and was accepted into its first-ever class of students—even the building itself was still under construction when we started.

St. Xavier's was a prestigious member of the association for Jesuit colleges throughout India and all over the world. It became known not only for its excellent academics but also for its competitive sports teams (although I was not athletic and cannot take any credit). The college was run by Jesuit fathers and brothers, who were very unlike the nuns from my previous Catholic school. These men smiled, enjoyed a laugh, and preferred a fun-loving atmosphere over a militaristic one.

Twelve years later, in 1968, I would join Harvard's Boston Lying-in Hospital as a fellow in the Anesthesia Department.

The department was small and intimate. I was a few days into my fellowship when Dr. Lee, one of the staff members, asked me where I was from. I said that she was probably not familiar with Ahmedabad. It is India's fifth-largest city, but most people don't know much about it. Her reply surprised me. She pronounced Ahmedabad correctly and then told me that she had donated one thousand dollars to the construction of a new college there, St. Xavier's. What a small world! I discovered that the Jesuit fathers had an affiliation with Boston College, and I enjoyed meeting some of my professors who were visiting from Ahmedabad.

Back to 1956. I was very excited to start at St. Xavier's, and I kept myself busy by shopping for new clothes. No more school uniforms! Finally, classes started in June. The campus was very close by, so I took the public bus and then walked a short distance. Some students who lived farther away either biked or took the bus; very few (maybe 1 percent) came by car.

There were more than one hundred twenty students in my class; 20 percent of them were girls. I was very lucky to have my long-time friend Ragini with me as well, and we both found a new friend in a girl named Thrity from Poona, near Bombay, who was going to college while staying with her aunts. The three of us had the best time together. Since all three of us had come from all-girls schools, it was our first time interacting with boys. We found a good group of friends, boys and girls, and many of us have stayed in touch throughout the years. (Three years ago, we hosted a fifty-six-year reunion with five male classmates and one female classmate. Ragini couldn't make it but made me promise over the phone not to forget about her while we all chatted.)

During our time at St. Xavier's, we, of course, indulged in some college craziness, but mostly we paid attention to our studies and worked hard. Every day I would go home and tell my family anything new or exciting that had happened.

Our curriculum was much harder than a Liberal Arts education. Most of the boys were working toward an Engineering major, the girls Medicine. Besides classwork (didactics), we also had labs in Botany and Zoology. Botany was easy, but Zoology was hit-or-miss for me. In the Zoology labs, we dissected earthworms, cockroaches, and lobsters. I did not like dissecting the dirty cockroaches and earthworms, but the lobsters were all right. The lobsters came by air from Bombay, and they were a beautiful red on the outside with nice white flesh on the inside. At the time, lobster was not considered gourmet food in Gujarat, even by the meat-eaters; no one had developed a taste for it yet because it was not part of our regional cuisine. One of my friends in the lab, however, was always delighted to take home any leftovers; she was a Parsee from Bombay, so she enjoyed lobster. Times have changed in Gujarat, and now lobster is considered a delicacy.

Sometimes I would have to stay late at school because the lobsters would be late coming from Bombay, and our lab hours had to be extended. Bauji was used to me being home before him. If I wasn't, he would come to St. Xavier's to either give me a ride or monitor my actions, so all my friends knew who my (overprotective) dad was. My transfer from an all-girls school to a co-ed college was an adjustment for everyone!

While keeping an eye on me, Bauji was also busy in 1957 overseeing the construction of our new home, which he had custom designed. Bapaji had known Bauji was not happy at our current place, The Bhatia Building, so before his death, he had bought three-quarters of an acre in the suburbs for Bauji and, in his will, had given The Bhatia Building to Chachaji.

Since business was doing so well, the plan was to make our dream house, big enough for the whole family to live together. I was lucky to grow up with so much support, respect, love, and diversity all under one roof. We were truly one big family. You don't see that anymore in India today.

The house was three and a half stories, twelve thousand square feet, with a wide marble staircase, a huge family room to accommodate many guests, and five bedrooms, each with an attached bathroom and a private balcony for sleeping on at night April through September, during the warm weather. There was also a garage with an adjoining servants' quarters, and the grounds were beautifully manicured with a six-foot wall around them. Bauji and Chaeji's suite was on the first floor and had two bedrooms, a walk-in closet, and a veranda. Chachaji and Auntyji's suite was identical but on the second floor. My room was above the living room (drawing room), twenty by fifteen feet, and I shared it with my sister Nirmal. I was going to miss my own private ten-by-twelve-foot room in our current house.

Construction on the house was going full speed, and sometimes on Sundays we went to see the progress. In all my other spare time, though, I was studying hard for early admission to med school.

In March 1958, I took my inter-science final exams at St. Xavier's. There were still riots and rallies going on for an independent Gujarat, which caused a great deal of disturbance, but I still did well on my exams. Unfortunately, the exams were leaked beforehand, and some students, mostly boys, cheated and got higher scores.

Despite my good grades, I was denied early admission to medical school in Ahmedabad. I was very disheartened because I would have to complete my BSC and then reapply after two or more years. My dreams were shattered. Thankfully, there was a silver lining. After some research, I discovered that I could apply to medical colleges in Delhi and in the city of Indore, where Aunt Chaeji's sister lived. All hope was not lost. I immediately ruled out Indore because I would have to live with family, and I focused my efforts on Delhi.

I had three options for medical school in Delhi: Maulana Azad, a new school, which would open that very same year; the All India Institute, also a fairly new school, started in 1956 but well-known and growing; and Lady Hardinge, a prestigious school opened in 1916 and named after the wife of Lord Hardinge. Lord Hardinge was the viceroy of India when it was under British rule, and his wife was a proponent of women's education. It was an excellent college and still is one today, but it had one strike against it in my book: it was women-only. After spending two years at the co-ed St. Xavier's, I did not want to go back to an all-girls school.

With Bauji's support and encouragement, I applied to the medical schools of All India Institute (AIMS) and Lady Hardinge (LHMC). As part of the application process, I had to do an oral interview at my choice of one of four centers in India. The closest one to me was an overnight train ride to Bombay. The AIMS interview was scheduled for April 26, and the LHMC for the next day, April 27. Meanwhile, our new house was almost done, so we started planning a big housewarming celebration. The date of the party was set for April 26.

This was a dilemma for me. Should I go to my AIMS interview on April 26 or attend my family's party? I was mature, but not enough to sacrifice what was sure to be a very fun party. So, I decided to put all my eggs in one basket and apply only to LHMC. I would go to the housewarming and then leave early to catch the night train to Bombay for my interview on the morning of the twenty-seventh. Bauji's cousin Brijlal (our business account manager) would accompany me.

The day of the big party arrived, and I wore a saree for the first time. Until then I had only worn dresses, skirts, and blouses, occasionally a salwar kameez. I borrowed the saree from Chaeji and paired it with a blouse from Auntyji, who helped me drape the saree. Bauji was surprised when he saw me. A big smile spread across his face—I was his little girl all grown up.

I had invited a dozen or so of my closest friends to the party, both boys and girls, and we all had so much fun. I was sorry when it was time for me to cut the celebration short and leave for Bombay.

Unfortunately, the trip did not go as smoothly as I had hoped. The train was supposed to arrive in Bombay at eight the next morning, but we were delayed due to heavy rainfall, which caused flooding on the train tracks and throughout the city. Such a deluge isn't necessarily unusual in Bombay, but it hadn't occurred to me that I might have to deal with it.

We finally arrived in Bombay at ten o'clock, two hours late. By then, I was nervous and very upset; I was worried that I would miss my interview in spite of all my efforts and sacrifices. As soon as we pulled into the station at Dadar Junction, I left straightaway to the interview center at Tata Memorial Hospital. I had sad memories of this hospital—it was where Baji had had her surgery. I prayed to God and Bapaji the entire way there, asking for help to make it on time. Finally, I made it around all the city's flooding and arrived at the hospital—a big sigh of relief. Once there, I realized I needn't have been so worried; everyone had been affected by the flooding.

I sat down in the waiting area with about thirty other girls. A few of them stood out as a touch more fashionable than the rest. Bombay was modern and nicknamed Bollywood because it was a favorite location for filming movies. One of the girls in the room was wearing a black blouse and a striking bright yellow skirt with black playing cards patterned all over it. Her name was Amina, and she had already completed her interview. She said she was happy with how it had gone. The interview panel had asked her who had won the Oscars, which was an easy question for her. (I would not have known the answer.) We would go on to become close friends.

Another girl in the interview room I would befriend was Fazila. She stood out with her impressive figure—thin and tall (five feet ten inches). We are still good friends today. Her daughter is a professor at Brown University, so Fazila frequently flies to the States.

When it was my turn to be interviewed, I stepped into a room with four women and one man. They introduced themselves, but I managed to remember the name of only the college principal. After asking me a few simple questions, they asked me an important one: What is my hometown, Ahmedabad, famous for? I replied that it was the Manchester of India. They seemed impressed.

I headed back home to play the waiting game. In June 1958, I returned to St. Xavier's for my junior year. This college, which I had so thoroughly enjoyed, now held no interest for me—I was in too much suspense. I attended class every day, because I had no choice, but my mind was elsewhere, constantly praying I would be admitted to LHMC. I wanted it so badly that I told myself I would go even if it were a hellhole of a medical school (although I knew it wasn't). I convinced myself that I had been rejected and that I had failed not only myself but, more importantly, Bapaji, and I would have to put my dream on hold for two long years.

For three weeks I lived in this misery, and then I got a letter from LHMC. I had been accepted; classes would start the first week of August. My joy was boundless. Bapaji used to say, *If at first you don't succeed, try, try again.* He would also say that all things work out for the best. I had been accepted into the most desirable, prestigious school in Delhi. LHMC was, and still is, the Harvard of India.

I immediately began preparing for my move to Delhi. Having never lived away from home alone, I was naïve and had no idea what to pack. Chaeji helped me with the necessities—new clothes, bedsheets, towels—and before I knew it, it was time to leave.

My trip was scheduled for the first week of August. We had decided that I would go alone on the twenty-four-hour train ride to Delhi, and Bauji's uncle would meet me at the station and take me to LHMC's campus. I knew him from past family visits and had memories of him crying during Baji's operation. I had been confident throughout my packing that I would be fine on my first-ever solo trip, but when it came time to say goodbye to Bauji and Chaeji at Ahmedabad's train station, I suddenly felt apprehensive, and tears pooled in my eyes. I was only seventeen, heading out on my own. Bauji and Chaeji gave me detailed instructions to correspond regularly with them by postcard. Later, in Bauji's first letter to me, he wrote that when he saw my tears, he wished he had accompanied me and not let me travel alone.

Luckily, the trip went smoothly, and Bauji's uncle brought me to LHMC. He did not need to hang around long, as I found my footing quickly.

# Chapter Six

My first day at LHMC was a quick orientation and tour of the campus, which included four cafeterias, each offering different cuisines. I filled out more paperwork, got directions to the bookstore, and received my room assignment. Being a first-year student, I was at the very bottom of the nice-rooms list and had to have a roommate. The rooms for third years and above were in modern wings, and the fourth and fifth years got their own rooms with verandas.

My room was straight out of a nightmare. Imagine a prison cell: high ceilings, yellow walls, two dark-brown, floor-to-ceiling closets, two beds, and communal bathrooms thirty feet down the hall. Everything looked like it was the original decor from back when the dorms were built, in 1916. A case for immediate depression if there ever were one. My first thought was something along the lines of *I wish I could go back to my life of luxury.* But I quickly replaced that thought with ones of courage and determination. Bapaji had succeeded in spite of some primitive surroundings, and so could I.

The campus itself was beautiful. The buildings were old and majestic, with British architecture, surrounded by manicured lawns, and in the middle of them was a statue of Lady Hardinge. The statue had a plaque with the college's founding year, 1916, followed by the college's motto in Latin, *Per ardua ad astra*, which means "Through adversity to the stars."

It was a sprawling campus to accommodate the five hundred students, plus residents and interns. It had tennis courts and a swimming pool as well as housing for professors and two teaching hospitals, the Smt. Sucheta Kirplani Hospital for Women and the Kalawati Saran Children's Hospital. It was like its own city. I was impressed.

The campus was in the heart of Delhi, surrounded by street-food stalls and restaurants, both fast food and gourmet. It was an extremely fashionable part of town—like New York's Fifth Avenue—and there were boutiques selling custom-made everything. We were also next to the renowned Hanuman Temple in Connaught Place.

Connaught Place, often shortened to CP, is one of the top heritage structures in Delhi. It was developed to be both a showpiece as well as a prominent business district. Construction began on it in 1929 and was completed in 1933. It was named after the British Prince Arthur, the first Duke of Connaught and Strathearn. Today it is the fourth-most-expensive office location in the world and the fifth-highest-priced market.

Regal Cinema was the first movie theater in Connaught Place, opening in 1932. It was only three blocks from campus, and because Regal had at some point installed air conditioning, we often went there to escape the heat (and, of course, to enjoy a movie).

Students at the other two medical schools in Delhi envied us for having the best location. We were safe and protected within LHMC's city-like campus yet still within reach of all the glamour.

The medical students in their first two years were a mix of boarders and day students, but the third- through fifth-year students were 95 percent boarders.

With the start of first-year classes, we were the fresh kids on campus. There were five girls in my class from Kashmir because of the quota system, which required five Kashmiris be admitted every year, no matter their grade-point average. So there were plenty of Kashmiris on campus, and the newcomers in our class were much more comfortable than the rest of us because they already had connections among the other Kashmiris.

Some of these quota students were good students and deserved to be at LHMC; others were just plain lucky and barely got passing grades. One Kashmiri student in particular stands out in my memory. She had the lowest grades in our class and had somehow earned a backsliding caste status despite belonging to a wealthy family. She got a substantial amount of financial assistance every month, which she used to buy expensive clothing and other indulgences. If I had been her, my conscience would never have allowed me to act in such a way.

The students in my class came from many different continents and countries—Africa, Singapore, the Philippines, and all over India. It was a bit of a culture shock for me, and every day I was growing and learning something new. Above all, I was learning to see the world from different perspectives—some of which I respected, and some I only tolerated.

Some of us were more privileged than others, and over time I realized the many financial hardships some of my classmates had to overcome to make it to medical school. Because of these experiences, I became a better person, and I frequently reflected on Bapaji's teachings and values to continue guiding me toward empathy and kindness. There was one student, however, whom I could never respect, despite my best intentions.

She was a brilliant student, but that's where the buck stopped. She had somewhere between four and six siblings, ages four to ten, who would visit her every Saturday and Sunday, and she would always take them to the mess hall to eat. The food at the mess was less than mediocre, but the British mannerisms of the waiters along with the presentation of the food was a touch above. The waiters dressed up in white uniforms and brought the food in dishes, family style, to the table. There were no self-serve buffet lines. Plated dessert was always a part of the evening meal.

When this student brought her siblings to the mess hall, the waiters were very polite but would understandably try to limit the number of dessert plates she was taking for her siblings. She would insist, however, that they give her the desserts of the students who were away for the weekend. I saw her siblings morning and night, following her to and from the mess hall; it was not a pretty sight. I knew her family had limited resources and that she was trying to give her siblings a treat, but I still could not agree with her—I felt she had inexcusably compromised her self-respect.

I still think of her every now and then, and I wonder how she could have approached the situation differently, or if her parents could have raised her differently so she would have acted more appropriately. In the end, she did do well in medical school and had a successful life, but she was the only person I could not respect, despite Bapaji's teachings of compassion (and I think even he would have agreed with me).

As the new class on campus, we did get the traditional hazing from third-year students. They mostly stole our snacks and homemade sweets behind our backs. I do not agree with hazing, but we all tolerated it and quickly moved on when it was over.

A few of us students, including Amina and Fazila and some others from Bombay, wore dresses or skirts and blouses. We were in the minority at LHMC—perhaps in the tenth percentile. Everyone else wore salwar kameez, a few sarees. By the third year, though, we had all given up dresses because our patients were not used to seeing doctors in dresses.

Classes began in August 1958. We had two subjects: Anatomy and Physiology, which were our majors for the first two years, with minors in Physics and Chemistry.

The anatomy lectures were great, but we all got our first rude shock in the labs, dissecting human cadavers. None of us were prepared for that. It was scary and disturbing to be looking at another human being who now smelled of formalin and was being attacked by us, part by part. It felt like we were invading their privacy as they lay on the tables day after day. We dissected them over a span of months, covering the details of nerves, muscles, and bones. We started with the upper limbs, progressed to the lower limbs, on to the thorax, abdomen, and, lastly, the brain. It was stressful, but we all got through it.

None of the other subjects were exceptionally difficult or mentally taxing; they required only concentration and effort.

With time, I adjusted to my new surroundings at LHMC and felt motivated to work hard. I developed a good circle of friends who knew how to balance their studies with their social lives. I am still in touch with many of them who were boarders like me (except for those who have passed away); three of them even made it to my son's wedding in Boston (Fazila's daughter represented her).

One of my closest friends was Amina, whom I met during LHMC's interview. She was a happy spirit, colorful, always full of smiles and laughter. She was also very slim with measurements of 40-24-34. She said that whatever she ate went right to the top. I remember a custom tailor in Delhi once mixed up an order and made some dresses for Amina rather than for our friend Ila, who was very "healthy" (a word for overweight). Once the dresses were finished, they could not be altered because Ila's body type was so different from Amina's. Of course, Ila was upset at first, but she got over it.

Amina's family was originally from Saudi Arabia but had moved to Bombay and owned date farms. Being a Muslim, Amina would sneak into the Hindu temple next to their condo in Bombay to get *prasad*, an offering of food to God which is shared among the worshipers.

Amina's father had passed away, and she lived with her mother and two sisters, one who was older and divorced and another who was younger, very pretty, and going to dental school in Bombay.

Her older, divorced sister would come visit us and ask (or rather *tell*) Amina to buy her *bidis*—skinny, cheap cigarettes made of unprocessed tobacco flakes rolled in a tendu leaf and tied with a colorful string. Bidis were smoked by poor people, and it was looked down on for educated girls to be seen buying them, but since I was Amina's friend, I accompanied her to the bidi shop behind campus, hoping nobody would recognize us.

Amina also had another older sister who was still living in Saudi Arabia and was married to one of the few Saudi men who had a college education. He was the Saudi Arabian ambassador to four European nations. This sister always wore the traditional burka while in Saudi Arabia (even then people could still discern who was who based on the feet and gait), but when she visited her family in Delhi—which she often did—the burka would be off as soon as her feet hit the tarmac, and the smoking and drinking would begin. She was very beautiful, modern, and fashionable in her miniskirts and Western elegance.

Since Amina had connections to the Saudi Arabian embassy, a limo would pick her up at the train station to take her to Bombay for school breaks. She also got to go to the annual gala at the Saudi embassy in Delhi, and I was lucky enough to be invited to come along, too. I loved going; the gala was very formal, and it was interesting to see all the Saudi men greeting us in their traditional national costume.

Amina's younger sister got engaged to a Saudi man who was only a high-school graduate but had a rich family business. So, after finishing her dental degree, the plan was for her to move back to Saudi Arabia, which seemed strange to me. Amina, however, had decided she was not going to marry any Saudi, as there were no educated matches.

Amina visited my family in Ahmedabad, and they were delighted to have her. She even invited my brother Vijay to visit her in Bombay, but she told him to wear shorts so he could pass as a little boy, since her mother did not allow teenage boys.

Amina was kind and helpful but also very outspoken. She and another dear friend, Saroj, went with Bauji and Chaeji to my engagement ceremony carrying lavish gifts to my future in-laws at the Tilak Bazaar. As custom goes, I did not attend. To get to the ceremony, Amina and Saroj had to squeeze their way through the bazaar's traffic jam of shoppers and cargo and street hawkers, all while being overwhelmed by the constant pollution. We had all heard about the craziness of this business bazaar but had never actually seen it. Amina, never one to hold back her opinion, told Chaeji that I had very high standards for my environment and that I would be miserable living in this dump. Even though my fiancé, Raj, was very desirable, Amina said the engagement should be called off. Bauji and Chaeji reassured Amina that my in-laws were planning on moving to the suburbs.

Amina also preferred fun over work, so she graduated six months after me. We stayed friends, though, even after my wedding (which she could not attend due to her exams). After Amina finished medical school, she moved back to Bombay; a year later, I left India, and we lost contact. As time went by, many of us were able to reconnect, but Amina was lost. Whenever we had a reunion in the U.S. or India, no one knew how to get in touch with her. At one of these reunions, we found out she was working in an emergency room somewhere in the Middle East and had performed CPR on Ila's brother. Like me, she had become an anesthesiologist and was married. We all tried to find her using this new information, but no luck.

Fifteen years ago, I got the sad news, thirdhand, that Amina had died. I was extremely saddened. I called my classmate in New York, who had more details. It seems a mutual colleague of ours from the Middle East, an ob-gyn, had contacted this classmate to arrange for Amina to come to New York for medical treatment. Unfortunately, Amina did not make it. She died of ovarian cancer, one of the deadliest, fastest-growing cancers. I learned that she'd had no children and that her marriage had not worked out. I hope that she at least had her sisters by her side during those last few difficult weeks of her life. I miss Amina and hold dear the five and a half years we had together. She lived a life full of laughter and joy, which she shared with everyone who knew her at LHMC. Whenever any of us get together now, we always fondly recall our memories of her. Recently, I found a touching obituary of Amina on the Internet, written by the staff of Al Maktoum Hospital in Dubai, where she had worked. They honored her thirty years of dedicated service, and they mentioned that she was the first United Arab Emirates (UAE) woman to get a private pilot license, which she earned in Miami in 1979. She was also the first UAE female physician and the only UAE female anesthesiologist in the whole country. They wrote that she had a "great sense of fun" and was "above religion, caste, race, or creed"—both very true. The obituary also said that she'd left a daughter behind. If I could find this daughter, it would be wonderful to share old memories of Amina with her.

Another friend I loved dearly and who felt like family was Saroj. Like Amina, we met each other while in medical school, and we stayed in touch until she passed away from breast cancer in November 2012. She was not an A student, but getting top grades did not matter so as long as you were able to pass the annual exams in one or two tries. Saroj was always cheerful, helpful, and full of fun. She was from Delhi, so I visited her family many times and became very close to them during the five and a half years of medical school. One summer, she came with me to visit my family in Ahmedabad, and they all loved her and adopted her as a surrogate member.

Saroj got engaged and married a few months after me. She attended my wedding, and we attended her wedding, which was two weeks after mine. She married a doctor (an arranged marriage by her parents), and she moved to Indore, four hundred miles southwest of Delhi. We stayed in touch through letters at first and then by phone. During the last year of her life, she became a big computer fan and would send me lengthy e-mails about her latest news and health updates.

Both Saroj and her husband were successful doctors, and their three children all became doctors as well. In the late '80s,

Saroj and her husband visited Raj and me in Weston. We all had a wonderful time. Saroj had changed a lot over the years. She had once been easygoing and full of laughter. In her marriage, though, she had assumed many joint family responsibilities, and while she had taken them on gracefully and with a smile, she had become a more dedicated, serious, and caring person. I saw all of this change through our long-distance communication, but when she visited me in person, she became more of the same person I had once known back in medical school. Perhaps while on vacation she allowed herself to return for a short time to her carefree dream world of her past.

After her husband passed away, Saroj visited us again in the summer of 2008 with her sister, who lived in New York. This was Saroj's first solo visit to the States since her husband's death, and we encouraged her to come again. She promised she would return to attend our son's wedding. Unfortunately, three months before the wedding, her cancer had spread, and she could not make the long journey. We communicated until the end—our last phone conversation was two weeks before she passed away. My family and I continue to talk about Saroj and all the good times we shared with her.

Every day at LHMC was an adventure and a chance for me to further develop empathy. One of our classmates had to have an appendectomy. We were all in tears, deeply concerned; we felt like her family, and we surrounded her in her hospital bed. I had never before seen someone so young undergo surgery. The experience was an emotional one, but it also helped me mature.

In October 1958, I had my first fall break. I took the train to Ahmedabad to enjoy the ten days with my family. The twenty-four-hour journey did not bother me one bit. I traveled in the second-class cabin; third class was too crowded (with no AC), and first class was not safe as it could be half empty. I would go on this trip three times every year until my graduation—both in the summer heat and the December cold, no hesitation, only excitement to see family and friends. They were all keen to see me, too, welcoming me with open arms and offering me extra favors as their special guest.

On this first visit home, I excitedly told them about my first semester and my variety of classmates and all the amenities of LHMC's great location. By now, my family had moved into our new house. It was called Chhabil Villa, in memory of Bapaji. The name was inscribed on a plaque next to the entry gate, which remained there up until 2012, when the grounds were converted into condominiums. Even when the family moved to a smaller house in 1995, Chaeji would periodically ask his driver to swing by Chhabil Villa for old time's sake. I enjoyed the fancy new house, but in my heart, I still missed my own cubby in The Bhatia Building and the privacy of living on my own.

In Chhabil Villa, I shared a room with my sister Nirmal. She had the advantage of being the permanent resident, so she had more closet space than me, but I had matured enough at college not to let that bother me much. Moving away from home would slowly but steadily make me a better person.

I headed back to school in November and was as happy as ever. Delhi has nice winters, perhaps a bit on the chilly side. December through February, the temperature hovers around forty to fifty degrees, but it's nice and sunny, which means on campus it was cooler inside the classrooms and warmer outside on the lawns. There was no running hot water, either, so if I wanted a hot bath, I had to have hot water delivered in buckets for a charge. I eventually bought a heating rod, which I immersed in a bucket of cold water in my room, and, a half hour later, the water was warm.

On Tuesdays, some of my classmates and I would go to the Hanuman Temple near campus to pray and ask for good luck (we needed all the help we could get with exams). Even now whenever I'm in Delhi, I visit the Hanuman Temple to offer thanks and appreciation. Tuesday is a special day for the god Hanuman (other gods have their own special days as well). Back when I was at LHMC, most Hindus, even non-vegetarians, abstained from eating meat on Tuesdays, and the clubs did not serve alcohol, called a "dry day" (that's not the case anymore). I heard in the news that the U.S. president Barack Obama was given a small statue of Hanuman, which he carries in his pocket from time to time for motivation and good luck.

The first year at LHMC flew by, and I went back home for the summer and visited with old friends from St. Xavier's. In August 1959, I began my second year of medical school. I had a better dorm room, but I still had to deal with the mean red-faced little monkeys that would invade the room if the veranda door was left ajar. Whenever they did get in, they called all the shots. If I was in bed, I would cover my face with the sheets and let them take all my snacks and anything else from my shelves, without confrontation, and I wouldn't move until after they had left. These monkeys didn't weigh more than fifteen pounds, but they were destructive and could attack. They lived in the greenery around LHMC's Olympic-sized swimming pool (I've heard, though, that they've migrated to more desirable locations because there aren't as many trees and bushes around the pool anymore). They also were frequently seen at the Hanuman Temple, either working with street vendors, performing tricks and dances, or living on their own, asking for goodies from temple visitors.

These little guys were opportunistic, so if you weren't careful with your shopping bags, you'd find yourself watching all your goodies being parceled out and enjoyed by them.

Red-faced monkeys are typically found in northern India. In Ahmedabad, in the south, we had black-faced monkeys. They were much bigger—weighing around thirty pounds—but they were less wicked (and probably less intelligent) than their red-faced counterparts.

My future husband, Raj, frequently had to deal with these monkeys in the Tilak Bazaar, where he worked. Once he forgot his gold Parker pen under his pillow out on the terrace where he slept, and by the time he got back to his room, a red-faced monkey had already found the treasure and was enjoying chewing on it in a nearby tree. Poor Raj tried all sorts of tricks to get the pen back, even using an air gun, but to no avail. The monkey continued to happily gnaw away. Finally, when the monkey had chewed the pen to bits, he threw the pieces back at Raj. Even then, Raj couldn't bring himself to punish these monkeys. They were too amusing to watch, playing with their offspring and taking care of their troop.

For my second year at LHMC, I got to pick my own roommate. She was from Bombay, and we got along well. She was much more worldly and experienced than I was in dating and socializing because she had learned from her two older sisters. She gave me good advice and guided me along my way.

Most of my classmates, in fact, were one or two years older than me. They came from diverse backgrounds and varying income brackets. Divorce was rare back then, so they had stable home lives. Some were extremely rich, but most had modest upbringings and were good, hardworking students.

My time at LHMC made me a better person than I would have been if I had simply stayed at home in my cushiony environment, being catered to and lapping up my everyday comforts without realizing how differently many people throughout the world live. I also learned at LHMC that there is more than one way to be right. I began to open myself up to outside suggestions and practiced looking at situations from multiple perspectives. I developed an understanding for other people's needs—to be empathetic and to see the world through their eyes. I matured, became kinder, more sensitive, and learned to give others the benefit of the doubt. Above all, dealing with so many people every day taught me to overlook the faults of others; no one is perfect.

I had many colorful friends at LHMC. I remember one girl who was six or seven years older than me but was only a year ahead of me in school. She had failed too many times at another medical school and had transferred to ours (and she was still at LHMC when I graduated). She was very sophisticated and charming, always wearing a saree, and she received frequent guests in the lounge. Later I learned that she was dating a famous politician who was forty-eight years old. When one of the other students commented on their age difference, she replied, "He is only forty-eight." I once heard that she had also been fond of Bauji; I put two and two together and realized she must have tried to be friendly with him. To me, of course, Bauji was only my father, but he was forty-one years old, which was not so old by her standards.

This girl was a socialite as well. She told me on the day of my final exams, four days after my engagement, that she had met my soon-to-be husband. What a surprise! She was an interesting girl but also exceptional, one of a kind. Studies were not her priority.

Since LHMC and its dorms were women-only, visitors had to wait in the lounge while the Durban (orderly) brought the guest register with the visitor's name to the student's room. Some of the dorms were as far as .2 miles away from the visitors' lounge! Not all the students, though, were rule-followers. Some snuck through the locked gates at night, and all sorts of stories followed them back the next morning.

Every year in March, LHMC would open its campus to all visitors. It was the only day men were allowed on the grounds. Everyone would be abuzz with preparations. The lawns were manicured and the gardens pruned. Surrounding the Lady Hardinge statue was a bed of beautiful multi-colored roses in full bloom, and we students were forbidden to touch them; they were even protected by guards for the big day. The third-year students provided the entertainment with plays, dances, and other performances. Much to my disappointment, I had no important local relatives to visit my room. Bauji would visit me at least once a year, usually in March, at the end of his annual meeting for the Chamber of Commerce, which was held in Delhi. He would wait for me in the visitors' lounge, and a few times he quietly pointed out to me the students who broke the rules and tell me how he did not appreciate them.

Bauji would visit for a couple days, and we always had a wonderful time together. He had changed from being an over-protective father during my time at St. Xavier's to trusting me 99 percent at LHMC.

Of course I would take full advantage of Bauji's visits and do loads of shopping, an indulgence I looked forward to. Chaeji could not accompany him on these visits because of her responsibilities at home, so she had little idea of my extravagance and lack of control when it came to beautiful clothes. Lucky for me, Bauji had good taste, and he would buy sarees for Chaeji, Auntyji, and me (because I would sometimes accompany him to parties, so I had to be properly attired).

My second year at LHMC was difficult because of the university exam. My study habits revolved around getting the proper amount of sleep, which had been a priority of mine since birth. I had no problems staying up late, but I had never been an early riser. When Bapaji was alive, he was my alarm clock, with multiple snooze allowances, until finally I would give up and get up. He would say, "Sadhna, wake up. Time is money."

At LHMC, I was often behind in the morning, so I'd skip breakfast rather than be late for class. On the days when I needed to be up really early in the morning, my friend Saroj would spray water on to my eyelids gently (with my permission).

But being a sleep hog had its advantages, too. I was able to concentrate for long periods of time in class, and I was able to read my textbooks quickly. My classmates, on the other hand, who also worked hard but were sleep-deprived, would struggle to keep up with the schedule. They would often comment that I slept more, studied less, and traveled to Ahmedabad three times a year, but I still managed to get excellent grades. I had no answer for them. I was in the top 4 percent of my class. I was satisfied with my work, even though I could have done better if I had put in more effort.

In April 1961, I completed my second-year exams and passed all my subjects on the first try. I went to Ahmedabad for the summer and was back at LHMC on August 3 to start my third year.

In our third year, we began working directly with patients. This was different than simply studying textbooks; now we had to not only narrate the patients' signs and symptoms but figure out the next step. All the students were given rotation assignments. The LH hospital was a city hospital and for women only. Adjoining it was a children's hospital. To meet with male patients, we went to the close-by Wellington Hospital. These hours of patient contact opened my eyes to the difficult conditions some people have to live in—poverty, illness, suffering.

Early on, most of us developed Medical Student Syndrome. We became hypochondriacs and diagnosed ourselves with all sorts of illnesses (always assuming the worst, of course). A common cold became in our minds pneumonia or tuberculosis. An upset stomach, perhaps from eating street food, became appendicitis or an intestinal obstruction. Every self-diagnosis, though, was short-lived and ever-changing with our curriculum (but none of us ever thought we had contracted a venereal disease, because we all had a clean slate; and in those days, AIDS and HIV were nonexistent). As we gradually matured in our studies and work, our hypochondriac levels went down.

Unfortunately, I truly did get sick in March 1961 with Hepatitis A, probably from the street food or the swimming pool. At first I thought I had typhoid, but after looking at the patient wards, I knew I did not want to be a patient in the compromised city hospital. Luckily, Bauji's office manager was in Delhi on business. With great difficulty, I booked a trunk call (phone call) to Bauji from LHMC's visitors' lounge. I explained my illness to him, and he agreed that, after getting permission from the warden, I should go home. It was the best decision. I recovered in Ahmedabad for two weeks and then returned to LHMC. When the third-year college exams came around, I heard the usual comments from my classmates: I got sick, visited home, and still I did better than them. But I knew their comments were in good jest, so they didn't bother me.

Sadly, during this time, my close friend Fazila lost her mother to throat cancer; her mother was only forty-eight. I felt terrible for Fazila and became even closer to her. After her mother's death, her father moved to Karachi to be with Fazila's older sister, so

Fazila now traveled to Pakistan during school breaks. I have many wonderful memories of Fazila, and I even visited her in the UK in 1965. She was dating a man from Karachi then, and she eventually moved to Karachi herself, and we all lost touch with her.

Years later, in July 1996, I attended a conference for physicians of Indian origin. It was a three-day affair in Boston, full of lectures, entertainment, and shopping. While I was shopping, I met a nice, outgoing boutique-owner who was from Karachi but now lived in Florida. I casually mentioned to her that I missed my friend Fazila, who had moved to Karachi, and I and all my classmates had lost touch with her. The woman instantly replied that she knew a Bombay woman in Karachi who was tall, slim, and a Bohra (Sunni Muslim-community) doctor. Imagine my surprise and delight! (This was before the days of Facebook magic.) The lady said she visited Karachi every January and offered to try to contact Fazila.

Sure enough, she gave me an update: Fazila's daughter was at Wellesley College and her sons at Boston University, and Fazila frequently flew to Boston. I could not believe it! My excitement was short-lived, however, because I did not think I would be able to connect with her any time soon.

Then, in the middle of January 1997, Boston was in the thick of winter, with plenty of snow and cold. I had had a very tough day at work and had gotten into my car at 6 p.m., worn out from the day, when my beeper went off. I went back into the hospital and was told it was an emergency—I was needed at the other hospital seven miles down the road. When I arrived, I walked into a nightmare of a situation involving a little boy. The doctors were in desperate need of a break, too, so I relieved them for a while. I finally got home around 8 p.m. I was physically and mentally exhausted, and I could not stop thinking about that poor sick boy and his condition. Raj could see the state I was in, and luckily, he had some good news from me: a letter had come from my friend Fazila. I was completely surprised, overjoyed, and instantly happy.

Fazila's letter was long and warm (she always had a knack for letter-writing). She wrote that the woman who owned the boutique had delivered my card as soon as she had landed in Karachi. Fazila said she was so excited to hear from me that she responded immediately. She was a pediatrician for PIA (Pakistani International Airline), so she had the fringe benefit of nearly free air travel every year, and she had rented an apartment on Newbury Street in Boston for many summers. Her daughter, Vazira, was now studying at Columbia. Together Fazila and I planned for her and her husband, Yakub, to visit us in January. We were both looking forward to our reunion after thirty-two years.

We hosted Fazila and Yakub for five days. Before their visit, Raj and I were minorly apprehensive about hosting a stranger (Yakub), but our concerns evaporated as soon as we met him— he was likeable and easy to get along with. We all enjoyed each other's company.

Fazila and I had so much catching up to do that five days wasn't nearly enough time. For one of the nights, we went to our waterfront house on Cape Cod and invited over Booba, another one of our classmates. Fazila is outspoken, while Booba is rather quiet, but we all reconnected easily, talking about our college days, other classmates, Delhi, Bombay, Karachi, the UK, our husbands, our children, ourselves. I guess old friends always stay a part of you.

While at the cape, we visited the beautiful Spohr Gardens in Falmouth. Truly a hidden gem. It was early in the year, but already the daffodils were in bloom. The five-acre gardens were privately owned but open to the public. They were not, however, advertised, so even some of the locals did not know they existed. Our neighbor in East Falmouth, Eva, an eighty-year-old retired nurse, had discovered them and led us to the locale.

The gardens' owners were elderly—an ex-Navy officer and his wife, a nurse. According to Eva, they lived on a private section of the grounds and did not have children. The retired officer had collected many nautical treasures and Navy memorabilia throughout his career and had tastefully intermingled them with the gardens. There were many flowers and budding trees as well, and at the bottom of a hill was an oyster pond with swans.

All of us enjoyed the gardens, especially Booba. She has a passion for gardening, and being from Kashmir, she was born in a city full of daffodils. She was thrilled by all the varieties at the Spohr Gardens, and she even educated us on double daffodils, which have petals in layers.

Since our first visit to the gardens, we have returned many times, bringing along family and friends. Sometimes our visits coincided with the blooming of the daffodils, but even when they didn't, it was still beautiful.

After the gardens, we ate lunch at a nice waterfront restaurant, the Flying Bridge, which overlooks the Falmouth Harbor. Then Booba left and returned to Milton.

Fazila and I continued chatting about the good old days. She recalled how I would often wake up in the middle of the night while at LHMC to find her legs parallel to my face. I replied, yes, she would sneak into my room whenever she saw a lizard on the wall in her room. She said that was an excuse. The truth was, she wanted to sleep under the soft warmth of my velvet *razai* (cotton-filled comforter). We also chatted about some of our other classmates who were not as lucky as us, and Fazila mentioned how nervous she was about our reunion (her cousin had even suggested she get her hair done), but when we were finally face to face, all our apprehension melted away, and we were both our original, authentic selves.

This get-together was the first of many for Fazila, Yakub, Raj, and me. Since then, we have been meeting frequently in Boston. One summer, her daughter, Vazira, came to the cape with her two kids, enjoying the beach and the dock. And eight years ago when they visited, Chaeji was also our guest.

Chaeji was always looking for company, so it was a special treat for her—even more so since it was during Diwali and we went to a friend's house for a party, eating, drinking, and playing cards (they say it's actually lucky to lose at cards on Diwali; that way it brings you luck for the rest of the year).

Vazira is a professor at Brown now, so on any given day, I might get a visit from Fazila. Vazira and her husband attended our son's wedding and met some of Fazila's and my former classmates.

Because I got in touch with Fazila, she has now been able to reunite with many of our old friends in Delhi, and she frequently visits them. Regrettably, we kept having to turn down her invitations to visit her in Karachi, and she eventually stopped asking. (Many years ago, Chaeji and Raj were very keen on visiting D. I. Khan, which is north of Karachi, but they got over that dream long ago due to changing times.)

# Chapter Seven

*Back to 1961.* It was now summer, and I was glad to be back in Ahmedabad. I saw my dear friend Ragini, whom I met those many years ago in 1944 on my second day of preschool at Mount Carmel Convent. We always have so much to share whenever we get together. She is married to a very nice and prominent businessman, a mill owner and industrialist.

I was also glad to spend time with my siblings and extended family. We were still living in Chhabil Villa, so there was plenty of room for everyone. Unji Ben, our wonderful jack-of-all-trades housekeeper, kept everything running smoothly.

While I was finishing up my third year at LHMC, Chachaji and Auntyji had had another baby, a little girl. Chaeji was always Auntyji's support system during her labors—one of the many pros of living with extended family, which outweighed any minor disagreements. Bauji and Chaeji were busy as usual with their social engagements. They enjoyed hosting and entertaining guests—a normal part of their routine—and the rest of us participated as much or as little as we wanted. The summer was typically hot, anywhere from eighty to one hundred five degrees. We didn't have air conditioning, but plenty of fans did the job.

For the first time, we had a puppy in the house. She was a German shepherd, and her name was Gypsy. Chaeji was in charge of her care, although in reality, she only supervised the gardener and the other servants, who did most of the hands-on care.

Our grounds were completely walled-in, so it was fairly safe for Gypsy to roam around outside. Back then, I was not a dog-lover, but I have since been converted and am now dedicated to them (anyone can change, even me!).

In August 1961, I returned to LHMC for my fourth year. It was the same routine as the previous year, with lectures and practicals. We all had full schedules, with rotations in clinics as well as nonclinical rota-tions in pathology, social and preventive medicine, and psychiatry. For one of my psychiatry rotations, I worked for a week at the mental hospital in Agra, a three-hour train ride southeast from Delhi. Agra was a renowned, respected mental hospital, and patients came from all over India (although I do not know exactly what the hospital's treat-ments involve). During my rotation, I visited the woman from Ahmedabad who had sadly become mentally unstable when her husband had forced her to give up her baby to one of his relatives. I hardly recognized her in the hospital; she was no longer the young, beautiful woman she had once been.

Despite my demanding workload, I still made time to visit the Taj Mahal (my classmates and I always knew how to make the best of it and have a good time). The Taj was breathtaking, both in the light of day and by moonlight at night. There are simply no words to do it justice. Truly one of the Seven Wonders of the World.

In April 1962, I was back at LHMC and taking my fourth-year final exams. These were university exams, and I did pretty well. Then I spent another wonderful summer in Ahmedabad.

In August 1962, I returned to LHMC for my fifth and final year. It was interesting to see the fresh students coming in from so many diverse places and backgrounds. I counted my blessings and silently thanked Bapaji for teaching me to focus, work hard, and be happy.

Every year, we students got upgraded to better dorm rooms, so now I had my own room, and I shared a bathroom—a set-up I did not mind at all.

In the first week of December, Bauji was in Delhi to attend a conference and to do some business. It was a special trip because a war had unexpectedly broken out between China and India, and it was important for him to visit and reassure his clients. During his stay, I, of course, indulged in some shopping as well as some goodies he brought from home, and Bauji and I had many mature conversations. Our relationship had evolved to become open and friendly.

When it was time for Bauji to head home, we said our good-byes, and I went back to my dorm room. Three hours later, much to my surprise, the Durban came knocking on the door with the visitors' register. Bauji was back. I was confused and figured he must be doing some fatherly spying on me, but when I met him down in the visitors' lounge, he told me quite the story.

He had been at the bank when he bumped into the son of an old friend. The young man's name was Raj, and he was in Delhi because he was also concerned about the war and its potential impact on his business. Bauji immediately liked Raj and did a quick background check on him. Through mutual connections, Bauji found out that Raj was single and in business with his father.

Bauji was already well-acquainted with the family because they had given Bapaji his first job in 1907 as a teenager, and at first, Raj's family and Bauji's had stayed in touch, but due to some minor misunderstanding, they had not spoken in ten years.

Raj's family was prestigious, with a strong genealogical tree, old money, and a well-established business. Raj himself was impressive, too: settled, cultured, handsome, with a background familiar to Bauji.

So, this all led up to Bauji telling me that he had arranged for me to meet Raj tomorrow in the visitors' lounge. I was shocked.

Until now, my family had never even thought of my getting married. We had focused only on my education, and I still had a year of medical school and an internship to go before I graduated. I could recall only one time that Bauji and Chaiji even mentioned marriage, when I had said that I was not interested in marrying a doctor because I thought married life would be boring, talking shop at home. They had expressed surprise at my opinion but said they would respect it. I was only twenty-two years old and was certainly not running out of time by any means.

I openly resisted, saying that I would meet Raj when Chaeji could be present. Bauji replied that Raj's mother was out of town as well, so we'd simply have to make do with only Raj and his younger brother. Then he reassured me that it was only a meeting, nothing more.

Since Bauji had already made the commitment, I had to honor it, but I told myself it was a formality and that I could forget about the meeting—and Raj—as soon as it was over.

The next day Bauji and I met Raj and his younger brother Darshan as well as the intermediary who had brought them. For some unknown reason, Raj kept his sunglasses on the entire time (maybe he thought it was fashionable, or perhaps he wore glasses and hated them and wore the sunglasses as a cover-up). Afterward, I mentioned the sunglasses to Bauji, wondering aloud if Raj was trying to conceal something. Bauji said he had no explanation for it, but he was sure Raj's eyes were okay.

Even though Raj and Darshan were eight years apart, it still took me a minute to figure out who was who. Raj looked impressive and polished, and I knew his background check had come back clean.

The meeting was short, a simple introduction, and I didn't take it seriously except to honor Bauji's promise. We didn't have much to talk about. Raj was a seasoned player in the world of matchmaking, but I was a novice. This was my first encounter.

For some time after, the meeting was swept under the rug. I was certainly not in a rush to marry, and I thought it was only a passing fancy of Bauji's. In fact, when I went to Ahmedabad for December break, no one mentioned anything. But apparently Bauji was quietly digging even deeper into Raj's background. He found out more about Raj's friends, including girls (but no serious relationships). Raj was six and a half years older than me and came from an affluent family in the very cosmopolitan city of Delhi. He was a groomed, seasoned socialite, while I was in many ways inexperienced in the outside world.

In February 1963, Aunt Bhen and her husband, Jijaji, were on their way to Ahmedabad, so Bauji asked them to swing by 182 Tilak Bazaar while they were in Delhi and sneak a peek at Raj working with his father. Bhen and Jijaji agreed and quietly walked by, keeping their eyes on the shop. Their first time around, they mistook one of the staff to be Raj, but when they walked by a second time to confirm, they identified the right person. Afterward, Bhen visited me at LHMC and gave me her approval. I was not too happy about it; I was not ready to get married.

Next, I heard that another aunt had approved of Raj, too. I could no longer ignore that everyone was in agreement except for me.

In those days, matchmaking discussions were not carried out by phone—as long distance was primitive—only by letter. I don't remember much about how it progressed because I was very focused on my studies. The final exams were approaching fast, and I knew they would be tough. There were five subjects, each of which would be tested through essays, oral exams, and clinical exams. The clinical exams would take place at patients' bedsides in surgery, family medicine, and ob-gyn.

Bauji and Chaeji came to Delhi at the end of March. They were keen to make more progress on their matchmaking. The next step was to meet Raj's parents and family. A location was agreed upon—a restaurant called the Standard in Connaught Place, close to my college. Here I got to see Raj without his sunglasses. I also got to meet his mother, Mataji, and his sister, Munni. Munni was one year younger than Raj; she was beautiful and charming. His mother was forty-seven years old, a well-known beauty. She was vain and had a big personality.

This meeting was more detailed than our previous one, and we had some interesting discussions. Raj asked me if I planned to work after marriage. I replied, "Of course." He said, "Who will take care of the kids?" At this point in my life, I was not thinking that far ahead, and besides, working was an absolute priority for me, with no exceptions. And Bauji and Chaeji agreed with me on that. Well, Raj and I exchanged some honest words (translation: we had an open disagreement). Mataji and Munni said nothing.

Afterward, I told Bauji that I needed to meet Raj alone a few times before coming to any decision. Chaeji thought our age gap was too wide. Three to four years was more appropriate, she said. In many ways, Chaeji was being more pragmatic about the situation than I was. She encouraged me to think openly and realistically about the options and not to get impressed with these beautiful people and their riches.

Perhaps Chaeji was able to be more objective than me because she was familiar with Raj's world. She, too, had grown up with wealth and affluence, and she had even grown up calling Raj's father "Chachaji," uncle. Her maiden surname, Baablas, was the same surname as Raj's father, whose first name was Radheyshiam, but I called him Pitaji. The Baablas were a subdivision of the Bhatia community, and Chaeji's childhood home and Pitaji's ancestral home were on the same street in D. I. Khan, in the Bhatia Mohulla (residential complex) inside the entire Bhatia community. (The Bhatia Mohulla still exists today.)

The talks between our two families continued to progress. Bauji and Chaeji drove to Tilak Bazaar to meet Pitaji and Mataji in their home. There, Bauji made clear that my decision to continue working after children was nonnegotiable. Pitaji responded positively, saying that I was a professional, so there was no question that I would continue to pursue my career (and I believe Raj, after some thought, came to that realization as well). Bauji was reassured. With this issue now smoothed over, even I was starting to warm up to the idea of marriage.

Since I was the bride, the wedding would take place in Ahmedabad. Mataji wanted a wedding in June 1963, but that was not practical. I needed to first complete my internship and then graduate in December 1963.

Raj's wedding party would consist of eighty people traveling by train. At Mataji's request, when the train stopped at important cities along the way, provisions were brought on board such as gourmet meals, desserts, and snacks provided by Bauji's business clients. This was quite the task for Bauji to work on (more on that later).

All the plans were laid out. It was the end of March now, and my finals were only six days away. The pressure was immense; it felt like my life was on the line. It was decided that four days before my final exams, the *sagan* ceremony (the engagement ceremony) would take place. There was no option to reschedule—Bauji and Chaeji were already in Delhi for it. I was concerned that the timing of this ceremony would distract me from my finals. I made it clear to Bauji that, if I failed any of my subjects, I would hold him personally responsible. He completely understood my point, but they were already in Delhi so they wanted to at least start the marriage process.

Luckily, with everything I already had on my plate, I did not have to be present for the *sagan*, which serves as the first commitment from both sides that the marriage plans will continue. The ritual is that the bride's parents and family go to the groom's house and bring baskets of fruits, nuts, sweets, and more. They offer a short *puja* (prayer) for the groom and then shower him with gifts of money. The rest of his family receives gifts as well, and it is customary for the bride's mother to do the giving. Chaeji felt embarrassed giving the gift to Raj's father because she had called him "uncle" for so many years that their relationship was not on equal grounds. They asked Bauji's uncle to perform the ceremony.

Once the ceremony was over, Bauji and Chaeji left for Ahmedabad. My dear friends Amina and Saroj went with them. Afterward, Amina told me every detail of the ceremony from start to finish. Amina had also been to my suburban home in Ahmedabad, so she was able to give me her opinion on the inner-city home of the groom's family. She was detailed, including both positives and negatives. She mentioned that the building was two hundred years old and that it felt like the steps leading to the front door were at a ninety-degree angle. A tough climb even for someone as young and healthy as her. But both Amina and Saroj were greatly impressed by the family's good looks.

Two days before my finals, I had visitors. Raj's sister, Munni, came to my room to bring me to the visitors' lounge. She wanted me to meet her father, Pitaji, and her husband, RG—and, of course, Raj was there as well. RG was a captain in the Indian army, a prestigious position; he was handsome and articulate, and had a sense of humor. I exchanged only a quick "Hello" with Pitaji, and then Raj gave me my ring. The second step of the wedding process was complete.

Word got around fast among my classmates that I was engaged. I was only the second person out of the sixty-five of us to be engaged. That was certainly not planned on my part.

The first day of exams I was eating breakfast when a frequent visitor on campus, Sam, came up to me and congratulated me on my engagement. Sam was the friend of a senior classmate, the one who was dating a politician and liked older men (Bauji did not approve of her). I was shocked that she was talking to me because, even though I had seen Sam many times on campus, we had never even exchanged a "Hello." She said Raj was her friend and my senior classmate's friend, and she added that Raj was a nice guy. Considering my senior classmate's social reputation, I was now a little concerned about Raj's social life, too, but I had no time to think about it. I had to bury it in the back of my mind; I needed to focus on the exams. I could not afford failure.

It was now the middle of April, and the exams were over. One can never be sure of the results, especially with the examiners demanding answers to diagnoses, treatments, etc., while at the bedside of a real patient. I was meeting Raj, Munni, and RG for coffee. RG was always welcome company; he helped me feel at ease, like a breath of fresh air in a stifling room. Over coffee, I got to know Raj better. We had a few similarities, but otherwise, we were worlds apart. He was a cosmopolitan Delhi boy; I was a small-town girl. He was a member of clubs, a tennis player, had a wide social circle, indulged in motorbikes, and enjoyed partying. By Indian standards, he should have been married by now. I mentioned to Raj my conversation with Sam, but he didn't reply. It didn't matter to me. His past was of no consequence to me. What I cared about was our future. And I was confident in it.

He told me he had distributed our food gifts from the sagan ceremony to his friends, and they were all overwhelmed by the generosity and lavishness of my parents. (Unfortunately, all the fresh fruit that could not be eaten in time by his family and friends had to be thrown away.)

In the summer of 1963, I was back in Ahmedabad, anxiously waiting for my exam results and wondering what my future would look like. Finally, I got the wonderful news: I'd passed! I had become the first doctor in our family. I was very happy with my grades, and Bauji was relieved that he did not have to feel guilty about timing my engagement so closely to my finals. He said he knew from the beginning that I could handle everything on my plate.

The exam results had been published in the local Delhi newspaper, so Raj's family called to congratulate me. Saroj called as well to give me more details. She said I had finished fifth in our class of sixty-five. I was thrilled. I received an outpouring of congratulations from many other friends and family members. Everybody was celebrating. I wished Bapaji could have been one of them; he would have been even happier than me. My becoming a doctor had been his biggest hope and dream. I had not let him down.

Next on my calendar was an internship starting on June 15 and ending December 14. Graduation would be December 15; I would be awarded an MBBS degree, and then I was on my own.

The family priests exchanged our *kundalis* (birth horoscopes) to ensure marriage compatibility, and after that, the wedding was set for January 19, 1964. Mataji wanted the wedding earlier, but I insisted that I first needed to complete my internship and get my degree. I was in no rush. I needed to get married in my own time.

Now began the shopping in preparation for the wedding. Chaeji offered to do my shopping in Benares, but since I could not be there to give my input, I declined. Benares, also known as Varanasi or Kashi, is a city on the Ganges River, five hundred miles southeast of Delhi. It is believed to have been settled around 2000 BCE and is one of the oldest continually inhabited cities in the world. It is also the spiritual capital of India, the holiest of the seven sacred cities.

Like the city of Haridwar, Benares has bathing ghats (platform steps) for ablutions, and it has Aarti, the ceremony of light with lamps floating down the river, which has existed from the ancient past to today. Today it is famous as well for its beautiful handwoven sarees, ranging in price from a thousand to more than one hundred thousand rupees. Chaeji frequently visited Benares because her father and brother had settled there after the partition. I would have gotten more for my money to shop in Benares than to buy the same sarees in a Delhi designer store, but I wanted to see and choose them for myself.

Bauji was my shopping companion, as he had been the past five years. This time, however, we had difficulty agreeing on what to buy. Bauji loved one saree in particular, which I did not like. It was handwoven, pink, with detailed, real-silver threads and a dark-red border—a masterpiece from Benares. I told Bauji that although he had excellent taste, contrasting borders were not fashionable in Delhi right then. This saree was made in an Ahmedabad style. (I must admit, I have been complimented for my taste in clothes; I may not wear the most expensive things, but they are elegant and coordinated.)

Before starting our shopping, Bauji and I had agreed on a budget for my sarees and jewelry. We had also agreed that I would be able to choose what to buy within that budget. But Bauji had his heart set on this pink saree. He said it would be an extra gift for me, excluded from our budget. I quickly agreed! In later years, this type of saree became extremely fashionable, and I was the envy of many when I wore it. Of course, Bauji could not help but remind me of his insistence and attempts to persuade me. I have taken special care to preserve this saree over the years—the price of silver is high nowadays, so only synthetic silver is used in today's sarees. My saree has a few tarnished streaks in the silver due to oxidation, but that only makes it look mature, like a rare wine, and it represents all the ways I, too, have matured over the decades. Whenever I wear it, the memory from fifty-three years ago feels like yesterday.

June came around, and it was time for me to start my internship. I moved into the intern building at LHMC, which was very different from the usual dorms. It was freestanding but still a part of campus and within easy walking distance to the hospital. The building itself was new and modern, and it was outside of the no-entry zone, so visitors could come and go freely. Plus, each room had an attached bath and a nice veranda. I was happy with my room and furnished and decorated it tastefully.

One day I had an unexpected visitor in my new room. Munni had been in the area, so she stopped by to say "Hello." I was excited to see her because I had just received a gift from a friend in the U.S.—a pack of six lipsticks that stacked one on top of the other. Impressive and unusual. I showed it to Munni and was shocked when she told me to divide it so she could have half. I replied that with the way the lipsticks fitted into each other, it could not be divided, so I offered all of them to her. She accepted without hesitation. I had to blink back tears—after all, I had owned the gift barely long enough to give it away. But my tears were happy tears, too. My spur-of-the-moment decision to give Munni my special gift made me think of the many times Bapaji had taught me generosity. I knew that he would he have been proud of me in that moment.

Life went on, and I was busy with my internship, which consisted of two-month rotations in surgery, family or internal medicine, and ob-gyn, followed by graduation on December 15. My initial plan was to become a surgeon, but Bauji discussed it with me, and we decided it would be better to be an ob-gyn, since they each had a gender preference: female surgeons were few while male ob-gyn's were few.

Some of my other classmates were now engaged. Saroj was engaged to an ENT doctor (ear, nose, and throat) who was from Indore, 400 miles south of Delhi. It was an arranged marriage. I was sad that Saroj and I would be separated. Also, another classmate, Meena, was engaged to a wealthy businessman (again, arranged).

My meetings with Raj became more frequent. He was still getting used to the idea of settling down. I, however, was already busy planning our future. To be honest, I was in love with him. Raj's best friend and social sidekick, Vinod, was happily married, so Vinod was probably influencing Raj to do the same, but Raj was taking his time, still enjoying his social life with the likes of Sam. I was not worried, though, because I could see that he was slowly coming around to the idea.

On September 3 Munni again visited me. This time she brought me *mithai* (Indian sweets). It was her birthday, and because she was the only daughter in her family, Pitaji always made it a very special occasion. I wished Munni a happy birthday and mentioned that we were both Virgos, since my birthday was September 15. Munni was five years older than me and had two children—a three-year-old son and an infant daughter, both very lovable. After that day, I always remembered her birthday. In these early years, I always sent her a card, but as technology progressed, I called her instead. (I took it upon myself to remind Raj of the birthdays and anniversaries on both sides of our family.) Munni is no longer with us, but I still think of her every September 3.

September 15 came around, my birthday. I was twenty-three years old. This was my first and only birthday I would celebrate as a fiancée, so I wanted to make it special. I invited Raj, Munni, RG, and Kailash (their friend) to my room for an evening party. I went shopping and filled my table with pastries, snacks, and goodies. I also wanted to have *ras malai* (a rich cheesecake of sorts), but I did not have a refrigerator, so I made a quick trip to the store right before the party. I came back in time to be ready to receive my guests, but when I opened my door, I got a big surprise. Raj, Munni, RG, and Kailash were already there.

They had crashed my party, sneaking in through the window while I was out, and they had already eaten most of the treats. They were impishly smiling for what they thought was a great accomplishment. Meanwhile, I was at a loss for words. All I could manage was, "Today is my birthday." I wasn't angry so much as surprised at their dismissive attitudes and actions. They did not understand how I felt, but I said nothing more about it. I kept calm and simply told them to enjoy the ras malai. (From the brief get-togethers we'd already had at coffee shops, I knew they were foodies, so with the food gone, I knew the party was over before it even began.)

After that, Raj and I did not meet up much, and when we did, we did not discuss any future plans. He was always late, too, blaming the traffic, while I was always punctual (it was second nature to me).

In October, Bauji and Chaeji came to Delhi to do more wedding shopping, and it was then that I got another surprise visit (although, to be fair, all visitors were pretty much a surprise to me because I didn't have a phone for them to reach me on). I was working at the hospital when my friend, Amina, full of excitement, ran in and told me that she had met Mataji and Raj. She was excited because Mataji was well-known in the community as an exceptionally beautiful woman. Mataji looked like a model or a movie star, always dressed up and wearing lots of jewelry. Amina told me to come quickly because Mataji and Raj had brought a nice gift basket with goodies for me, and they were waiting in my room.

When I got to my room, however, I realized that there was more to the visit than a simple gift basket. Mataji told me, "Tomorrow is Karva Chauth." Karva Chauth is a one-day Hindu festival celebrated by married women. They fast all day for the welfare of their husbands. The festival is about ten days before Diwali, so it varies anywhere from late October to early November. The fast starts before the sun rises—no food, no drink, not even water—and it does not end until the moon rises (if it is cloudy, the fast ends based on the expected time of the moon). In the evening, before the conclusion of the fast, the family gathers together for a *puja* (prayer).

Mataji had brought me the gift basket to enjoy in the early morning hours before the fast began (the mother-in-law is also supposed to receive a gift of a saree from the daughter-in-law). She added that I did not have to fast, but Raj interrupted her, saying I would, of course, fast and do great.

I was familiar with the details of Karva Chauth—I had grown up watching Chaeji and Auntyji observe it in Ahmedabad— but I was still technically not married. Raj, however, was set on it, so I agreed. Before this, me fasting was unheard of. I had never attempted anything like it, and I was not looking forward to it.

The next day I went shopping with Chaeji and Bauji, and I told them about my plight. Chaeji had already observed Karva Chauth in Ahmedabad three weeks before (since festivals are determined by the moon and stars). They were both surprised I would be fasting this year—I was only engaged.

As I had expected, the fast was very taxing for me, especially the lack of water while out in the brutal hot weather. But I survived, thank God. I will never forget my first Karva Chauth. Since then, I have observed Karva Chauth regularly, missing only three out of the past fifty-three years. The first miss was due to my pregnancy, and the second and third because of traveling (I also had to modify the date of Karva Chauth once because I was on a twenty-four-hour hospital rotation).

Raj, against my better judgement, has been fasting with me for the past ten years. So far we have fulfilled the fast 100 percent. In the future, though, we might have to modify it; time will tell.

Karva Chauth has become commercialized over the years, even in Boston. It's grown from being a simple fast to all glitz and glamour, with *puja* (prayer) being held on a large communal scale in the Hindu temples.

After one week, Bauji and Chaeji completed their wedding shopping (according to tradition, the bride's family bestows gifts on the groom's wedding party), and they went back to Ahmedabad to start on all the mega-wedding plans. Now it was my turn to focus on my own wedding shopping. Working around my hospital schedule, I went shopping with Mataji and Raj. Luckily, we all had similar taste, so the decisions were easy.

During the wedding planning, Bauji received a no-compromise request from Mataji: Raj had to sit on a mare at the start of the wedding procession. In northern India, the groom rides a white mare to the bride's house, encircled by his family and friends. In Gujarat and Bombay, on the other hand, the groom arrives in a car decorated with flowers—usually a convertible or sometimes a vehicle equivalent to a limo. Since Mataji was from Delhi, the white mare was a must.

This request was tough for Bauji. If he had simply needed to find any horse, he would have been fine, but it had to be a white mare. He ended up having to drive with a friend's son twenty miles outside of Ahmedabad to a village where a contact of Bauji's had told him he could find a mare. Well, turns out the mare was the size of a donkey and very sorry-looking—undernourished and perpetually exhausted. Bauji was disappointed, but he had no other choice. He explained to the owner that he needed the mare for a groom to ride in a wedding procession. The owner asked how big the groom was, and Bauji replied, gesturing at his traveling companion, "The same size as my friend." Like Raj, this young man was six feet tall and one hundred eighty pounds. The problem was evident.

Bauji had to find a solution, so he asked the owner to feed the mare very well for the next three months at Bauji's expense, adding that the mare only needed to sustain Raj's weight for five to ten minutes. This was a win-win for the owner, and he quickly agreed. Bauji was relieved.

Bauji narrated this adventure to the family, and we were all amused (he shared the story partially just so everyone would know he had done his best under the circumstances). When the wedding day came, Raj did ride the little mare for the five required minutes, and then he immediately switched to a waiting car. The owner probably pocketed the extra feeding money from Bauji because the mare looked just as sad and sorry as she did on the day Bauji first looked at her. I wish we had thought to take a picture of Raj riding that poor *ghodi* (pony)!

This tradition of riding a white mare runs strong in Ahmedabad these days, so I don't think it is nearly as challenging to find a mare to rent. In fact, in Delhi and northern India, the demand is so great during the peak wedding season that mares are imported from surrounding areas. And these mares are majestic, with their pure white coats and saddles beautifully decorated with colorful throws and bells.

In fact, for the past ten years, it has been fashionable here in New England to have the groom arrive on a mare, even if the groom is Jewish, Catholic, or Protestant, not Hindu. Passersby are mesmerized by the procession, some of them having never seen anything like this before.

Back in Ahmedabad, Bauji was neck-deep in wedding preparations. With such a detail-oriented, persistent personality, he was working on the plans many hours a day. In Delhi, I was solely focused on my internship.

Finally December 15 arrived: my graduation. Unlike the States, where graduations are big, glittery affairs, my graduation was modest. The students traveled by bus to the Delhi University campus, where we were handed our diplomas. A few of the local students had their families present, but for the rest of us, the ceremony was simply a long-awaited formality to moving on with our careers.

It was time for me to say goodbye to Lady Hardinge Medical College and goodbye to five and a half bittersweet years. Little did I realize when I first arrived at LHMC how much I would grow and mature here. I had become a compassionate, sympathetic, and resilient adult, and I was so proud of fulfilling Bapaji's dream for me. He had sown the seeds, and I had brought them into fruition. I missed him now more than ever. With his teachings as my guide, I would always have the courage to follow the right path for me and never to have regrets about it.

I packed up most of my belongings, leaving only a few essentials with Saroj to collect after my wedding, and I said goodbye to my classmates and friends. We were all going in different directions, just as we had come from different directions in the beginning. I was returning to Delhi after the wedding to live with Raj, so I would be able to stay connected with some of my classmates. Others, however, were moving back to their homelands, satisfied with their memories at LHMC and ready to move on.

# Chapter Eight

*I had one last train ride back* to Ahmedabad before it would no longer be my home. Raj took me to the train station (I reminded him to be on time because he was consistently late, and I didn't want to miss my train). Luckily, our wedding was set for January 19, 1964, so I had one month to relax and mentally prepare. There is a blackout period for Hindus when auspicious occasions, such as weddings, are not to be performed. The blackout, called *Tara Duba* ("stars are drowned"), is based on astrology and typically falls between mid-December and mid-January. For those who believe, there is a puja for all ailments and problems. Like everything else, Tara Duba has been modified over the years. Many weddings are now held during Tara Duba because brides and grooms are coming to India from all over the world, and one of the easiest times to get away is at the end of December. So the quick fix for them is to get a special *puja* (prayer) performed by the pandit, the family's designated priest, to abort and cure the inauspicious stars.

When I arrived in Ahmedabad, the entire family was very excited for my upcoming mega-wedding, and by early January, the preparations were in full swing. Every evening, we would gather to exchange ideas and review wedding duties (all of Bauji's office staff had been assigned jobs related to their expertise).

The family also decided on the menu for the big dinner on January 18, the evening before the wedding, when Raj's wedding party would arrive. It would be a special Gujarati dinner. Bauji assigned his brother-in-law the job of supervising the chefs in the backyard, where the meal would be prepared. Bauji's brother-in-law was a good man and performed his duties well and with great pride.

We had a constant flow of relatives at our door. Bhen and her family had come, Chaeji's family, too, and aunts and uncles from all over were arriving as planned. Devi Singh, the old chef from Bauji's office, was in charge of our kitchen for the day-to-day meals, and he was helped by our jack-of-all-trades multitasking housekeeper, Unji Ben. Everyone was excited to pitch in; nobody complained.

The venue for the wedding was going to be our own home, Chhabil Villa. The grounds were prepared with decorations and lighting, and the front gate was draped in fresh flowers. The last wedding in our immediate family had been Bhen's, which had taken place shortly after the death of Baji, my grandmother, so the mood had been somber. And the wedding of Bauji's brother, Chachaji, which had taken place in Delhi, was also soon after a death in the family (an uncle's). So with my wedding, Bauji was excited to have only to entertain, entertain, entertain.

The night before the wedding came, and it was time for our lavish Gujarati dinner. This pre-wedding dinner was customarily held at the groom's home, but Bauji wanted all his Gujarati friends and business associates to be invited to the festivities.

The dinner was a sit-down *thali* dinner with multiple courses. A *thali* is a big plate with six to ten small bowls on it, and in our bowls was gourmet Gujarati cuisine at its best. (These days, many restaurants offer all-vegetarian Gujarati food.) There were five hundred guests at the dinner, and thankfully, everything went smoothly. Bauji was especially happy that he had finally had the chance to show his gratitude to a community which had supported him for more than twenty-five years.

Meanwhile, Raj and the *baraat* party (groom's party) of eighty people had begun their twenty-four-hour train journey from Delhi to Ahmedabad on the morning of the eighteenth. As requested by Mataji, they stopped along the way in different train stations to be treated to meals, snacks, tea, and refreshments by Bauji's business clients. Again, everything went smoothly; the journey and everyone's hospitality along the way were perfection.

Bauji and his friends greeted the baraat party at the train station on the morning of the nineteenth, the day of the wedding. He had cars waiting to transport them. In those days, Ahmedabad had only one nice hotel, so Bauji's friends had generously loaned Bauji their houses for the wedding party. The houses were newly built (some of them not even occupied yet), and they were in a gated community about two miles from our house.

Bauji pulled out all the stops for our guests. Along with the indulgent, lavish meals, he also provided on-site services for all of their needs: a shoe polisher, a barber, a valet service for ironing, and a tailor for any last-minute alterations. Bauji even provided them with transportation for a tour of Ahmedabad. Ahmedabad has the best weather in January: sunshine, no rain, and comfortable temps in the sixties and seventies. The entire baraat party was overwhelmed with such generous, VIP treatment.

The wedding procession began from the baraat party's location at 8 p.m. on the evening of the nineteenth. The weather was beautiful, the trees and flowers in glorious full bloom. Weddings in India typically take place in the evening because it feels more glamorous for the groom's procession to walk the streets with lights, music, singing, and dancing.

Raj began the procession as Mataji had wanted, riding that poor undernourished mare. This part was understandably short, and I'm sure both the horse and Raj were relieved when Raj hopped into the waiting car covered in fresh flowers.

The groom's party arrived at Chhabil Villa on time at 8:30, the band playing and everyone singing and dancing. Bauji's exhaustive planning had so far gone off without a hitch.

Next, Raj and I exchanged garlands, a tradition called *jaimala*. Then the wedding dinner began, and all the guests mixed and mingled. Everyone was putting on a fashion show, displaying their wealth with sarees and jewelry. Raj liked British fashion, so he was wearing a Western suit, along with a turban which had a very heavy silver *mukut* (it was so heavy, it felt almost like a punishment). *Mukuts* were worn in ancient times by the kings during their coronations. Through the changing times, old values have resurfaced, and most grooms do not wear Western suits anymore; instead, they wear an *achkan* (a long, heavy, festive silk coat), and they pair it with *churidar* (tight, pajama-like pants), and they wear a turban called *pagdi*.

After the gourmet dinner and desserts, it was close to midnight and time for most of the guests to leave. Usually only close family to the bride and groom attend the actual wedding ceremony, which is conducted by the family pandit and lasts about an hour. A wedding pagoda is typically built on the lawn for the ceremony, but in our case, our entry hall was large enough for both the pagoda and all the seating for our guests.

Bauji asked our pandit to keep the ceremony fairly short. The pandit mostly spoke in Sanskrit, so I only understood the small part said in Hindi. Then the ceremony ended, and I was married.

Baji and Bapaji were with us in spirit and in all of my family's thoughts throughout the festivities. Bapaji's dream of my becoming a doctor had come true, but I do not think even he could have guessed that one day his granddaughter would marry the grandson of his very first boss. Bauji told me that Bapaji had remembered Pitaji, Raj's father, when Pitaji was only five years old. Pitaji was well-disciplined, while his older brother, Chachaji, was bit more wild, always running around.

Everything in the celebration had gone perfectly, and Raj's family was very happy. Bauji, too, was satisfied; he had put his heart and soul into this extraordinary, lavish affair, and all his hard work had paid off. Many other weddings would take place at Chhabil Villa in the future, but Bauji later told me that none of them meant so much to him or commanded so much of his time and effort than my wedding and my little brother's.

Munni, Raj's sister, was given the list of all the gifts we were giving to her entire extended family. As was the custom, we gave sarees to the women, suits to the men, and silk material for salwar kameez (shirts) for the elderly grand-aunts. There was no reciprocity of gifts from their family to ours, but no one made an issue of it. Every family has their own customs.

The next morning, Raj and I left for Delhi. Luckily, we had our own two-berth private cabin on the train. For me, the journey was nothing unusual—I had gone back and forth many times from LHMC to Ahmedabad.

When we arrived in Delhi, it was freezing cold—in the low forties—and no sunshine. Now it was on to Tilak Bazaar, my new home. I had heard about this place from Amina, my outspoken friend, after she had attended my engagement ceremony at Tilak Bazaar. Per tradition, I had not attended the ceremony, but Amina told my parents I would not be happy in such a crowded, polluted place. Bauji and Chaeji, however, reassured Amina that Raj's family was planning on moving to the suburbs. Well, they hadn't moved yet, and Amina had been right: this place was going to be tough for me. It was almost like camping, long-term. Raj's and my room was simply a partition off the living room, seven feet by five feet, with no privacy. The toilets were also on the opposite end of the house from the bathrooms, which did not make sense to me, and it took me some time to adjust to the constant back-and-forth flow of traffic. This was poverty in the house of the rich. Raj assured me that soon a room would be built on the upper floor for us. *Fine*, I said to myself, *I can endure this.*

Meanwhile, Raj's wedding party had begun departing from Dehli. It was then Munni realized we had given her a surplus of sarees and salwar kameez material, and she conspired with Mataji to keep eight to ten of the sarees and hand out instead the rest of the salwar kameez material. All the sarees were identical, so she and Mataji kept one each for themselves and planned on returning the rest to the designer store for cash. Since I was now living with them, they shared their plan with me and asked me to keep quiet if my family asked about the gifts. I was very disturbed by their plan—shocked, in fact, by their petty deceit—but I agreed to say nothing.

Luckily, at least Munni's husband, RG, always had a cultured, welcoming air about him, and he suggested to Raj that we go on a honeymoon. This turned out to be a wonderful idea. Raj suggested Mussoorie, a town at the foothills of the Himalayas. I had never seen snow fall before, so I was very excited.

Growing up, Raj had frequently visited Mussoorie with his family when it was warm. One year he spent the entire summer there while recovering from typhoid. Another year, they visited in the winter because they wanted to see snow fall, but they got more than they bargained for when they got hit by a blizzard, and all the roads were closed for a week. And during the year of the partition, when the entire country was in turmoil, Pitaji rented a house in Mussoorie for the safety of his family while he commuted to Delhi for work. Lucky for them, they were wealthy and could afford such luxuries.

Mussoorie is about a six-hour drive from Delhi. Raj and I took the night-train to Dehradun and then a one-hour cab to Mussoorie. The town sits at an altitude of six thousand feet and is beautiful—clean and heavily influenced by British culture. It has many hiking trails, some of which lead to small waterfalls, and it is home to many elite boarding schools and summer cottages owned by the rich. In the warm months, Mussoorie is all abuzz, a welcome respite from the Delhi heat. All the hotels are booked, the indoor skating rinks are packed, and walking down the main road is like walking down the red carpet alongside the who's who of famous people. The winters, however, are pretty quiet, since few people are crazy enough to risk the snow and all its complications. (I later learned that Bauji wrote to Pitaji to say that Pitaji should not have encouraged Raj and me to go to Mussoorie because it can be dangerous in the winter. Luckily, our trip was uneventful.)

Raj and I stayed in a four-star hotel. Breakfast was served on the grounds under sunny skies, and our favorite restaurant was Kwality, where we alternated between ordering Chinese and

Indian food (Chinese food in India is very different from the Chinese food in the U.S.). There was also a fast-food place that Raj had loved ever since he was a kid; it served potatoes, *puri* (puffed fried bread), and mouth-watering mango pickle.

The temps hovered in the thirties the entire time we were there, but sadly, no snow. (I would not see snow fall until 1966, when we lived in London.) We could only stay for a week in Mussoorie because my friend, Saroj, was getting married in Delhi, and it was important that we support her and attend her wedding.

Even though our honeymoon was short, it was still perfect. It gave Raj and me the time and space to establish a foundation of understanding and a warm relationship, which would serve us for the rest of our marriage.

We returned to Delhi refreshed and happy. Little did I know that the next chapter in my life would be very difficult. As the years have gone by, I have been able to deal with my emotions, but still, the time from February 1964 to September 1965 left me with lifelong scars.

But first, some background on my new family. Ruby was the family dog, a big German shepherd. Raj was her main caretaker, and he took her for walks in the morning and evening. She greeted me by jumping up on me, which I tolerated even though I was not a dog-lover (but years later, I would change my mind). Ruby was a strict vegetarian—absolutely no meat for her. Mataji and I were the only vegetarians among the people in the house.

Pitaji, the family patriarch, was a tall, slim man in his early fifties. He had no mentors. His father had died young, and his older brother, Chachaji, had suffered financial loss and was being subsidized by Pitaji. Chachaji lived with his second wife, Chachiji, across from us in a modest apartment. Chachiji was born Muslim and, from what I knew of her, was a very nice person. She had class, was slim, and must have been beautiful in her youth. She often visited Mataji in the afternoon. (Chachiji's first wife was a Hindu and now lived in Haridwar, having taken a sanyas, the life stage of renunciation. We visited her, and, from what little I saw of her, she seemed like a very nice person, too. She and Chachaji had a daughter together who was beautiful and had a TV personality.)

Chachaji had once enjoyed—and then lost—a life of luxury and indulgence, but both he and Chachiji were still kind, loving people (although I did not know them extremely well).

Soon after Pitaji married Mataji, his mother died of breast cancer, and then his younger sister died as well. So, at an early age, Pitaji inherited both a lot of responsibility and wealth. He was an active man, a member of two country clubs, and he played tennis six days a week until he was over eighty-plus years old. Tennis was his social life, and he had good friends.

Pitaji also drove himself everywhere. He was an aggressive driver. Raj was an expert driver, too, as he had been driving years before he was a teenager. Even before Raj could drive, though, when Pitaji was the only driver in the family, he still had two cars: a convertible Packard (an imported luxury car) and later on, a Vauxhall. These cars were comparable to Cadillacs and Mercedes in the U.S. Back in those days, there were very few cars manufactured in India. There was a boxy Ambassador (similar to an Austin), a Fiat 1100 (which had a waiting list of more than eight years), and a Triumph Sport. And even then, the parts for these cars were still imported.

Pitaji parked his cars not by choice in a garage a quarter of a mile from his home. It was tandem parking (cars parked one behind the other), and the spaces were measured down to the inch. The walk between the garage and home was a crowded, messy maze of animals and people.

Pitaji was fun-loving but also very disciplined and hard-working. Six days a week, he worked downstairs at his business from morning until 7 p.m., taking a break only for lunch and a short siesta. He was a self-learned man, fluent in Urdu, Pushto, Hindi, and English. He was an excellent provider for his wife and children, frequently indulging them in luxury vacations to different towns in the foothills of the Himalayas. He had plenty of cousins, and they all worked in the cloth business, either in Delhi or Bombay. He was not very warm with them, however, because he tended to be self-centered (although I did learn later that he helped some of his relatives who were refugees from Burma, giving them room in his house during their transition, and he helped a few others who turned to him as well, so he did show kindness).

Mataji is more difficult for me to describe. I have mixed feelings about her. She was exceptionally beautiful—the whole Derawal community raved about her—but she was vain, very much aware of her beauty. Her marriage to Pitaji had been arranged, and Pitaji was far too protective of her. Unlike my parents' marriage, theirs was founded on joint family decisions. Mataji had the heart and brains to become someone wonderful, but it was like she lived in a glass cage. She was to be seen and admired but not to have an identity of her own.

There is a saying in Hindi: "A frog's whole world is the well in which he resides." Mataji's well was tiny. She had no relationship with anyone in her family except her father and her brothers and sisters. She had no friends. She attended weddings and celebrations only on Pitaji's side of the family, but, even then, she had minimal interaction and remained emotionally distant. She had no parties or social gatherings at her own home, entertaining only her immediate family. Pitaji, it seemed, never encouraged her to find her place in the world. As a result, she was seen as snobbish and proud, even though she was actually a good person.

To be fair, Pitaji probably had to be protective of Mataji earlier in their marriage, especially during the partition, because they lived in a predominantly Muslim area. Later on, though, he could have encouraged her to get out and be part of the world. But he never did. Instead, Mataji's life consisted of going to the temple in the morning (chauffeured and accompanied by Pitaji) and then returning home and spending the rest of the day cooking. All their meals were made from scratch. It was Mataji's way of showing her love for her husband and children. The only other occasional part of her life was shopping, but, of course, she did not go on her own. She was accompanied by either Pitaji or, in later years, Munni.

Raj was Mataji's firstborn and quite clearly the favorite. Pitaji and Mataji's second son died of tetanus around age seven. According to Raj, he was a good, pleasant kid. This tragedy took a severe toll on Mataji. She felt helpless, so she turned to religion, becoming even more devout.

Munni was one and a half years younger than Raj, and the two of them got along. She was the only daughter, so she had a special place in Mataji's heart. When Munni reached adulthood, she became Mataji's advisor. Mataji never questioned Munni's judgment, right or wrong.

Mataji adored Munni's husband, RG. He had the charm (and plenty of compliments) to win her over. In fact, I'd be hard-pressed to find anybody who wouldn't be impressed by his agreeable personality and demeanor.

I suppose you could say that RG "conspired" to marry Munni. He became Raj's friend for the sole purpose of getting to know her. And his plan worked: she fell in love with him. At first, Pitaji was against their relationship, but he eventually relented. (Munni and RG are still a handsome couple today.) When I moved in to Raj's family's home, RG was deployed in a combat zone, so Munni was living with us, along with her three-year-old son and one-year-old daughter.

The third son, Darshan, was the black sheep of the family. He was eight years younger than Raj, and their personalities couldn't have been more different. Darshan was the baby, and he stayed that way his whole life. Ironically, though, he had an impressive stature—six foot one, and on the heavier side compared to Raj. He was more social than Raj, too, and easier going. I could converse with Darshan on light topics, like entertainment and social happenings.

At the time I married Raj, Darshan was a senior at a liberal arts college, but that was only a front for his more enjoyable pursuits. His favorite and only pastime other than playing tennis was going to the movies. Every time he went to the movies, he would try to hide it, but Munni always caught him in the lie. She could smell the cigarette smoke on him (movie theaters were full of smokers back then).

Columnist Ann Landers wrote, "Class bespeaks an aristocracy that has nothing to do with ancestors or money." If you have class, you've got it made. If you don't, no matter what else you have, it doesn't make a difference. Every member of Raj's family had a PhD in the art of receiving but had never learned the ABC's of generosity (or even *reciprocity*). Their version of charity began at home, with the only recipients being themselves. Pseudo class, yes; real class, no. They were slum millionaires, and I was now a part of them.

With the honeymoon in Mussoorie over, it was time to get back to reality. Soon after, I had my first run-in with my new sister-in-law and mother-in-law. We had our own family *dhobi* (laundryman) for our clothes, as was the practice in all households. One day I gave him some of my towels and sheets to do as well. Munni was not happy that I was unloading my designer towels and sheets to the dhobi, and she complained to Mataji about it. I was dumbstruck. What else could I have done? They didn't own a washing machine, and they didn't have any help at home for handwashing delicates. I was hurt and frustrated; still, I kept a respectful silence on the issue.

I realized then that my dream wedding was over and that it was time to move on with life. And it did not look inviting: a jungle of thorns with only a single rose bud—my marriage to Raj—which would bloom only if I put in a lot of effort. That night I shared the laundry incident with Raj. I was deflated and in tears. It felt like my hopes for a wonderful future had been shattered. Raj was sympathetic and tried to console me.

Every day Raj and I were getting closer, learning more about each other. We had different values, priorities, and upbringings, but we were slowly adjusting through compromise. He would become my protector and shield between me and his family. This incident was only the beginning of our clashes.

Saroj's wedding came soon enough—in Delhi, in early February. It was nice to be a part of her wedding, and since Raj's family was my family, they were also invited for a two-day celebration.

Then in mid-February, I went back to Ahmedabad to visit my parents for the first time since the wedding, a custom in India called *fera*. Per tradition, I visited them alone first. Raj would join me after a few days, and we would leave together to our new home in Delhi.

The visit was a much-needed break from all the stress I was dealing with in my new family. Of course, everyone in Ahmedabad presumed I was very happy with my new life. When Raj arrived, everyone gave him a royal welcome with open arms, catering to his every whim. We were overrun with invitations from relatives and friends to eat breakfast, lunch, and dinner with them. And at home, Chaeji, Auntyji, and our housekeeper, Unji Ben, were busy preparing gourmet meals for whenever we were around. They even planned a daytime outing for us to Kankaria Lake, where Raj enjoyed rowing (one of his hobbies), and we meandered among the beautiful gardens.

My brothers, sisters, and I also planned a short trip for us to visit Mount Abu. Raj had never been there. It was a four-hour car ride; Raj and Vijay were the designated drivers. The weather was perfect, in the sixties and seventies. We availed the hospitality of Bauji's old friends and showed Raj all of our favorite places and things to do: watching the sunset on the mountain, horseback riding, boating on Nakki Lake, and a lot of sightseeing.

Mount Abu is famous for both its Dilwara temples and the IAS School (Indian Administrative Service). The school was started back in the era of British rule; it is highly prestigious and very difficult to get into. If you have an IAS degree, you've got it made. Graduates from IAS hold key positions in the government and often pursue Foreign Service jobs. Since we were having such good weather during our visit, we went to the IAS grounds and watched some officers training their military horses. These horses were truly majestic, parading around.

We also visited the Dilwara temples. There are five of them in Mount Abu, built among the mango trees and wooded hills. They are Jain temples, the most important place of worship for its followers, and it took more than fifteen years to construct them in phases. These temples are considered to be the best architectural example of carved marble between the eleventh and thirteenth centuries. The detail in the temples is absolutely mesmerizing; some even consider it on par with the Taj Mahal. In fact, the intricacy of the carvings was considered so important back when the temples were being built that the wages of the artists working on them were determined by the weight of the dust they had produced each day. The more fine dust they made, the harder and more intricately they had worked.

My family and I had been to Mount Abu many times, but it was wonderful to introduce the place to Raj. More importantly, this visit allowed Raj to feel the warmth and affection of my siblings and parents, and it gave my family the opportunity to establish a comfortable, intimate relationship with him. But, all good things must come to an end, and before I knew it, Raj and I were headed back to Delhi.

The euphoria from our visit to Ahmedabad quickly vanished, and I was left trying to find my way in my new reality. I would be starting my residency in July at the M.A.M. college, attached to the Irwin Hospital (now the Lok Nayak Hospital). It was considered a very desirable position. In the meantime, though, I had a six-month sabbatical from work. I'd be spending it in my new home, working through family issues, mostly clashes of culture and values. Luckily, I was mentally prepared, and I was confident in my ability not to waver in my beliefs and never to compromise something I would later regret. My upbringing, the teachings from my childhood, and my genetics were my greatest sources of strength.

Bapaji had been only sixteen when he had set off on his own, without even a mentor to guide him. Bauji had also had to wade through difficult times before earning rank and prestige in the business world. At the young age of thirty-four, Chaeji shouldered the responsibility of the entire household after the death of Baji.

And Bhen had left our home to live in a much more inconvenient and uncomfortable one, but she was still as optimistic and happy as ever. I had been gifted with an extraordinary set of genes. I needed only to be persistent, and I knew I would succeed.

I felt Bapaji especially had anointed me with his wisdom. We had been so close for so many years. I was confident in my ability to adapt and find sustainable solutions that would allow me to maintain my dignity and integrity, and still achieve my goals in a peaceful, silent manner. Because of Bapaji's upbringing, I would not do anything—even for the sake of my new family—if it meant upsetting my conscience. I would not be intimidated or influenced in any way. On the other hand, it was also important to me to show respect, no matter how others chose to act, so I held to my code of silence, never exchanging any negative words with my new family. I kept my head down and my mind focused on my goals.

Thankfully, I did not have to face my new situation alone. Raj was beside me to offer comfort, assistance, guidance, and advice. Two brains are always better than one.

One day after returning from Ahmedabad, the temple where Mataji prayed regularly hosted a special lunch for our family to show appreciation for the donation she had made. When the servers came to offer us seconds on the appetizer, I was full and declined. Raj's family was unhappy with me. They thought I should've taken the extra fritters and brought them home. I was shocked. How could someone do that, especially in a temple? But they did not understand my problem at all. I was disturbed and told Raj about the incident when I got home. I had become the optimist in this family, the one who appreciated what we did have instead of lusting after what we didn't. As Bapaji always said, if you want to move up in life, you have to see your glass as half full, not half empty.

Besides the ideological clashes, I also struggled with the lack of help in my new home. The household help was meager and only part-time (far below the average). They could have afforded much more help, but no one wanted to work for Mataji. She was an intolerable micromanager. So, we had only a part-time sweeper who cleaned the toilets and rooms, and the rest of the work was up to us. It was my responsibility to help, but I did not have much experience at only twenty-three years old, and I was trying to manage a professional career on top of all these menial, time-consuming tasks.

I especially struggled in the kitchen. Even though I was a fast learner, there was a lot to learn. I started at the bottom of the totem pole, chopping onions (which made me cry), while Mataji and Munni instructed me. I did not like the situation, but I tried to accept it gracefully. At the very least, Mataji and Munni were both good cooks, and I did learn a lot from them. Day by day, my cooking improved, but I still had a hard time kneading flour into dough by hand. I had never kneaded dough before, and I made a right mess of it, smearing it all up my arms. I hated it. The first kitchen gadget I purchased when we moved out on our own to London was a Kenwood Kitchen Machine. It was so versatile and could do all the jobs I despised, especially kneading. These days, I have a Braun Kitchen Machine, but I seldom use it anymore for making bread. I'm much better now at kneading dough without smearing it everywhere.

As much as I disliked making bread back then, the absolute worst job for me was washing the dishes—my own personal hell. There was no sink in the house, so I had to sit on a step stool and wash these big pots and pans under a spigot. I'd try to protect my clothes from getting dirty and wet, but it was still a messy job.

Sometimes while I was cleaning, I would think about the disparity between my new world and my old world, the one my siblings still lived in. I had essentially become a maid, while they were still enjoying a life of carefree comfort. My only consolation was that at least I was not being discriminated against. Mataji did her fair share of the work. And, despite my less-than-ideal circumstances, Raj and I were still getting along great. Unfortunately, though, he had no solution for my housework predicament. I had to accept that this was my life for the time being, and there was no change in sight.

Finally, I caught a small break. Raj's and my bedroom was complete! It was on the third floor and modest, ten feet by fifteen, with no attached bathroom. We bought some drapes, a dresser, and a beautiful bedroom set that we enjoyed for many years. We were one step closer to privacy, but my kitchen situation had not improved.

One day Munni and Mataji wanted potato cutlets, so they had me do the rough, menial work. Then, when I was done prepping the potatoes, they asked me to leave, saying they'd call me back when they needed me again. I couldn't understand why I needed to go, and then Munni bluntly told me that they did not want me to know the secret ingredient for their potato cutlets. I was hurt (even though I couldn't have cared less what the ingredient was). How many times had I shown them my integrity? How many times had I bit my tongue and kept their underhanded secrets? But again, I controlled myself, refusing to engage in a rude exchange. I obeyed their orders, leaving the kitchen and returning when called to finish the rest of the job.

This was only one of many instances when Mataji silently endorsed Munni's rude, hurtful behavior. They were truly partners in crime. But I kept my suffering to myself, crying only in the privacy of my room and sharing my feelings only with Raj. The poor man was stuck between a rock and hard place: me versus his family.

Even though Raj and I were getting along, we still had our minor disagreements. For example, Raj had been working with his father, Pitaji, for the past eight years, and they both shared the same schedule. Raj, though, was more easygoing and would sometimes show up late to work. This was unacceptable to me, and I told him that he should be punctual and should be working even harder than Pitaji, not taking extra breaks.

Before I knew it, it was summer, and we all went on a short vacation to Agra, three hours away by car. It was a welcome respite. It gave me time to think outside of my grueling routine at home, and I again enjoyed the beauty of the Taj Mahal both during the day and at night.

But before we had even finished our drive back to Delhi, the home problems had already started up again. Darshan was a constant troublemaker, but being the baby of the family, he never was punished—all his faults were swept under the rug. Ironically, he was always complaining that Raj was the favorite and that he was deprived of everything.

I had accepted that Darshan's and my relationship would never be anything more than shallow (as a friend of mine once told me, "You are born with relatives. Friends, you make by choice."). For one thing, college was a joke to him. He had already flunked the university exams once because he refused to study. Furthermore, he liked to spy.

One afternoon, Raj and I were intimate in our room. After all, we were married. There was nothing immoral or illegal about it. That evening, though, Mataji asked to speak with me. She told me that I should not be making love in the afternoons. If I got pregnant, my baby would be a demon. She gave the example of the demon king Ravana, who was conceived in the afternoon in the epic *Ramayana*.

Needless to say, I was shocked. How did Mataji even know about something that had happened between Raj and me behind closed doors? I later told Raj about Mataji's sermon, and he, too, was surprised. Turns out the culprit was Darshan, who had been spying through the drapes of our window. As they say, an empty mind is a devil's workshop. To this day, I am amazed that I remained calm, bit my tongue, and let it go.

In July 1964, my six-month sabbatical from medicine ended and I began my residency at Irwin Hospital. I was anxious to get back to my real work, away from home. I wanted to specialize in ob-gyn, but I knew a residency in internal medicine would help as well, so I started there. I got orientated at the hospital, received a list of my duties as well as my call schedule, and then got started on my first batch of a dozen patients.

I enjoyed the work, and I was lucky to have such wonderful co-workers, too. They divided up the house calls at night, and we hung out together on the weekends. Even Raj enjoyed socializing with them.

Most families would be proud to have a MD daughter-in-law, but that was not the case for me. Darshan loved to brag about how he had once turned down a wedding proposal from a female doctor. And for Mataji, my professional career meant only that she had lost her help in the kitchen. Now I was gone all day at the hospital.

Unfortunately for me, Mataji was not going to let her little kitchen maid get away so easily. After I started my residency, she suggested that I wake up earlier so I had time to make the despised dough before leaving for the hospital. I complied, as usual, and got up early every morning to complete my chore. This meant I was running on fumes for most of the day, but slowly I adjusted to my new workload and found a balance between home and hospital. Of course, problems were always cropping up, but Raj and I always worked together to find solutions.

The only member of my new family other than Raj who seemed to be proud of my professional accomplishments was Pitaji. I overhead him at a party telling his friends that his daughter-in-law was an MD, and he later brought me over to introduce me.

At any rate, after I prepared the dough in the morning, Raj would drive me to the hospital on his scooter, and usually, in the evenings, I would ride an auto-rickshaw home. The family owned a Fiat, a Vauxhall (a British-made car), and a couple of scooters, but I had never learned how to drive. I had taken a few brief lessons from Chachaji in Ahmedabad, but I had no need to continue learning once I was at LHMC. Now I planned on picking up my lessons again with Raj.

When I started my residency at Irwin, the Vauxhall was old and needed to retire (in the past, it had been a prestigious possession, a status symbol). So, Pitaji purchased a new car, a spacious Ambassador, and the family decided to take it on a road trip to Mussoorie. We all set off. Mid-journey, however, we discovered that one of the rear passenger doors would open on a whim, even while driving. Obviously it was not safe to sit next to it, and it was too late to turn around. The decision was made to keep a little empty space between the door and me. All the occupants in the car were heavy except for Pitaji and me (I weighed only ninety pounds), so Mataji suggested I sit on her lap. I agreed and moved. The only positive side of my new predicatment was that my concern over the car's safety was greatly reduced—I was too squished to be concerned about much of anything.

But it was all worth it when we arrived at Mussoorie. As soon as I saw the place, the sweet memories of Raj's and my honeymoon came flooding back to me. And even better, this time, we were visiting in the summer. Mussoorie was beautiful: breathtaking mountain vistas, greenery everywhere, and the smell of fresh pine. When our visit was over, we headed back home, stopping in Haridwar on our way (which had been their tradition throughout the years).

We were back in the sweltering heat of a Delhi summer, but at least I was enjoying my residency. I was learning under excellent senior staff doctors and renowned professors of medicine.

Before I knew it, it was September 3, Munni's birthday. Everyone in the family wished her well, and she had a nice day. Twelve days later, it was my birthday, but nobody remembered. I was sad and disappointed. I told Raj it was my birthday, so we went out together, and I purchased a saree for my present. I haven't worn it in fifty years, but I still have it, for memory's sake. Raj can be a slow learner, but after my reminder that first year, he has always remembered my birthday since then and given me something thoughtful. (But I have always been the one in charge of remembering everyone else's birthdays and anniversaries, on both sides of the family, and I always send our best wishes promptly.) Munni never remembered my birthday, even later when we became close.

It was now October 1964, and Diwali was quickly approaching. I suggested to Raj that we celebrate it in Ahmedabad because, from what I had gathered, there wasn't much of a celebration at his house. Darshan heard about our plans and asked if he could come along. Raj agreed (Raj was always kind to Darshan, no matter his antics).

This year's Diwali with my family was festive and joyous, as usual. The weather in Ahmedabad was beautiful, and the excitement was contagious, like Christmas. Raj, Darshan, and I had a wonderful time at the parties, both at home and at Bauji's office. It was especially a treat for Darshan, who had never vacationed in Ahmedabad before. Of course, even with all these exciting events, Darshan still could not keep himself out of trouble. Many years later, my sisters told me that Darshan was showing off his secret talent of being able to perfectly forge Raj's and my signatures. He would come to abuse this "talent" many times over the years.

## Chapter Nine

*After a perfect holiday* in Ahmedabad, we returned to Delhi and continued with our usual routines. Come December, I had completed my residency in internal medicine.

When New Year's Eve rolled around, Raj surprised me with a night out at a five-star restaurant, just the two of us. It was incredibly expensive—an entire month's worth of my salary—so I was hesitant at first, but it ended up being a great treat. We still remember the ambience and the intricately plated gourmet food.

In January 1965, I started my residency in ob-gyn, my specialty. I was in the operating room, performing minor surgery under the supervision and direction of senior doctors. I was also delivering babies on my own and assisting with C-sections. This was more to my liking than internal medicine, and it was as close as I was going to get to surgery (which had been my first choice of specialty until I spoke with Bauji). My teachers during this residency were Dr. D, the head instructor, and Dr. K, the assistant professor. They were both excellent, and I enjoyed learning from them, despite my heavy workload, which included many night calls (it felt like the number of babies born at night versus during the day was way off).

One of my other professors, Dr. DS, was also the department chair and the principal of the medical college. She was infamous for her toughness—even the male medical students were afraid of her. Luckily, she had been my professor at LHMC, so I'd already had some exposure to her. Dr. DS's sister had been one of our professors, too (for physiology), and, ironically she was the gentlest of ladies (although both sisters were equally accomplished). Just goes to show that sharing the same genes does not guarantee any similarities (look at Raj and Darshan, two brothers worlds apart).

Dr. DS was tough, but she also had a sense of humor. She once visited my family in Ahmedabad while at a conference, and they enjoyed a wonderful lunch together.

This new residency had been very competitive to get into, and it was a privilege to train under these doctors. I worked hard and came prepared every morning for my rounds, constantly perfecting my skills and my diagnoses. I was lucky to have supervisors who appreciated me; Dr. D and Dr. K frequently complimented me on my work. I felt proud, and their words gave me the confidence that one day I, too, would be a good ob-gyn.

During this residency, Munni was pregnant, and she was very unhappy about it. It was an unplanned pregnancy, and she wanted me to help her arrange an abortion. In her mind, she was a princess, and she did not deserve to be so uncomfortable. She even tried to convince me that Mataji agreed with her decision. But back then, we did not perform "therapeutic" abortions, so, instead, I took her to my superior, Dr. K, for her prenatal care. Since I had a personal connection to her doctor, Munni got extra-special attention, and her pregnancy progressed uneventfully. I was relieved to be done with solving her issues, but I still had other family medical problems to deal with.

Mataji was always complaining of one illness or another, usually several of them at one time. In the beginning, I believed her and thought she had serious health issues, but as time went by, she visited doctor after doctor who said that the ailments were self-diagnosed, except for some arthritis in her right knee, which was partially due to her weight. Mataji's real problem was that she was vain. She was forty-eight years old and afraid to look as if she was aging. Pitaji, on the other hand, was disciplined and slim, with no health problems or complaints. A married couple with two very different personalities.

In May 1964, Raj's family went on vacation to a beautiful hill resort, Nainital. Raj and I, however, stayed back because I was saving up my vacation time for Nirmal's wedding. As much as I would have liked to see Nainital, it was nice to have the house to ourselves, a rare few days of privacy.

The next big event in the family was Darshan's exam results. They were published in the local paper, and we were elated to see his ID number in the pass list. We celebrated, and per tradition, shared *mithai* (Indian sweets) with Chachiji and Pitaji's office staff. Two days later, we got a big shock.

The ever-deceitful Darshan had actually failed his exams, so he had told us the ID number of his friend, who had passed. He knew he had no chance of passing, even on his second try, because he never studied. His one and only priority was to play tennis and watch movies, and then come home and relax for the rest of the day. By then, I was already well-aware of Darshan's abuse of his family to serve his own selfish purposes.

One evening, Raj had come to pick me up at the hospital at the end of my shift, when, at the last minute, Dr. K asked if I could assist in an emergency C-section. Raj told me to go ahead and that he would meet me in the call room, but Dr. K had an idea. She asked Raj if he would instead like to come to the OR and watch the C-section. Raj was excited and eagerly accepted.

Raj stood at the head end of the table, away from all the blood and mess below (luckily he didn't faint), and he watched the anesthesiologist work. Dr. K was an excellent teacher and a talented doctor, and Raj enjoyed this once-in-a-lifetime firsthand experience. After the surgery, Raj said I might want to consider becoming an anesthesiologist. So I analyzed the pros and cons, and I decided it was worth exploring further. One of the big pros was that all elective surgeries in those days were scheduled in the mornings, to avoid the midday heat. Only emergency surgeries were done in the afternoons. So being an anesthesiologist would give me a more structured life than delivering babies, and it would still allow me to participate (albeit somewhat passively) in surgery. I continued to mull over the possibility.

Meanwhile, many of the young doctors at the hospital were leaving in droves. They were moving abroad for specialized training and better learning opportunities. Every day my peers were making plans to move, mostly to the UK (a few to the far-off U.S.). Listening to them tempted me, too, so I brought up the idea to Raj. We both gave it some serious thought and began exploring our options. The more we researched, the more optimistic we became. There were obstacles, of course, but with plenty of planning and initiative, we could clear them. We focused on the UK because doctors were in high demand, and we could both get jobs while I completed my graduate training.

Raj had always wanted to study in the UK, but Mataji had never let him pursue it because she was worried he would marry a Brit. Now she wouldn't have to worry about that. Raj and I were both young and ready for adventure. The plan was to live in the UK for one year and then return to Delhi so Raj could continue working with Pitaji. Initially, we faced some resistance from his family, but their hesitations were weak and short-lived. The plan was set: we were going to the UK.

I wasn't the only one in my family with big plans, though. On July 2, my sister Nirmal was getting married to her classmate VR in Ahmedabad, and then they were both leaving in September to complete graduate studies in the U.S., and my brother Vijay was going to move with them and get his master's in engineering. They were all going to Knoxville.

I couldn't miss my sister's wedding, but I took off as little time as possible from work—only one week. Those seven days, though, were enough to catch the ire of Dr. DS. She was disappointed in me, and, even though I had been intensely dedicated throughout my residency, she gave me demerits, which was sadly ironic because she had been planning on giving me the award for best resident but changed her mind when I was absent on the last day of residency. Dr. K knew how hard I had worked, and she tried her best to help Dr. DS understand the situation, but to no avail. Dr. DS had her principles, and she had her limits.

Once back from the wedding, Raj and I were in full swing planning for our adventure. We consulted with friends who had already made the move, and we received our first-ever passports. Our excitement was boundless; we were living the dream. One drawback, however, was that India does not allow its citizens to take more than eleven dollars' worth of currency out of the country (crazy politics). So we worked through a contact in London to arrange a short-term loan on our arrival. Looking at the easy availability of jobs there and the fact that many of our colleagues had survived it, we were confident our finances would pan out. Now everything was in place. Raj, Nirmal, VR, Vijay, and I were set to depart from Bombay around the second week of September. I had only one last thing to do before we could leave.

Munni was due in early September, and I had promised to help her with her labor and delivery (not that I had much of a choice in the matter). So on September 5, Munni went into labor, and I stayed by her side from the very beginning to the very end. Luckily, her husband, RG, was also home on break from combat duty. He was always good company, and it was nice to have some backup. Munni had a very low pain threshold, and we were all acutely aware of it.

Dr. K would be delivering her baby, but first we needed to get through the labor. Dr. K was a little disgusted by Munni's exaggerated pain, screaming at the earliest stage of labor. It was during this early stage that Dr. K got a call to perform an emergency C-section, so I was left to care for Munni. It was late at night, I had already had a long day, and it looked like I was going to be up for many more hours. Suddenly, Munni's labor progressed very rapidly, and before I knew it, I was delivering the baby. I had delivered babies before during my residency, but I had never done it on my own for my family. I shouted for the nurse to assist me, but, by then, it was over. A beautiful, healthy baby girl was born around 3 a.m. After completing all the necessary checks, I brought her to RG, who had been waiting in the visitors' lounge. Both Raj and I were proud that I was able to handle the delivery, and when Dr. K returned from the C-section, she thanked me for a job well done.

The next day, I went back to the hospital to visit Munni and to thank Dr. K for her patience and kindness throughout my residency. During our conversation, Dr. K mentioned that my sister-in-law was truly one of a kind. It was certainly not typical for Dr. K to have a patient start screaming right out of the gate. Dr. K had even said to Munni, "If you were Sadhna, you would not be behaving like this." Munni's response was shocking. She told Dr. K, "I am my parents' only daughter, so my pain level is different than Sadhna's. She can tolerate more because she has three sisters." I was disappointed in Munni and had no way of justifying her response to Dr. K. I could have confronted Munni, but I refused to stoop to her level. It was something I had been taught since childhood.

Throughout my short time in this new family, I had tolerated what I felt was intolerable, and I had done so without creating a scene. I told myself to always rise above their petty issues (as painful as some of them were). Of course, at times, I did waver (I am human), but I always found strength in Bapaji's words of wisdom and his can-do attitude.

I had fulfilled my promise to Munni—she was home with her new baby—so it was finally time to start packing for my dream adventure. I told Raj about Dr. K's conversation with Munni. We were both glad to be getting away, out on our own. We had no apprehension, only euphoria.

The second week of September finally arrived. I was leaving my new family and my suffering behind. My mantra was, "What happened in Tilak Bazaar stays in Tilak Bazaar" (well, at least until now; this is the first time I've spoken about it with anyone other than Raj). That year had taken a severe toll on me, but I never even considered telling my parents about it. Raj's family was now my family, and I did not want to air their dirty laundry, nor did I want to alarm my parents. I knew that if I put my mind to it, I would be strong enough to get through it amicably and forget about it when the time came. And the time had finally come: we were leaving!

First, we had a short flight from Delhi to Bombay. This was my first time ever in a plane and only Raj's second (his first was a short flight over Delhi on a private plane). We were both thrilled and enjoyed the one-and-a-half-hour flight. Once in Bombay, we met up with my brother Vijay, my sister Nirmal, and her husband, VR, who would all be flying with us by Swiss Air to Geneva. This was a big affair for my family. Everyone had come from Ahmedabad, including Chachaji and Auntyji, and Bhen and Jijaji had even traveled from Morinda. It was a royal send-off, with bouquets of flowers and everyone dressed up. Much unlike today, flying back then was a formal affair, and all passengers followed the dress code. The women wore dresses, and the men wore suits and ties. You would never see jeans or shorts. So, with our family and friends at the airport, we said our tearful (but still joyful) goodbyes. Again, unlike today, flying was fairly new, and we had no idea when or if we would see each other again. Bauji in particular was under a lot of stress. The war between India and Pakistan was heating up, and it was clear it would be long, undoubtedly with casualties and repercussions. He was concerned about our flight, but Swiss Air was considered a safe airline.

When we boarded the plane, I still could not believe this trip was actually happening—a dream come true. For me, it signaled the end of a treacherous beginning, a chapter in my life I was so ready to close and would not think about again for many years. Instead, I was focused on my future, on this giant step forward Raj and I were taking together. The flight attendants gave their safety spiel (which, back then, we actually listened to), and then we were off.

Soon enough we had landed in Geneva, where we would stay for two days before getting on another plane bound for Paris, where we would spend another two days. Then we would say our goodbyes to Vijay, Nirmal, and VR, who would be off to the U.S., and Raj and I would fly to London.

Our time in Geneva was short but unforgettable. Geneva was well-known for its breathtaking Swiss countryside. We had all seen its beauty in movies, but to see and experience it in person was incredible—the greenery, the mountains, the lakes. It felt like we had stumbled into Wonderland. The roads and the sidewalks were exceptionally clean. There were no beggars, no homeless. Everyone seemed to be happy and comfortable. (Of course, this was our first time outside of India, so today's travelers might find Geneva less impressive.) Together we took a city tour and a boat ride, and then it was off to Paris. In Paris, we took another city tour and visited the Eiffel Tower as well as the river Seine. We said our goodbyes to Vijay, Nirmal, and VR, and then Raj and I headed off for London.

We were met at Heathrow Airport by a single guy, a contact of Darshan's (about the only good thing that happened to us through him). This man took us to his apartment building, where we sublet one of his rooms for a week. The room itself was small and simple, but we had access to a common kitchen and bathroom. This man was very hospitable, and I still think of him fondly today.

One surprise for me at our new place were the showers. The hot water came from a geyser (a gas-fired water heater; the water gets heated as it travels through it). The hot water was time-controlled and paid for through shillings, like a parking meter. It wasn't a problem for me. I enjoyed learning new things every day.

After a few days' rest, I lined up an interview in internal medicine for a temporary job. The residency helped my orientation to the U.K., and I began looking into the possibility of a residency in anesthesiology. I knew absolutely nothing about anesthesiology, but I wanted to at least give it a try.

Soon I landed a SHO (senior house officer) anesthesiology position in southeast London. Raj and I started apartment-hunting for a place close to the new hospital. Our choices were meager. We ended up in a room with a kitchenette and no connected bathroom. It wasn't the best, but we knew it was only temporary. During this time, I observed my third Karva Chauth, fasting and watching the full moon.

My first day at my new residency, I met my anesthesiologist consultant, Dr. Brett. She was a beautiful, dignified woman in her early thirties. Besides working in London, she had also spent two years in Philadelphia, so she had the best training and experience. She was an excellent teacher, and I was incredibly lucky to be learning from her. (Of course, my other supervising consultants were good, too, but none of them compared to Dr. Brett.)

In the beginning, I knew very little about anesthesiology, but I bought books, and I shadowed Dr. Brett for a few days. She taught me the ABCs of the specialty, including how to use the anesthesia machine. I learned quickly, and, before long, I was administering anesthesia to patients under the watchful eye of Dr. Brett. One patient in particular I remember clearly: a young lady who reacted unexpectedly to a muscle relaxant and stopped breathing. There was only one ventilator available, so Dr. Brett and I had to take turns hand-ventilating her for twenty-four hours. We were delighted when she finally started breathing on her own again. Over the years, I've had several patients react similarly, and the outcome has always been uneventful, but this was my first time, so the memory has stayed fresh.

Raj and I were again packing, getting ready to move to better living quarters. It was our third move in a month. Luckily, we had few belongings, so the moves were fairly painless. We had found a modest apartment close to the hospital, and it had a kitchen and a bathroom. We stayed in this place for eight months. Meanwhile, Raj got a job working in a department store, which he commuted to via the tube (subway).

We weren't always working, though. We had time to enjoy the city, too. We had so much fun exploring it, getting a crash course in English culture and making a few friends along the way. We loved how easy it was to get around on the tube. We were especially impressed by Oxford Street and Bond Street. After we started earning some money, we frequently liked to indulge ourselves at Marks & Spencer, buying all our clothes there. Life was good.

I was now six months into my training and eligible to apply for my diploma in anesthesiology by taking the DA exam, which was administered by the Royal College of Physicians of London and the Royal College of Surgeons of England. So, along with working long hours, I was now studying hard, too. The exam was in July, and I needed to pass it before going back to India.

During this time, I got a promotion. Since I had been working as an SHO for six months, I was now a registrar in anesthesiology. If I could land a job, I would have not only the title but also an increase in salary.

Lucky me, I found a job opening twenty-five miles away, in northwest London. I scheduled an interview and rode the tube on the Bakerloo line to the last stop, the suburb of Watford. I left the interview happy: I had a new job. And to top it off, the hospital had just built brand-new, ultra-modern apartments for its residency program, and Raj and I could rent one.

I couldn't wait to move, but first I needed to pass my DA exam. I knew the essay part would be easy for me, but I was nervous about the oral and hands-on sections. I was worried I'd mess up all the different kinds of breathing tubes and hardware required in anesthesiology. I got through it, though, and soon found out I had passed. I was in heaven. Of course I couldn't help but think how proud Bapaji would have been.

It was July and time to move into our new apartment—it would be our final move here in London. The apartment was small: a galley kitchen, a bedroom, a nice living room, and an attached bath. But it was all well-constructed and beautiful. The walls had grass cloth wallpaper, and the entire place felt open and airy, with plenty of glass and windows. Most importantly of all, the apartment had central heating, which was uncommon then, even in the older, expensive homes in London. Raj and I were overjoyed.

One of our big plans before heading back to India was to buy a car. Raj decided on a Fiat 1400. It was a mid-size car, fancy-looking, and it had a heater, which was an unusual, extra luxury back then. Luckily, the hospital campus had a covered parking garage. Raj drove the car to the tube station, and then he'd park it and take the tube into London. I was working in two hospitals that were fairly close together, and my employer covered my cab expenses. I was happy in my new job, and now that we were finally done with moving, Raj decided to take some computer courses in London in addition to his work. The computer was the size of a mega-refrigerator.

We outfitted our apartment with some new kitchen gadgets. My first big purchase was a Kenwood Kitchen Machine. I loved it. It did all the messy jobs, especially making the dough for *roti* (flatbread). Raj had always had a fancy for the Cona Percolator, a vacuum coffeemaker that looked like a chemistry flask. He had admired it ever since having his coffee brought in it at Gaylord, a fancy restaurant in India. This was our second kitchen splurge, and we purchased it at the department store Selfridges. Raj had wanted to purchase the four-cup-size percolator, but it was very expensive, and I talked him down to the two-cup. We paid five pounds for it—quite the indulgence in 1966. We enjoyed this coffeemaker for many years, occasionally replacing the top or bottom pieces. Raj still reminds me to this day how I convinced him not to buy the one he wanted, and I always remind him that we were students on a budget. But we also both knew how lucky we were to have a secure future. Our plans were to return to India, where Raj would work with Pitaji, and I would get a good job with my British diploma and high level of training.

We were so content in our beautiful little apartment, and we felt safe. Even though we never locked it when we were out, we didn't have to worry about break-ins or thieves (very unlike India). We enjoyed inviting our circle of friends over, and they were all surprised to see our cute, modern apartment. I remember one evening in particular, when I invited my new consultant and his wife over for an Indian dinner. They were completely taken aback by our luxury apartment. Even in their expensive home, they did not have central heating. In fact, when Raj's cousin and her brother-in-law, who was also a very well-paid consultant, saw our apartment, he said that he lived like a Queen's servant but we lived like the Queen's guests.

The apartment building itself was called Shrodell Sisters' Home. Nurses in Britain were called "sisters," which wasn't new to me because it was the same in India (due to British influence). But what did surprise me was that all specialized doctors were not called "doctors." In fact, to call them "doctor" was considered offensive. Even after they passed their difficult specialty boards (FRCS for surgeons, and FRCP for general medicine), they were addressed as simply "Mr. So-and-so." But funny enough, it was the junior doctors who were addressed as "doctor" (a habit that was difficult for me to break after moving to the U.S., where consultants are usually called only by their first names).

On the weekends, Raj and I continued to explore London and its surrounding area. We took many day trips, including to Stonehenge, Windsor Castle, and Blackpool, and we hosted some of my family as well.

My sisters Varsha and Veena were moving to the U.S. to get their graduate degrees in nuclear physics and economics. What a perfect opportunity for them to swing by London! Raj and I were excited and immediately began planning for a two-week road trip around Europe. We also invited Darshan to join us. Of course, he was delighted to accept.

Darshan arrived a few days before my sisters. He was overwhelmed by our apartment and commented that the maids were keeping the bathroom sparkling and the sink spotless. Our response stunned him. We didn't have any maids, we told him; all the work was self-service elbow grease. A couple of days later, Darshan also mentioned that Bauji had sent Raj's family his annual summer gift basket filled with delicious alphonso mangoes. Darshan added that everyone in the family was surprised because they figured Bauji would not bother sending any gifts this year, since I was not living with them. Darshan could not comprehend the value Bauji placed on dignity, class, and family.

Once Varsha and Veena arrived, we were ready to hit the road. Luckily, all five of us fit comfortably in the Fiat. (In fact, the front seat was a bench, so we could have even fit a sixth slim person.)

We were on a modest budget, but it was still a wonderful vacation, and we learned so much about so many different cultures. Darshan shared in the driving (somewhat shockingly, he was a safe driver), and we visited Amsterdam, Geneva, Zurich, Florence, Rome, and Paris. I had my first taste of pizza in Rome

(I had it again when we moved to the U.S., and ever since, it has been a regular meal for Raj and me).

While driving in the French countryside, we picked up some bread and what we thought was butter. We were later disappointed to discover it was actually chocolate and that we would have to eat our bread plain. Of course, language was an obstacle throughout our vacation. Veena had actually taken French as a second language, but it was no help. We were also chagrined by the unpleasant discovery that we had to pay to use the restroom at gas stations. This had not been factored into our budget. Darshan especially was upset by this, cursing in Hindi at a gas station parking lot. On the whole, though, it was a fun, memorable trip.

We were lucky that the weather cooperated with us. It was sunny and comfortable the entire time. In fact, at one point during our trip, we decided to picnic on the side of the highway using our portable gas stove. We were soon interrupted, however, by the Highway Patrol, who pointed out our ignorance of highway regulations.

Two weeks later, we returned to London, full of happy memories. It was time for Veena and Varsha to leave for the U.S. Darshan was going to stay with us for a while longer. Raj and I decided to let bygones be bygones and give Darshan a fresh start. We welcomed him into our home with open arms.

Darshan had a couple of friends and acquaintances in London to visit, and he had the wonderful opportunity to pursue any studies of his choice during his stay. The hang-up, though, was that the Indian government did not allow money to be exchanged for education. I had always been taught in my upbringing the importance of learning, so I offered to work overtime and drop all my vacation time to support Darshan's studies. From my point of view, this was an opportunity of a lifetime for him. Darshan, however, did not see it that way. Ever the playboy, he wanted only to enjoy meandering around London for a while before heading back to his life of luxury in India. After three months of nothing but fun, he returned to Delhi.

Raj and I were considering going back to Delhi, too, but first we wanted to persuade Bauji and Chaeji to visit us in London as well before visiting my siblings in the U.S. They not only agreed to visit, but they also took it a step further: they were going to tour the world. They delved into the initial stages of planning. They were going to visit Europe (including the UK), the U.S., Canada, Japan, and Hong Kong (which at the time was a British colony).

Once Raj and I knew Bauji and Chaeji were going to visit the U.S., we wanted to go as well. All of my siblings now lived there, except for Pradeep, my eleven-year-old little brother.

It was during all these exciting plans that I got a call one day from Raj while I was at the hospital. He told me to look out the window. Snow falling! I was so excited. It was only a flurry, but this was my first time ever seeing snow fall. Little did I know then that I would soon be living through many blustery winters with mountains of snow.

# Chapter Ten

*W*hile *Raj and I were talking* through the details of our visit to the US, I had an epiphany. I told Raj it would be wonderful to live there for a year and make it a working vacation, because we did not have the money to do much otherwise. But how could we make it happen?

First, I would have to sit for the ECFMG exam (Educational Commission for Foreign Medical Graduates). In the UK, the exam was given about twice a year (in some other countries, I think it was only once a year). Luckily, London was one of the centers where the exam was given, so it was convenient, although I knew it would not be easy. The exam was an all-day affair, consisting of one section in English proficiency (this was the only easy part for me), and the second part covered every specialty in medicine, including psychiatry. I knew it would be a challenge, but I decided it was worth the effort. So, no more vacations for me. Only work and studying. I sat for the exam—and passed.

Now the next decision for Raj and me was where to move to in the U.S.—East or West? I looked into job postings and applied to two. My first choice was a job at Harvard University in Boston. The second was in Syracuse, New York. I had already completed two years of anesthesiology, and I wanted credit for it rather than having to start again as a first-year resident.

The wait was long, but finally I got an offer to be a second-year resident at the Deaconess Hospital in Boston, a Harvard University teaching hospital. Raj and I were elated.

Meanwhile, Bauji had been encouraging Pitaji to go on a world tour as well, and Pitaji and Mataji were actually seriously considering it.

Before I knew it, Bauji, Chaeji, and Pradeep had finalized their traveling plans. They were lucky that Pradeep wasn't twelve yet. Back then, children under twelve flew for half price.

So, in May 1967, they began their world adventure, vacationing around Europe for two weeks and then arriving in London. They stayed with us for one month, and the memories we made then would last us all a lifetime. After that, they were off to the U.S.

Raj's and my U.S. plans were gaining momentum as well. Back and forth I communicated with my new employer and looked for apartment rentals. I was also working with my current employer to tie up loose ends and set an end date.

Meanwhile, in August 1966, Pitaji and Mataji had finalized their world tour (after getting much encouragement from Bauji on his return to India). Pitaji and Mataji first spent a week around Europe, and then they arrived in London. They were both very happy. Mataji was especially content to see that her darling son looked well-fed and that I had finally mastered the art of cooking (or at least she was satisfied with my progress).

Of course, it wasn't all smooth sailing during their visit. Mataji was still a hypochondriac, so even though she was the picture of perfect health, she was sure something was wrong.

We made appointments with many doctors on London's famous Harley Street, known for its large number of private specialists who deal with complex cases. Mataji got a thorough workup, including X-rays and labs. To our relief (although not to our surprise), all the results came back clean. The only small finding was her arthritic knee, which she was advised to lose weight to alleviate some of the pain. We were all satisfied with the results, except for Mataji. We continued on, though, with our sightseeing and shopping.

By now, Raj and I had had plenty of practice and were great tour guides. Mataji was happy to keep our trips relatively close around London because of her health limitations, but we knew Pitaji could handle more. In fact, he had had to cut their Europe trip short because Mataji was not feeling well, so we suggested he head out again to see Italy and some other areas. He agreed. We planned a trip for him, and he had a wonderful time. Mataji was happy staying back, so it all worked out.

Meanwhile, Raj and I were still ironing out the details for our move to the U.S.: getting our visas in order, submitting the required notice to my current hospital, and continuing to fulfill my work obligations.

After getting some advice from my siblings who lived in Knoxville, our plans were set. First we would fly to Montreal to see the World's Fair, and then we would fly to New York to see its sights for a few days; our last stop would be Boston. (Although we didn't know it then, Boston would become our permanent home. We could not ask for more, and we are proud to call ourselves Americans.)

Finally the day came. In mid-September 1967, Raj, Pitaji, Mataji, and I flew to Montreal. With fall in full swing, the weather was beautiful, and the fair itself was amazing, with countless attractions. Of course, it was also extremely crowded—line after line after line. Mataji, however, simply ignored the lines and cut in front of everyone. She wanted me to join her, but I refused. I tried in vain to tell her to follow the rules. Back then, there were no special lines for the handicapped. Nowadays, with the Baby Boomer generation aging, things have changed.

Next we were off to New York. The flight was short, the plane flew low, and it was a beautiful sunny day, so we all enjoyed looking at the scenery below. Mataji became very excited, pointing out her window and telling me to look at all the trees exploding with fruit. She said I could eat as much as I wanted with such an abundance (well, we all knew she was a foodie). A few days later, we realized that those weren't fruit trees. They were all the leaves changing colors, getting ready for winter (although Mataji was right, there is always an abundance of fruit here, no matter the season).

Once we were in New York, we dropped off our bags at the YMCA. We needed a place to sleep, and the YMCA fit our modest budget. Then we did the usual touristy things: going to the top of the Empire State Building, seeing a show at Radio City Music Hall, and, of course, shopping at the giant Macy's store.

It was here in New York that Mataji faced a once-in-a-lifetime shock. One day, we all went back to the YMCA to shower. After I finished showering, I walked into the ladies' dressing area, where I found Mataji extremely disturbed. She was literally shaking. It took her a while to calm down, and then she finally told me that she had seen a nude, morbidly obese woman. This was a genuine culture shock for her. She could never have imagined, even in her wildest dreams, seeing someone in that condition. For her, it was like seeing a human who had three eyes and two noses (after all, Mataji had lived a rather protected life).

Our time in New York was soon over. Next stop: Boston. Raj and I were leaving before Pitaji and Mataji, and taking the Greyhound to save money. After living in the suburbs of London for two years, we were well-acquainted with public transportation. Pitaji and Mataji were flying to Boston because they had their round-the-world plane tickets. We planned to meet up with them in Boston at our new apartment on Francis Street. We had also coordinated with Bindu, my old college friend from Ahmedabad, to meet Raj and me at the bus stop, and she would drive us to the apartment.

As our bus pulled into the Greyhound terminal, we saw her smiling face. It was so reassuring to see an old friend in a foreign place. Our joy was mutual.

Bindu and I hadn't seen each other for three years. She was studying at Boston University and had lived in the area for more than two years.

Raj and I settled into her twelve-year-old Ford and began our first drive to our new home on Francis Street. We got lost, though, and ended up on Francis Street in Brookline, which was a nice suburb with nice houses. It was then we learned that different suburbs in Boston sometimes share the same street names. Finally, we made it to Francis Street in Boston. We were disappointed to see that the apartment buildings on this street were rundown and crowded. (Today, this is the address for the Brigham and Women's Hospital, one of Harvard's largest teaching hospitals.) At the very least, though, we got a warm reception from Dr. Dagli (also a second-year resident) and his wonderful wife, Dr. Sheila Dagli.

Since Pitaji and Mataji had flown, they had already arrived and were waiting for us, and they looked disturbed. They told us one of their bags had been stolen in the lobby of the Y in New

York just as they were leaving for the airport. Mataji had lost not only all her beautiful sarees but also all the shopping she had done in London. Raj and I felt terrible, and we felt responsible for not warning them, although we were naïve ourselves. We had all become accustomed to the honesty we had found during our time in the UK and the rest of Europe.

Raj and I brought our bags into our shabby one-bedroom apartment. Dr. Dagli had held it for us as planned while he and his wife moved into a two-bedroom apartment in the adjoining building. Their living next door was a big morale booster for Raj and me, and, to this day, we fondly remember their warm hospitality. Over the next two years, we would become close friends.

Bindu came back the next day to help us get acquainted with the area and pick up some necessities. She drove all four of us to the Stop & Shop. When we walked in, we were taken aback by how huge the store was and how many choices there were in every category. The supermarkets in London were mini-marts compared to this. Many years later, in 1985, Raj and I watched the movie *Moscow on the Hudson*. We completely understood how Robin Williams' character felt when he walked into a grocery store and saw shelf after shelf of different varieties of coffee. He mumbled over and over, "Coffee, coffee, coffee," until he fainted. Although we didn't faint, we were still overwhelmed by all the decisions.

We also realized during this first shopping trip that everything in the U.S. is huge: the supermarkets, the department stores, the cars, the refrigerators and other appliances, and even the fruits and vegetables. So it was ironic to us that the standard voltage in the U.S. is only 110, while the rest of the world is 220.

As the days went by, Pitaji was very unhappy in our new apartment. It was quite a step down from our luxury apartment in London. He felt sorry for us and suggested that we come back to India with him. He said he would even handle the finances for the move. We declined and said we would follow through with our plan to stay for one year before returning to India permanently. So, Pitaji stayed with us for one more week, and then he left to finish his eighty-day trip around the world: the West Coast, Hawaii, Hong Kong, Japan, and then safely back to Delhi. Even if Pitaji hadn't been disappointed in our apartment, he still had to get back to his business and his schedule.

Mataji had decided to forgo the rest of her world trip. Instead, she stayed with us, and she was actually a good sport about our apartment, content to sleep on the sofa bed in the living room.

The following week, the weather was gorgeous, and Bindu offered to take us sightseeing. (Having a friend with a car was a big plus.) She came in the morning and told us we were taking a day trip to see the fall. We drove for thirty or forty miles and were enjoying the beautiful scenery, when Raj asked how much farther the fall was. Bindu, surprised, replied that the foliage was all around us (Mataji's "fruit trees"). The rest of the world calls fall *autumn*, so Raj and I had thought we were going to see a *waterfall*. Not that we were disappointed. We had never seen such vibrant colors in nature before; it was magical and breathtaking. Now every year, we look forward to another spectacular Northeastern fall; we know exactly the stages of change the trees in our backyard will go through— from green, to red, orange, and then yellow. Colors so unreal they look like a painting.

By now I had started my second-year residency at the Deaconess Hospital. Raj was staying at home with Mataji, helping her settle in while he started his job hunt. Mother and son were both happy with the arrangement.

The one good thing about our shabby apartment was that it was only a three-minute commute to my work. I was shocked when Dr. Dagli informed me that work in the OR started at 7 a.m. This was very unlike my schedules in India and the UK. Seven in the morning was morbidly too early for me. The only other time I'd had a similar schedule was in medical school. Back then, I'd had the choice to either eat breakfast or skip it and get fifteen more minutes of shut-eye. I usually chose the latter. Luckily, this time around, I had Raj. He offered to help me by making me coffee and toast every morning. I quickly agreed. But he had one rule. I could not complain or give any "helpful pointers." The only comments allowed were, "The coffee is perfect" and "The toast is excellent." This arrangement turned out to be a wonderful start to my day. And even after my retirement, Raj has continued to faithfully make my breakfast and I continue to enjoy my permanent addiction to sleeping in late.

My orientation to this hospital and its procedures went smoothly. The nurses were all friendly and helpful. The anesthesia machines and most of the other equipment was universal, so I was already familiar with it. I did, however, encounter one new thing during my orientation: donuts. Every day there was a pile of them in the break room. I had never tasted a donut before or even seen one. Now donuts are popular all over the world, but they have never grown on me. Perhaps if I were stuck in an extreme survival situation, I'd take a nibble of one, but that would be it.

I quickly found my routine at the hospital, which included trying to break my London habit of calling the consultants "doctor." The only thing that frustrated me at this new job was the slow pace. I had gotten much more done in a typical workday in the UK than I was getting done here.

Bindu dropped by our apartment again on another Saturday, and she invited us to go with her to the famous Filene's Basement, the oldest discount retailer in the U.S. We needed some more pots and pans in the kitchen, so we agreed. All four of us (Raj, Mataji, Bindu, and me) headed off to The Basement, as it was fondly called.

We walked into the store and got a huge shock. There were half-dressed women everywhere, trying on and taking off clothes in broad daylight. Mounds of discarded clothes were strewn all over, and the women were rushing around them, clinging to more piles of clothes on their heads. I turned to Raj and told him he'd better leave. I was worried that this floor of the store was for women only and he'd get arrested for being a peeping Tom. We frantically scanned our eyes across the store, looking for an elevator (in the UK housewares were always located in the basement; we eventually realized this store had no housewares). I noticed then that among the mob of women were a few beleaguered, battle-worn men. I was relieved. My heart rate slowed, and I told Raj not to worry. Men were allowed (whether they liked it or not!).

Despite our chaotic introduction to The Basement, we enjoyed shopping there and made many return trips over the years. I could go on for pages talking about all the treasures I found there. When Bauji and Chaeji would come to visit, they would always have to make a trip there, too, as though it were a pilgrimage site. I had thought that, once my salary topped $50,000, I would stop shopping at The Basement, but I never quit. It was The Basement that quit on me. Sadly, it had to file for bankruptcy during the economic crisis in the early 2000s.

With my week of orientation over, and I was now carrying out my share of responsibilities. It was almost winter, all our moving boxes had arrived from London, and we were feeling more settled. Dr. Dagli and his wife, Sheila, always took us grocery shopping, as we still did not have our own car. We were lucky to have them as friends, and Mataji enjoyed their company, too. I was content.

One day at work, I heard about one of the hospital's cardio-thoracic surgeons (I think he was from Pakistan). He was appar-ently very handsome and extremely competent. Everyone talked about good he was at his job, but they also said he was arrogant and proud, fully aware of his talent and his movie-star looks, walking around with a chip on his shoulder. I hadn't met him yet; only experienced residents were allowed to work on cardiac cases because the anesthesia was more complex. Residents had to get an entire year's worth of experience before they could be assigned to these high-risk surgeries. Since I was still establishing myself and doing routine cases, I didn't give much thought to this doctor. Before long, though, the Chief of Anesthesia realized how much work experience I already had, and he assigned me to do a case with this doctor. I mentally prepared myself to work with an egomaniac whose name was Dr. Ashraf.

Sure enough, this doctor had plans to take me down a notch— the fresh resident assigned to the VIP surgeon. He started out by asking me where I had graduated from in India. When I told him LHMC, immediately his face changed from aggression to surprise to warmth. His tone softened, and, it turned out, his sister, Booba, was an old classmate and friend of mine, and, even more surprisingly, his cousin had been another of my classmates and was still one of my very close friends.

Quickly this doctor aborted his mission to chew me out and instead fully accepted me. We went on to become good friends for the rest of our lives, sharing many more operations together.

In fact, he frequently told his friends and family how his plan to skewer me had failed. He turned into a mentor and a helper to both me and my family, and his warmth and affection lives on in us to this day.

So, after winning him over, this doctor invited me and my family over for dinner. But when I came home from work and shared the good news with Raj and Mataji, I didn't get the response I thought I'd get.

I was very keen to go to Dr. Ashraf's house; in fact, I was honored to be invited, but Mataji was adamant that she would not accompany us. With her strict religious beliefs, she ate only Hindu kosher vegetarian food prepared in a vegetarian kitchen. Raj, too, was hesitant.

I tried to explain that Dr. Ashraf was a very pleasant, warm person, but Mataji had always been stubborn. I knew I had to come up with something, though, because we couldn't just abandon her at home. Then I got an idea. I suggested that Mataji tell Dr. Ashraf she was fasting—then she would have an excuse not to eat.

Success—Mataji was finally on board! I was relieved and excited. These were not modern times, and with my upbringing, I had to respect Mataji's decision.

Dr. Ashraf picked us up in his luxurious Lincoln Continental Mark III and drove us to his mansion in Weston. It was early November, so the days were short, and it felt like a long drive in the wooded dark.

Dr. Ashraf's mansion was newly built, impressive and beyond lavish. His wife greeted us warmly. She had cooked us a delicious Indian meal with the assistance of some maids.

As per the plan, Mataji said she was fasting and would skip dinner. Dr. Ashraf did not look surprised; he had passed the school of etiquette with an A-plus. He assured Mataji that he had washed his hands three times with soap and water before preparing the vegetarian meal, a scrubbing more thorough than even pre-op to avoid any adulteration with non-vegetarian cuisine. How could Mataji refuse? Beneath all her stubbornness, she had a soft heart, and she quickly agreed to join us.

We had a wonderful time, and, at the end of the evening, when Dr. Ashraf drove us back home, he said that his wife, who had a small car of her own, would like to take me grocery shopping; he added that I should not hesitate to accept her offer. I figured his wife's "small car" had to be a station wagon of some sort, as all American cars were huge by my standards. I couldn't contain my curiosity and asked what she drove. A Mercedes Sports model, he said. Ah, yes—I should have known better after seeing their mansion.

Raj and I became good friends with the Ashrafs. They were generous and kind, visiting our Francis Street apartment and complimenting Mataji on her cooking. And Mataji, for her part, never again claimed to be fasting when we went to their home for dinner. In fact, she became very fond of Dr. Ashraf. He had mesmerized her with his charm and unflappable demeanor. Professionally, I often turned to Dr. Ashraf for medical advice, knowing he would not chastise me for it, and he always went above and beyond to be helpful.

As time went by and Mataji got settled into our apartment, her health concerns cropped up again. As usual, she was concerned about aging and fearful of losing her beauty. But the only real medical ailment she suffered from was minor arthritis in her knee, which we already knew about after schlepping from one doctor to the next on Harley Street when we lived in London.

Mataji was insistent, though, that she needed another full medical workup in the U.S. before returning to India. She argued that one should always get a second and third medical opinion. Raj and I already knew nothing would come of it, but we had to play by her rules.

So, Dr. Ashraf arranged for Mataji to see an orthopedist at the Deaconess Hospital. The total bill came to one thousand dollars. We had been in the U.S. for only two months and were still trying to find our financial footing. My yearly salary at the time was seven thousand, two hundred, and Raj was still job hunting.

Mataji, however, was completely ignorant of our tight finances. Her needs had always been taken care of by Pitaji. She had never handled finances, or even pocket money, and all of her shopping had been done for her.

Fortunately, her medical tests came back negative, as expected, so no follow-up was needed. The only procedure she got was a cortisone injection in her knee, with an advisement to lose weight. Mataji was not happy. At fifty-two years old, she weighed one hundred ninety pounds and had never even heard of dieting. She was a food lover, particularly of desserts.

I felt sorry for Mataji. I had never considered dieting, either, but I didn't necessarily have to; I weighed ninety-five pounds.

Luckily, Raj somehow persuaded Mataji to follow the treatment plan of diet and exercise, perhaps because Raj himself went on a temporary diet—a good son keeping his mother company.

Mataji began walking around the neighborhood. As she became acclimated to Boston's winter, she increasingly enjoyed the exercise and gradually increased her time to an hour, covering two miles. Her feelings about dieting, though, never came round.

Funny enough, even when she did start watching what she ate, she thought it was a one-time deal: she'd lose the pounds and then return to indulging in her normal foods. She was shocked when I told her that the diet was permanent, she needed to keep off the pounds. She lamented that she'd never be able to enjoy parties again. I often think of her reply now that I have to watch my own weight these days.

Mataji ended up losing ten to fifteen pounds, and she continued to enjoy her walks, unchaperoned. In fact, the longer she stayed with us in Boston, the more confident she became. She was living in a much bigger, very different world from the four walls of her home in India.

Raj and I didn't have much at the time, but Mataji enjoyed every day with us, becoming more and more independent. She went out and about by herself—exercising, exploring the neighborhood, enjoying going to stores like Stop & Shop and Sears in Fenway. She also enjoyed the company of our friends. I slowly began to realize that Mataji wasn't an airhead or heartless; she simply had never been given the opportunity to discover who she was or to develop social skills. She had been cut off her entire life from reality, but here in Boston, on her own, she had turned over a new leaf, and she was flourishing.

During this time, Raj landed a job, giving us financial security, and we were ready to move into a better apartment. But right after this decision, we experienced our first snowfall of twelve inches, and we immediately changed our minds. We decided to stay in our current apartment until the spring, when the weather would be more cooperative.

The next purchase on our list was a car. We were still planning on returning to India, so we decided to get the big Chevrolet Impala. In India, it was a prestigious luxury car. We specially ordered the tropical model (a standard shift), and it took three months to arrive. In the meantime, we continued getting rides from Bindu and Mr. and Mrs. Dagli, and it was actually nice to be able to enjoy our first winter without having to clear any snow from either a car or a home.

One of the places we frequently drove to was the Boston Haymarket, a centuries-old outdoor market with tons of fresh produce. It felt very much like India's farmers markets: crowded because of the low prices, and the rule of no touching any food. We visited Quincy Market as well, another chaotic, old Boston market (it was actually scheduled for demolition but was saved at the last minute and renovated in 1976). We also liked the North End of Boston, the city's oldest neighborhood, home to many restaurants and stores.

We were surprised to discover while milling about the North End that bulk almonds were nearly the same price as peanuts. In India, peanuts were cheap because they were local, while almonds were imported and expensive. Raj and Mataji were particularly aware of the price difference because their family business was selling wholesales nuts imported from Kabul and other parts of Afghanistan. In fact, Raj's whole family was addicted to nuts; they ate them every day. I would joke with Raj that he'd get nut toxicity. Of course, studies today now tout the myriad health benefits of nuts, but, in India, we've known about these benefits since ancient times.

Mataji said we should indulge in the inexpensive gourmet almonds and she'd make *almond halwa*. It was unbelievably delicious. Most people in India have never even tasted almond halwa. I was eager to learn the recipe, and, unlike in the past, Mataji was eager to teach me.

Even now I still make almond halwa a few times a year for family and friends, and I get many compliments. It's also part of our yearly Diwali menu, out of respect for Mataji and her memory. (I also make *daal halwa* for Diwali as well, a gourmet recipe from Chaeji, and it reminds me of my wonderful childhood and Chaeji's warmth and unconditional love for me.)

Besides almond halwa, Mataji was also enjoying cooking other foods for us. She made particularly delicious tandoori roti in our stove/oven (back in those days, we had only gas burners in India).

And as we continued to explore Boston, we learned more and more American vocabulary. For example, *ladies' fingers* is "okra." *Aubergine* or *brinjal* is "eggplant." *Why so?* is "Do you know?" *Standing in a queue* is "standing in line." The *tube* is the "subway." A *lift* is an "elevator," and *getting a lift* is "getting a ride." I'm sure there are still more words even now for me to learn.

In March 1968, our long-awaited dream car finally arrived. All three of us were excited. The Impala had air conditioning as well as some other extras, but it was a manual transmission, which luckily I could handle after driving the Fiat around London. Gas was twenty-one cents a gallon; by now, we knew the local roads, and we relied on maps for any unfamiliar areas. Unfortunately, though, we had no other option but to park our new car on the street.

Mataji had been with us for six months now and was still thoroughly enjoying herself. She did not miss Delhi or Pitaji, and she didn't seem in a hurry to go back. Raj and I, however, were worried about Pitaji being alone for so long, so we convinced Mataji to begin planning her return. As a going-away gift, Raj and I bought her a stove and had it shipped to Delhi so she could continue making her favorite rotis, a kind of flatbread. She was delighted. Raj and I also did some extra shopping for Darshan so he would not feel deprived.

These gifts for Raj's family were a mutual decision between Raj and me. We had been married for four years by now, and, from the beginning of it, we had agreed that it was not "his family" and "my family" but "our family." There would be no biases. All our decisions would be based on the needs of the individual, not on our relationship to them. This understanding has served us well over the years, helping us stay true to what is most important in life.

Mataji would also often remind us that our family was small and that we all needed to be in harmony. I agreed with her readily, because I had been taught to value family since I was a child. With each passing year, my conviction in this has only grown stronger.

Before Mataji's departure, we planned a sightseeing trip to Washington, DC, then on to New York for her flight from John F. Kennedy Airport. With how much her self-confidence had grown since living with us, she was comfortable flying back alone. She reached Delhi safely, and so did her stove a few months later.

Raj and I had assumed that everyone would be happy to see Mataji's new trim figure, so we were rudely surprised when we received a letter from her saying all the relatives were disappointed and complaining. Why? Because when Indians go on vacation, they're expected to enjoy themselves and return "healthy" (a euphemism for gaining weight). Ironically, she had actually returned home healthier in the literal sense of the word, but no one appreciated her efforts. Raj and I were disappointed. I guess you can't win them all.

Spring arrived, and it was time to look for a new apartment. All around us, the trees were budding with new leaves, and flowers were blooming. We felt so lucky to live in a city with four real seasons, each with its own glory and charm.

Raj and I found a decent one-bedroom apartment on quiet Tetlow Street, close to my work. And much to our delight, our next-door neighbor was the Isabella Gardner Museum. Back then, it was a hidden gem, and admittance was free.

We frequently visited the museum, bringing along friends and family whenever possible to soak in its beautiful gardens and European ambiance. Even today, we still visit, and it serves as a sweet reminder of our early days in Boston.

The move went smoothly. We could fit two sofas in our new living room, and they could each sleep one person, which was lucky for us because, during our eighteen-month stay in this apartment, we ended up hosting, on short notice, some acquaintances of Pitaji's from India, a business friend and his wife, whose son had settled in the Midwest.

They were from Delhi, and they were wealthy and nice. The husband expressly wanted to visit Cambridge and MIT campus, as his brother had studied at MIT many years ago. This was an easy enough request.

The next day, we drove across Harvard Bridge, explaining to them that the Charles River divided Boston from Cambridge, and, within a few minutes, we were at MIT campus. For whatever reason, though, this gentleman could not be convinced that it was this easy to get to Cambridge. He thought we were trying to fool him. After repeated assurances from Raj and me, I think he finally accepted that we were truly in Cambridge.

Around this time, I also had a new job opportunity pop up. The Brigham and Women's Hospital (then called Boston Lying-in Hospital, or BLI) offered me a fellowship in Obstetric Anesthesia. This was an incredible offer, a dream come true. Even better, the hospital was only a two-minute walk from our new apartment, across the playground of Roxbury Latin School.

My goal was to specialize in Obstetric Anesthesia and then return to Delhi, where I would be one of the first to offer epidurals and spinals for pain relief during labor and delivery. The year was 1968, and epidurals were available in very few hospitals. BLI was at the forefront of the movement, the best in the world, with state-of-the-art technology and equipment. I was nearing the end of my second-year residency at Deaconess, and so, after some persuading on my part, they agreed to release me to BLI.

In July 1968, I started my fellowship at BLI on Longwood Avenue (the renamed Brigham and Women's Hospital is now on Francis Street). I had done spinal anesthesia at Deaconess, so I was confident in those skills, but I had yet to learn epidurals. My initial incompetence shocked me.

My first few attempts were complete failures. With spinals, I was used to working with an 18-gauge needle on patients who were lying still. I had a 100 percent success rate. But with epidurals, I was working on labor patients. In short, they were in pain and moving targets, unable to follow my instructions (which wasn't entirely their fault, since, in those days, women in labor were given scopolamine for amnesia, or "twilight sleep," so it was like they were on a different planet). For spinals, I also had to use a 26-gauge needle (the smaller the gauge number, the smaller the outer diameter). The 26-gauge was a tiny, non-disposable, flexible needle that could break inside of the patient!

My first three attempts were failures. What a disgrace. I blinked back tears, hoping to sink through the floor.

Meanwhile, Dr. Weiss had been observing me from the glass-partitioned theater balcony meant for medical students to watch procedures. He was the department chair and the grandmaster of regional anesthesia (i.e., spinal and epidural). He had even designed an epidural needle known as "the Weiss needle," which would become my all-time favorite needle.

Dr. Weiss saw my miserable state and came down to calmly reassure me that, if I kept at it, I'd be fine in two days. This was difficult for me to believe—I had completely lost faith in myself—but I also knew that Dr. Weiss had years of experience and had trained many before me, so I agreed to keep trying.

Of course, Dr. Weiss was right. In two days, I had mastered the technique. We did twenty deliveries a day with spinal anesthesia and fewer than five deliveries a day with epidurals.

I was incredibly lucky to get my training at one of the largest, most prestigious obstetric centers not only in the U.S. but the entire world. Over the years, the department has become big and sprawling, but at the time, it was small and intimate.

When I started at BLI, there was another fellow along with me, Martin (Dr. MC) from the UK, who had completed his residency at Massachusetts General Hospital. Martin and I became good friends; he was a few months my senior and always ready to help.

We also had a couple nurse anesthetists (CRNAs), who worked under our direction. One of the CRNAs, Pat Bruce, joined the team at the same time as me; we worked together well and quickly bonded. She was from Nova Scotia but had become a U.S. citizen and had even served in the U.S. Army over in Europe. She was older than me, with a very warm disposition, and was much more experienced than I in American customs and traditions; thankfully, she was kind enough to teach them to me.

Our department also handled one-month rotating residents from Massachusetts General Hospital, Peter Bent Brigham Hospital, Boston University, and Tufts. Watching each resident during his or her first week reminded me of my own steep learning curve. Although I was now the teacher, I still learned from them, too; they were a diversified bunch of doctors and second-year residents with training that spanned the globe. I would latter miss this reciprocal teaching-learning relationship when I switched to private practice.

Although I enjoyed my work, night calls were difficult. There were deliveries at least every hour. I would administer a spinal and then immediately move on to the next suite, handing over the current patient's care to be monitored by the CRNA.

Within the following year after starting my fellowship, the number of patients receiving sedation with scopolamine ("twilight sleep") dropped noticeably, while epidurals skyrocketed. Epidurals went from a few hundred a year to more than three thousand a year. Innovation had made delivery pain-free, and BLI was the global leader. Even doctors from neighboring hospitals would bring their wives to BLI for childbirth. Needless to say, with all the practice I was getting, I had a very high success rate and was content with my performance.

I did, though, have some performance anxiety at first, which I quickly remedied. We had a very diverse patient population, and some of the patients were wives of the rich and famous: Boston Brahmans, sports stars, politicians, and professors, among others.

Invariably when an elite patient walked through our doors, my co-workers would begin playing telephone, whispering to each other, and, since I was still young, as soon as the attending nurse told me the patient was a VIP, I would get nervous about my performance. So, I told the nurses to stop giving me the who's who before I administered the anesthesia. After I completed the procedure, however, they were free to share. This worked most of the time, but sometimes I still figured it out beforehand because the nurses were overly cautious attending to VIP patients.

In later years (1978 and onward), our son Mohit had started an independent middle school in Brookline called Park School, and, so, I frequently was the anesthesiologist for many of its mothers in labor. Every time I'd think, *I hope she had a pleasant labor experience.* Normally an OR anesthesiologist plays only a peripheral role in patients' memories, as most are on sedatives and anti-anxiety medications. Even when we visit them the day after surgery and they thank us, they probably only have a vague idea of who we are.

Labor patients, however, spend a few hours with their anesthesiologists, so we tend to have more of a relationship. An obvious con here is that these labor patients might not be totally comfortable and will surely let their anesthesiologists know.

So, whenever I ran into previous labor patients, either in the hospital or out, my situation was a bit precarious. Had they been happy with their labor and delivery? If so, they might not even remember me. But if they were unhappy, they'd most certainly remember me (and if a mother had more than one baby, she'd be keeping a running mental tab).

At any rate, Dr. Dagli, our old neighbor and one of my first friends in Boston, had completed his assignment at Deaconess and was getting ready to return to India. But before he left, he wanted to work as a fellow for a few months in obstetric anesthesia because he knew how valuable and desirable this skill would be in India. So he joined us at BLI for three months to learn the art of spinals and epidurals.

Now our roles were reversed: I was the pro, and he was the new kid on the block. In the beginning, he shadowed me while I worked, and I was glad for the opportunity to be of some help to him.

Soon the time came for Dr. Dagli and his wife to leave. They were taking most of the household items they had accrued while in the U.S., but he was not taking his window air conditioner. Customs in India's airports were very strict at the time, with heavy duties on all imports and the rule of only one air conditioner per family. Since Dr. Dagli was not taking his unit back to India, we asked if he would transfer his leftover quota to us, and he happily agreed.

Raj and I had been concerned about our one-air-conditioner limit: how could we sleep in cool comfort knowing that Pitaji and Mataji were still suffering in the heat a few doors down? We were very grateful to Dr. Dagli, and, to this day, we've stayed good friends with him and his family.

Dr. Dagli will come up again later on, but I'll say now that he did return to India, and he established an anesthesia practice in Bombay. He eventually narrowed his scope to mainly OB anesthesia and became the celebrities' anesthesiologist. Bombay is the film capital of India, nicknamed "Bollywood," and Dr. Dagli delivered the babies of film stars, politicians—basically anyone who was rich and famous. So he became a kind of celebrity himself, although he always remained humble and down-to-earth.

At any rate, Raj and I were excited to buy our additional air-conditioner export unit, and we made a day trip to Canal Street in New York to purchase it. Two famous shops for international appliances were Bondy, owned by a nice lady, and another called ABC. Both of the owners were Jewish and catered to all international customers. Their inventories ran the gamut, from small appliances like our air conditioner to larger items, including refrigerators, washers, and dryers. Since then, we've made frequent trips to Canal Street for 220-volt appliances.

As time went by, Raj and I were becoming more and more comfortable with our American life, but we still had a lot to learn about the culture. Then, in the summer of 1968, I was shopping at Lechmere when a lady in her fifties wearing sneakers and casual clothes walked up to me and introduced herself as Mrs. Madeline

Marshall. She started talking to me about India, because her son and his wife were currently living there. (In those days, it was not common to see Indians in the U.S., so even fellow Indians who were strangers would greet one another warmly. Nowadays, most Indians pass each other without acknowledgment.) Madeline's son was working on his PhD, and she and her husband, John, were planning a trip to visit him, so she was wondering if I had any advice for her. Madeline was very warm and friendly, and we exchanged phone numbers and addresses to meet up again.

Not long after, the Marshalls invited Raj and me over for dinner. Madeline's husband, John, was big and sturdy, but he carried his weight well. They lived in the nice suburb of Belmont, and John was the school administrator of Belmont School. Their house was historic, surrounded by mature trees and full shrubs. They also had a beautiful garden, thanks to Madeline's green thumb and tender care.

Inside, the house had wood floors; some of them were slightly uneven due to the age of the house, and the living room's floor was covered with a 9-by-12 braided rug. All their furniture was early-American antique, but Raj and I thought they simply lived modestly! We later found out they were fond of antiques. They had a beautiful collection, which we learned more about as we returned to their home for subsequent get-togethers. John, for example, owned at least two or three antique cars; they were his pride and joy. One of the cars was a 1932 Model T with a rumble seat, and he was kind enough to take us out on joyrides, near and far.

But what meant the most to Raj and me was not the Marshalls' house but the warmth and affection with which they invited us into it. We all had a wonderful time together that first evening and instantly became friends.

They told us more about their son, who was also named John, and his wife, Judy. They were living in a small village near Delhi while John worked on his PhD in Anthropology. Surprisingly, their village had no electricity, even though Bhen's village had gotten electricity in 1954, fourteen years before.

Raj and I were happy to help the Marshalls plan their trip to India, and, in return, they treated us like family and educated us on American traditions and celebrations. In fact, Raj and I spent our first Halloween with the Marshalls. It was amazing to see all the kids dressed up and trick-or-treating. We also celebrated our first Thanksgiving with them that year, and the following year, we went to Belmont to watch the Fourth of July fireworks with them.

Neither Raj nor I knew much about Thanksgiving, so we were lucky to be invited to the Marshalls'. The meal was 100 percent American, and was even started off with a traditional Thanksgiving grace. John and Madeline had worked very hard cooking all the food to perfection. There was turkey and cranberries, along with all the usual sides and several varieties of pie: the pumpkin was not my favorite; the minced meat was okay; the pecan was to die for.

John had a great sense of humor and told us that, whenever they had company over and were running low on a certain pie, Madeline would say to him, "F.H.B." He asked me what I thought the acronym meant and I said, "Father, have both." He replied, "Father, hold back!"

From then on, the Marshalls invited us to celebrate every Thanksgiving with them, and if I happened to be working on Thanksgiving Day, they'd invite us over for the next day. (They also invited two other friends every Thanksgiving, a nice couple from Worcester.)

So it's not surprising that Thanksgiving is Raj's and my favorite American holiday. We always say grace before the start of the meal and express our gratitude for all our family and friends, including the wonderful Marshalls, who have since passed away. Even our dog, Shayru, loved Thanksgiving; pecan pie was his favorite. His last Thanksgiving was in 1999.

Thanksgiving is my favorite holiday for two reasons. First, it is celebrated by all faiths. There is no discrimination in race, creed, color, or gender. Second, Thanksgiving has not been commercialized with gift-giving. It is simply a day of appreciation for all mankind (and animal-kind, as Shayru pointed out).

Every Thanksgiving is special to Raj and me, and we count our blessings. It takes most immigrants some time to understand the importance of this purest day of the year; Raj and I were lucky to get a head start from the Marshalls.

In between all the holidays we celebrated with the Marshalls our first year, we also went on picnics to enjoy the beautiful fall colors. John knew where all the most scenic places were. If we were in one of his antique cars, many drivers passing by would wave in admiration. The places John drove us to were mesmerizing: placid lakes reflecting the bright fall leaves, with brilliant green mountains in the background. Raj and I were truly lucky to have such knowledgeable and generous American tour guides; we always knew we could turn to them whenever we needed advice on any matter.

During these outings with the Marshalls, Raj and I helped them plan their dream vacation to India, which was coming up quickly in the summer of 1969. They had planned to spend some time with their son, John, and his wife, Judy, sightseeing in Delhi, Agra, Jaipur, Bombay, and Kashmir. We also invited them to visit Raj's family in Delhi and to visit and stay with my family in Ahmedabad. Ahmedabad had not been on their original itinerary, and they were excited to step outside the usual tourist hotspots.

Likewise, Raj and I were happy we could help the Marshalls enjoy India in ways most tourists could not. For example, Raj's brother-in-law, RG, was posted as the ADC (Aide-de-Camp) to the President of India, and he was able to arrange for the Marshalls a tour of Rashtrapati Bhavan, the Indian equivalent of the White House. Also, Pitaji had business clients in Kashmir who sold saffron, so he arranged for the Marshalls to stay with them and experience life in a typical Indian home, including eating with their hands and sitting on the floor. And when the Marshalls were in Ahmedabad, they thoroughly enjoyed their two-day stay at Chhabil Villa. They were amazed to see, right in front of the house, a herd of camels, carrying their daily loads. To Indian natives, this was nothing unusual, but to them, it was unbelievable.

Bauji also took them sightseeing. John (the father) was an excellent photographer and had brought along his fancy camera with all its high-end accessories. He took hundreds of photographs, and on their return to Boston, Raj and I loved looking at them. It was interesting to see what stood out to a tourist—many things that Raj and I would never have noticed because we had grown up there.

The Marshalls had also bought memorabilia during their trip. One of their most treasured purchases was in Delhi: a sixty-pound granite antique statue of the Hindu god Ganesh (which they had to ship home since they couldn't very well fly it back). Ganesh, one of the most well-known Hindu gods, is the god of good fortune. From then on, the Marshalls continued to incorporate Hinduism into their lives, including coming over to our house to learn about and celebrate Diwali.

# Chapter Eleven

*N*ow back to my work at BLI, starting in July 1968. As I mentioned earlier, we started out as a small department. Dr. JW was the chairman, and he taught me regional anesthesia. He was in his fifties but looked young; even as an eighty-year-old, he had absolutely no receding hairline. He was the envy of many doctors in the locker room, brushing his full, luscious locks.

Although Dr. JW was soft-spoken, he had high standards. He refused to compromise patient care, even when pressured by the surgeons, and he passed this value on to me. (He once told me of a tragic accident that had happened at another hospital because a doctor had caved in to peer pressure. The movie *The Verdict* was later made based on this tragedy.)

Also on my team was Dr. HG. She was in her sixties, never-married, pleasant, single, and competent, and she always looked well dressed, even in her scrubs.

Then there was Dr. LL. She was oriental and married, with no kids. She was in her fifties but looked much younger; patients frequently mistook her for a resident in training. She was excellent at performing regional blocks; she could probably have administered one in her sleep. This was the doctor I mentioned earlier who had asked me where I was from, and when I answered "Ahmedabad," she replied that she had donated money to the construction of St. Xavier's, as she was associated with the Jesuit fathers. I had thanked her, adding that her generosity had paid off—St. Xavier's was a wonderful college.

With no social media in 1968, random connections like this one between Dr. LL and me were always surprising and fun. (Although, even back then, I still ran into some of my old professors from India here in the U.S. because they had come to visit Boston College. I've learned that everyone in the medical field has a connection to each other in one surprising way or another.)

Another one of my team members was Dr. DG. He was big, strong, and active, and preferred to work less and play more. (Dr. HG would complain that she had to pick up Dr. DG's slack.)

Dr. DG was smart and was studying for a law degree. He attended classes most evenings while continuing to work as a doctor during the day. He once told me that he kept a syringe in his refrigerator loaded with anectine, an anesthetic drug that causes paralysis, so if his wife was ever home alone and an intruder broke in, she could stick him with it. I still don't know if he was telling the truth or not, but it made for a good laugh.

Dr. DG eventually earned his law degree and went on to become a legal consultant for many hospitals.

The final doctor on our team was my associate Dr. MC. He was a fellow like me. He had completed his residency at Massachusetts General Hospital and had been at BLI six months before I had arrived. He was my favorite on the team, the epitome of a perfect gentleman. When I delivered my son, I requested that Dr. MC administer the anesthesia. Even though I went into labor on a Saturday and he was off duty, he came in with a smile. Sadly, he died young.

We also had two nurse anesthetists who worked under our direction. One of them was Pat Bruce, my friend forever. She was single, never having met the right man, and was full of life, perfectly balancing work and play. She also had a permanent tan. She told me that a summer tan is generic, but a winter tan is class and prestige.

Pat was a good person with good, strong values. She shared the responsibility of caring for her elderly, bedridden parents with her brother JK. Her father was independent and stubborn, a difficult man to care for. He had been born into poverty and thus lived in constant fear of falling into it again. He was frugal to the point of stingy. He once bought a dog clipper for his own use simply because it was on sale. Purchases like this were typical of him.

Pat's mother, on the other hand, was kind, she had multiple minor strokes and Alzheimer's and referred to Pat as "that girl." It was touching to see how dedicated Pat was to her mother's care and comfort. Pat worked double shifts at the hospital (two sixteen-hour days) so she could devote more uninterrupted time to her mother. Pat celebrated Mother's Day, and all holidays, as if her mother were fully aware of them.

Neither Pat nor her brother wanted to put their mother in a nursing home. Their plan was to care for her until she passed away and then put their very-demanding father into a nursing home.

As it turned out, their father passed away first. He had a heart attack while sitting in his chair. Their mother continued her slow decline for three years, and then she, too, passed away.

I respect and admire the unconditional love and dedication Pat and JK gave to their parents.

Throughout all the time Pat had spent caring for her parents alongside her brother, she had kept a secret from him—that she'd had mini-strokes. JK was a practicing Catholic, and Pat preferred to enjoy her sex life without the fear of unwanted pregnancy. So she secretly underwent tubal ligation, and I gave her anaesthesia.

Pat also had other siblings besides JK, and we'd all have a good time together when they visited from Nova Scotia. Then, in the late '70s, Pat moved to Texas. Raj especially missed her expertise at preparing lobster tails and other gourmet foods. After moving, Pat eventually did get married, but it was unfortunately not a good marriage, and we eventually lost touch with her in the '90s.

Back to my work at BLI. As time went by, new co-workers were added to our team. One of them was Dr. AL. She and I had only a professional relationship. One day, she walked up to me and asked if I could give her the name of my psychiatrist, as she needed to change hers. I was momentarily stunned. I didn't want her to feel badly that I didn't have one. Was it normal to have one? Later, as I got to know her better, I realized why she needed one (I'm joking mostly).

Another senior colleague, Dr. JC, was tall, slender, and happily married, with three children. She was also very confident and accomplished, but she had completed her medical training at Harvard under the iron fist of Dr. BL.

I never confirmed with Dr. JC, but I heard she had gotten pregnant during her training under Dr. BL. She had broken one of his unspoken rules. Luckily, she was saved by her family, who donated eleven thousand dollars to her training hospital so she could continue after having the baby. Money is power, and her family could afford it.

Another member to join our team was RE. He was initially our resident, and then he joined the staff. He was a man set in his ways. From the time I first met him, he never changed. He dressed like a farmer and was a penny-pincher to the extreme.

RE lived out in the sticks in Gloucester, so to get to work every day, he'd ride the train and then hop on the subway. He said that, when he'd started his commute in Gloucester, he was dressed like everybody else who lived out in the boonies, but, by the time he got to the subway stop, he stood out like a sore thumb. When he was a resident, he was so frugal that he'd actually get off the subway three or four stops early and run the rest of the way to work just to save twenty-five cents. When he became part of the staff, he could afford to pay the extra quarter, but he still couldn't bear to part with it. He did own a car, but it was an old, beat-up VW that could barely start up in the winter. Rather than buying a new car, though, RE instead came up with the idea of putting his cow in the garage next to his car. The space was so small that the cow practically hugged the VW all night, keeping it warm. Funny enough, his solution worked. The car didn't have problems starting anymore. RE had many entertaining stories like this one, but, unfortunately, I can't remember them anymore.

Besides RE, we had many other residents constantly rotating through our team. They came from all over the world, and I enjoyed learning about their different cultures and coaching them through a variety of issues. One resident in particular stands out in my mind, Dr. BC. A Navy veteran, he was bald, personable, and six feet four inches tall. With his commanding presence, many patients thought he was a staff member and would thus bypass the supervising staff and ask him to administer their anesthesia.

Dr. BC led an interesting life. He was single and had grown up in the South, where his parents and older brother were still living. His brother was married but had no children, and their parents kept hinting at both of them to get on with giving them some grandchildren. Dr. BC would jokingly tell us that he wished they knew how many grandchildren they actually did have all over the world. His parents didn't know, but he regularly donated his sperm for extra cash (and it paid well: twenty-five bucks a pop!). I ran into Dr. BC at a medical meeting several years after he'd left our team and, much to his parents' chagrin, he was still single.

Throughout the late '60s and early '70s at BLI, we had only one female doctor on staff and only one female resident in training. At the time, females comprised only about 15 percent of medical students; nowadays that number has jumped to more than 50 percent.

Dr. EC was our chairman. A retired Army brigadier general, he was six feet four inches tall and weighed two hundred fifty pounds, which he actually carried quite well. He was a competent and well-recognized doctor. In fact, all the doctors on the hospital team, whether passing through or permanent, were renowned and accomplished.

Dr. EC liked to a run tight ship (back then, the surgeon took pride in being the captain of the team). So, as soon as anyone on our third-floor staff saw Dr. EC drive into the parking lot, we were to start the induction of anesthesia. Patients were treated differently then. There was no written, informed consent and little dialogue between the patient and the doctor. Everything was done in good faith.

One day the OR nurse saw Dr. EC drive into the parking lot, so she said, "Let's get started." Although most of my senior colleagues followed this practice, I was not comfortable with it. I had my own standard of care.

I told the nurse, "All right." But instead of getting ready, I stood outside the OR, where the patient was waiting. When Dr. EC walked up, he was surprised to see me. He said, "You knew I was coming up the elevator." My heart was pounding; after all, I was only a junior staff member. But I managed to reply with a straight face, "What if you'd had a heart attack in the elevator?"

Dr. EC was taken aback. Luckily, he was also amused. He had a hearty laugh and agreed that I had done no wrong in waiting to give the patient anesthesia.

I had stuck to my principles, no matter the consequence, and I think Dr. EC respected me for that. Later on, he invited me to his VIP-only cookout. When Raj and I arrived at Dr. EC's beautiful house in the affluent suburb of Lincoln, we were the youngest couple there; all the other guests were senior faculty.

One of my favorite doctors at BLI was Dr. SL. He was a self-made man who never forgot his roots. He'd started out as an orderly and made it all the way to the top. He wasn't handsome, but he was charming and colorful. We could spot him from a mile away: he drove a convertible Mercedes and wore cowboy boots paired with a leather jacket. His tastes were quite different from the traditional conservative Boston doctor of the day.

Even Dr. SL's office had flair. Back then, doctors' offices were drab, old cubbyholes. But Dr. SL's new office at Brooke House in Brookline looked like a designer showroom, covered with art and glass. He was the envy of many of his colleagues.

Dr. SL was a great doctor, too, but I admired him the most because he treated his patients like princesses. I had heard about his exceptional bedside manner but had not seen it firsthand until he delivered my sister Veena's baby. His devotion to his patients and his way of communicating with warmth made him look superhuman. After seeing Dr. SL care for Veena, I recommended him to many of my friends, and they all sang his praises.

Dr. SL had a private nurse, DS, who was a consummate professional. She was young, vibrant, and vocal, giving the same level of attention to the patients as Dr. SL. In those days, fathers were not allowed in the delivery room. They could only briefly see the mother and baby for two minutes on their way from the delivery room to the recovery room. DS strongly believed that this moment was an important one for the fathers to bond with their new baby, one-on-one. So, she always found a way to separate the awaiting mother-in-law from the father, giving him that first moment alone with his baby. It was a sight to see DS's hand on the patient's face, keeping the mother-in-law out of sight.

Later on, when I was pregnant, I had a difficult time choosing my provider. There were too many choices. After reviewing more than thirty doctors, I finally chose Dr. TB. He was very professional and not too young. He was also the medical students' favorite, and he attended to many of their pregnant wives. He was so popular, in fact, that few actually knew his name. When wives called to make their initial maternity appointment, they simply called him "the doctor who delivers for medical students' wives." Dr. TB and I had a great doctor-patient relationship, and all went well during my delivery.

Around 1966, BLI merged with the Free Hospital for Women (commonly called the Parkway Division) and was renamed the Brigham and Women's Hospital, or BWH. Along with the merger came doctors from the Parkway Division, many of them with years of experience who had appointed themselves "doctor gods." Luckily, by then, I was fully confident in my capabilities, even as I continued to learn and incorporate new innovations in medicine.

One of the world-renowned surgeons from the Parkway Division who stood out in particular was Dr. K. He was known for his permanent tan, strong personality, and his invention of the birth-control pill. I was grateful to have had the privilege of working with him.

We had another doctor join our team as well. He was young and had trained in the Midwest. He was the first doctor to perform a surgery called laparoscopy, which is now very common. This procedure replaced a big abdominal incision with three tiny holes for telescopic surgery.

The first time I administered anesthesia during a laparoscopy was quite an event. The procedure required that the OR be dark, so, without even a warning, the lights were flicked off. Suddenly, I could not track my patient's color, nor could I even see the dials on my anesthesia machine. My panic spiked. I turned to the circulating OR nurse and asked her to get me a torch. Not only did she fail to understand my conundrum, but she couldn't even understand what I was asking for.

For a few minutes, it was a losing battle between my British English and her American English. Finally she said, "You mean flashlight?" I took a deep breath. Yes. I guess I still had more to learn here in the U.S.

Also on my team was Dr. Weiss, of course. He was my mentor, and I learned a great deal under his tutelage. Apart from imparting knowledge, he also taught me to hold a high standard for patient care and never to give in to pressure from the surgeons.

Even back then, Dr. Weiss was well recognized and respected throughout the world. As I mentioned earlier, he invented the Weiss needle; he was also president of the American Society of Anesthesiologists.

Dr. Weiss eventually retired and moved to Florida, but he later came back to visit and attend my Harvard alumni reunion. Then, when our department exploded in size, Dr. MA took over as chair. We had an excellent rapport. In my night calls with him, I had total autonomy.

As a practicing anesthesiologist in Boston, I was a member of the Massachusetts Society of Anesthesiologists. The last Friday of every month, the MSA would hold a meeting at the much desired restaurant Anthony's Pier 4, which was right on the waterfront. All Harvard faculty and residents, along with their spouses, were invited to attend.

Everyone eagerly looked forward to Pier 4's delicious popovers and lobster dinners—that is, everyone except me. I was a vegetarian and had to make do with the same old plate of boiled vegetables every time. The chefs were not flexible. In fact, in those days, all of Boston was very limited in its choices for gourmet cuisine. Chinese was pretty much the only alternative (unless you counted the universal Italian favorite: pizza).

Raj and I couldn't even find good bread to buy; sourdough was mostly unheard of then. And to get Indian groceries, for many years, we went to a Middle Eastern mini-market in Norwood called Homsy's. Nowadays, there are countless ethnic restaurants and grocery stores. Even Pier 4 eventually updated its menu, and Raj and I enjoyed going there on our own. But all good things come to an end, and in 2016, Pier 4 was demolished to make room for more waterfront high-rise condominiums and office buildings. I still get a little nostalgic thinking about it being gone.

As I continued learning and growing in my work, I had the opportunity to pursue a faculty position at Harvard. The job, however, required that I pass a two-day license test called the

FLEX exam. It was similar to but more difficult than the ECFMG that I'd taken back in London.

The problem was, since I had only a temporary visa, I could not take it in Massachusetts, as it was against state law. Luckily, there was a loophole. Vermont did allow test-takers with temporary visas, and Massachusetts had a reciprocity agreement with Vermont, so I'd end up with a license in both states.

I studied hard for the FLEX and then drove to Burlington to take it. The city was packed with FMGs (foreign medical graduates), many of whom were Indians and had come from many different states. The popular place for everyone to stay was the Howard Johnson Hotel, or the Ho Jo. After we had all finished taking the test, we went out to grab some dinner and ice cream. Our young waitress was timid and had a question for us: why had all the foreign doctors in the past two days exclusively ordered pistachio ice cream? To her, it was the strangest phenomenon. We laughed and explained to her that pistachios in other parts of the world were a gourmet food on par with lobster. (This reminded me of Mataji's love of nuts.)

I was notified that I had passed the exam, so now I had both a Vermont and a Massachusetts license, which meant I could work in any hospital in either state. I had elevated my rank and, most importantly, was now on the faculty of the Harvard Medical School, teaching anesthesiology. I was exalted.

But I wasn't done yet. My next goal was to pass the FRCP(C) (Fellow of the Royal College of Physicians of Canada). Because of my training in both the UK and the U.S., I was eligible to take it. It was the ultimate title in my field. I had chosen to take this exam instead of the equivalent American Boards because it allowed for an expedited schedule.

The American Boards had a required wait time of two years between the written and orals, but I needed to complete everything as quickly as possible, before I ran out of time and returned to India. This time crunch kept me extremely motivated. I was working hard and making a lot of progress.

During this time, I was also learning how to be a good doctor while keeping my nose out of other people's business. I remember, for example, when Dr. Weiss's daughter was in labor with his first grandchild. Dr. Weiss was very excited.

I was on call that day with Dr. MA, the current chairman. Dr. EC, head of the OB, was conducting the delivery. When Dr. Weiss's daughter was ready for her epidural, Dr. MA administered it while the rest of us waited in the staff lounge. Even though Dr. Weiss trusted Dr. MA, he was, of course, still nervous for his daughter. Even though Dr. Weiss was the doyen of epidurals, doctors aren't supposed to treat their own family members.

After the epidural, it sounded like she was still in pain; we could hear her in the staff lounge. I was distressed just seeing Dr. Weiss so helpless. Dr. SL turned to me and said, "Go make her comfortable." I replied, "Only chiefs, no Indians." We all shared a short laugh.

In the end, everything turned out all right. She delivered a beautiful, healthy baby girl. In later years, Dr. Weiss, his wife, and I shared these memories with each other, and ever since then, I've frequently reminded myself to stay out of problems I don't belong in.

On April 1, 1970, Raj and I visited India for the first time in almost five years. We were both full of excitement for the visit. Raj's little brother, Darshan, was getting married.

At the time, Raj was working on getting his accounting degree at Bentley University, so we had to coordinate this vacation with his advisor. We also had a truckload of shopping to do.

Because Raj and I were close relations to Darshan, we had an important role in the wedding, especially in the gift-giving. And since we were coming from the U.S., everyone had high expectations of their gifts. While India did earn its independence in 1947, its economy and luxury goods were still in their infancy even in 1970. Furthermore, India did not allow any foreign appliances or luxury clothes to be imported, so everyone was leaning on us.

At the time, all Raj and I had to our names were our new car and twenty-five thousand dollars in savings. But still, we were happy to do our duty.

We hit the stores with a detailed shopping list for relatives both near and far. Our first stop was Filene's Basement. We purchased more than thirty Arrow cotton shirts for men at a great bargain—two dollars and fifty cents a shirt. We bought woolen sweaters in sizes for men, women, and children. We also bought cosmetics for the women (even for Mataji's relatives) as well as sarees made with Japanese nylon (all the craze then) and French chiffon made in France and purchased in New York. We bought special gifts of pendant watches for the young daughters of Munni, Raj's sister. For the married couples, we bought pens and Swiss watches. And that was only part of our purchases. We wanted to please everybody.

When we arrived in Delhi, we received a warm welcome from all of Raj's family. It seemed Mataji and Pitaji had had a change of heart toward me. They graciously indulged me by taking me shopping for the wedding, a sweet, pleasant surprise. Maybe their stays with us in London and Boston had allowed them to understand my world.

I gave all our gifts except the pendant watches to Mataji to distribute to the relatives at her discretion. I wanted to give the watches to Munni's daughters myself and see their faces light up. I told Munni my plan, and she agreed.

Soon, though, I found out that Darshan had confiscated all the cosmetics I had given Mataji, and he was going to give them as his own gifts to his future wife and her family. Mataji and I were both dumbstruck.

Darshan had also nabbed the pendant watches and was planning on giving them to his new sister-in-laws. I strongly objected, but only after I put great pressure on him did he reluctantly return *one* of them. He was literally robbing little children. I could not help but think to myself what a mean, selfish devil he was. I told Munni what had happened and sent her a second watch in the mail after Raj and I returned to Boston.

Unfortunately, this was only the beginning of Darshan's despicable behavior. Next, he suggested to his parents that all the jewelry Bauji and Chaeji had gifted me at my wedding should be given instead to his witch fiancée, Alka.

Mataji told me that Pitaji replied, "If you touch Sadhna's jewelry, I will break your bones." That shut Darshan up for a little while.

Mataji also told me that Darshan, who was a big, strong guy, did not help Pitaji at all in the business. He was lazy. All he wanted to do was indulge in a life of luxury—playing tennis and hanging out with his friends.

The wedding itself was nice. We enjoyed socializing with all the relatives, especially with RG, Munni's husband; he was always in high spirits. Even Munni was fun to be around now that she had matured (although she still preferred to only receive gifts and never give them, but I had matured, too, so this no longer bothered me).

After the wedding, Darshan's selfish antics were back in full force, except now his new wife was in on them, too. Together they multiplied each other's insatiable thirst for greed and manipulation. For example, Darshan and Alka told me that the saree I had worn at the wedding was beautiful, and since I had already worn it once, I should part with it and give it to Alka. No, sorry, I demurred. But they were not to be deterred. Next they commented on what a lovely winter coat I had; perhaps I should give it to Alka. Although it would not fit her (she was well-endowed), she could pass it on to her sister. No again.

Their selfishness was nothing new to Munni—she had been around it for so long—but Raj and I were in shock. In the past, we had been forgiving of Darshan's shortcomings; now, though, we were disillusioned no more. Some people cannot be lifted out of the gutter, no matter how hard you may try to help them.

Luckily, our trip wasn't all bad. I had a wonderful time meeting with old classmates and visiting our old haunts. The neighborhoods and the street food brought back many memories. Not much had changed in five years.

Next Raj and I traveled to Ahmedabad for a few days. This was always a special treat for both of us. My family and friends always greeted us with open arms and treated us like VIPs. Raj was especially looking forward to indulging in many perfectly ripe mangoes.

The days flew by, and before we knew it, it was time to fly back to the U.S. The Russian airline Aeroflot was offering a special deal: if we flew in and out of the USSR, we did not need a visa. We decided to take advantage of the opportunity and visit Moscow. We stayed in Moscow for only two days, but the experience was unforgettable.

As soon as we landed, our passports were taken away by immigration. We stayed at the Moscow airport hotel, which was part of the travel package. Our room was freezing because the law required that the heat be turned off after a certain day of the year, and there was only one restaurant to eat at. I ended up needing to buy a toothbrush, which felt like it was made for a dog. The city itself was beautiful, but our tour guide never once smiled (it was forbidden).

After our first day, Raj and I were ready to leave, but Aeroflot did not offer daily flights. By the second day, we were more than ready to say *adios*. Things have changed in Russia since then, but we have absolutely no desire to go back.

Our next stop was Scandinavia. What a breath of fresh air! We had a wonderful time sightseeing in Copenhagen, Denmark, Oslo, Norway, and Stockholm, Sweden. We even met a former BLI resident in Stockholm, and he told us how Sweden had recently changed the roads from right-side driving to left. All traffic stopped for twenty-four hours; then, the next day, the the next day the switch was complete. Raj and I were amazed.

When we returned to Boston, spring was at the height of its glory. The flowering trees and crisp, bright air were so refreshing. Yet, even with the wonderful weather and all our comforts here, we still believed India was our home, and we both were homesick for a few days. The streets here seemed too quiet and orderly. There was little traffic, no animals sharing the road, and no constant hustle and bustle with horns sounding off in every direction. Our ambivalence, though, was short-lived, as we quickly fell back into daily life and were once again content.

While we had been away, we had left our new Impala on the street, and we hadn't had a second thought as to its safety. We were still naïve back then about vandalism and theft. I guess ignorance can be bliss. Luckily, our car was perfectly intact.

Raj and I heard even more good news on our return: the U.S. immigration laws had changed in our favor while we were in

India. We were now eligible for a green card: permanent-resident status. No Trump Test to pass. We were exuberant; this gave us total flexibility in our future plans. We immediately completed the necessary paperwork.

Then there was even more good news: Raj and I could afford to upgrade to a new apartment. After hunting around, we decided on Back Bay Manor, a high-rise off Huntington Avenue, which included parking and was only a five-minute walk to the hospital. Raj and I wanted to experience living in a high-rise before we returned to India, and this was the perfect opportunity. (At the time, only Bombay had high-rises, and we knew we'd be living in a house in Delhi.)

We had very few belongings, so the move was easy. Our new, spacious one-bedroom apartment was on the fourteenth floor and had a balcony with a good view of the city. It also had nice parquet floors and the luxury of central air conditioning. We were living in comfort and overjoyed. Now I was back to working hard and getting ready for the FRCPC exam.

In the fall of 1970, I went to Montreal for the written portion of the exam. It was a tough three-day, timed exam, but my hard work was rewarded, and I passed. I was very happy with my achievement, and I could not help but think how proud Bapaji would have been. The following year, I'd return to Toronto for the clinical and oral sections and be done with this final, ultimate test. My dream after that was to get pregnant. I wanted to wait until after the oral exam, because, in those days, women doctors were not common, and I did not want any more strikes against me.

Throughout the next year, I studied hard and attended all the weekly anesthesia conferences at the Countway Library of Medicine at Harvard University, staying abreast of all the latest research and developments in my field.

In the fall of 1971, I traveled to Toronto, feeling prepared and confident. My bedside clinical exam went well. Next came the orals. I was questioned by three examiners on many diverse topics for thirty minutes. I was satisfied with my performance and my answers, but somewhere along the way, I guess they were not. In the late evening, I received my results: I had failed. I was in shock. This was completely unexpected. Never had I felt so miserable.

I returned to Boston and immediately reviewed all my answers with the senior staff in my department. No one had an explanation for my failing. I couldn't even blame it on being visibly pregnant, as I had put off pregnancy for that very reason.

I continued to mourn for a while—it was a bitter pill to swallow—but I eventually recovered. As Winston Churchill said, "Success is not final, failure is not fatal; it is the courage to continue that counts."

Both Bapaji and Bauji had always taught me that if at first I didn't succeed, try, try again. Unfortunately for me, I could only attempt the test one more time, and then I'd be required to start it all over. I could not even bear the thought of it. Again I put off starting a family until after my second, and final, attempt at the FRCPC in October 1972.

Meanwhile, in December 1971, both my sister Veena and my brother Vijay were getting married, so Raj and I planned our second visit to India. In preparation, we did all the required shopping for gifts and requests from family members.

Veena's wedding was in Ahmedabad, and the baraat (groom's party) came from Bombay; they were a very festive group. It was the perfect getaway vacation for Raj and me. It was a very cold December in Boston, but the weather in Ahmedabad was perfect: sunshine, no rain, and temps in the sixties and seventies. We had a wonderful time visiting with friends and extended family members, sharing all our latest happenings in the U.S. Vijay, being the groom, went to his bride's city, Indore. That, too, was a fun, lavish wedding.

Of course, Raj and I also went to Delhi to see his family. The baby girl that I had delivered was now seven years old. While I was talking to Munni, she expressed her disappointment in Darshan and his new wife, Alka. Munni had come to realize how superficial her relationship was with them and how little they cared about her. She said that after Darshan's wedding, he had treated her and the rest of her family like second-class citizens.

Mataji also told me in private that Alka had stolen some of my clothes from her cedar closet. I chose not to confront Darshan about it, but Raj and I were both distressed and hurt by his and Alka's spiteful, selfish ways. We had hoped we could all be one happy family living in harmony, with plenty to share, but that was obviously never going to happen.

Mataji also told us that Darshan was not helping Pitaji with the business, and neither he nor Alka were helping at all around the house. They were on a permanent honeymoon. Even though Raj and I felt sorry for Pitaji and Mataji, there was nothing we could do.

The New Year rolled around, 1972, and Raj and I were back in Boston. Our latest big project was to buy our own home in order to save on rent. But we had strict criteria: the house had to be fifteen minutes or closer to my work, it needed to have central air conditioning (because we were spoiled), and it needed to be fairly new, requiring minimal maintenance.

After some time, we eventually found a nice house in the suburb of Newton. It had three bedrooms and a wonderfully private backyard. We made many happy memories in that house, enjoying good times with family and friends.

With this new home, I also needed a car to get to work. We bought a new Oldsmobile Cutlass. Unlike our big, stick-shift Impala, it had an automatic transmission, so I no longer needed to worry about rolling backwards on the hilly roads. I loved the change, and I've never looked back since.

Raj and I also enjoyed decorating our new home. I've always had a passion for interior design, so I scoured magazines as well as asked the Marshalls for advice. The results were both tasteful and rewarding. Also, in addition to our decorating, Raj bought a lawnmower, which he probably used a grand total of ten times.

My next priority after the house was studying for my second attempt at the FRCP(C) exam. I was completely focused; I *had* to pass. An important development in medicine was the *Roe v. Wade* case, legalizing abortion. It was slowly gaining momentum throughout the United States, but it was already legal in Massachusetts. The change was strong and immediate.

We were seeing patients at BLI who had traveled from many other states specifically for the procedure. The legal protocol was strictly followed as well as all the policies implemented.

We had young girls coming in every few months to get therapeutic abortions (meaning there was no medical reason for terminating the pregnancy). At first, it bothered me that these girls could not learn to avoid pregnancy. Later, though, I felt terrible when I realized that many of them had become pregnant without their consent, and often it involved a family member. These helpless young girls had been brutalized, and abortion was their only chance at rescue. I was still learning the harsh realities of the world, becoming more aware of the suffering other people have to face every day.

November came, and it was time for my second and final attempt at the FRCP(C). I was apprehensive and scared. I had followed all the rules—studied hard, hadn't gotten pregnant—but, still, there were no guarantees. Raj and I made our way to Montreal, a beautiful five-hour drive. We had been to Montreal a few times before, but only in the summer. This time we experienced our first snowfall, and we watched as the scenery turned into a winter wonderland. The leaves were still showing off their fall colors, and with the snow piled on top of them, it was a spectacular sight. The beauty helped reduce my stress, and we arrived at our hotel in the afternoon. The next day I woke up ready for the challenge.

Most of the exam went very well. One of my answers was readdressed and cross-examined, but I think my boldness and confidence in standing by it was well received.

Then I went back to the hotel and anxiously waited with Raj to receive our results in the evening. Yes, it was *our* results, not my results. It had been a team effort of hard work, discipline, sacrifice, and moral support. We were able to face the long evening together with more courage than if we had been alone.

Then came the best news: I had passed the FRCP(C). I was now promoted to the staff, becoming an Instructor in Anesthesiology at Harvard Medical School. It was a defining moment for both of us. Our joy and happiness were boundless. Of course, I immediately thought of Bapaji in heaven, beaming down on me with pride.

I had no more exams to pass. I had accomplished every one of my goals. I was prepared to return to India; this exam was equivalent to the American Boards, and it was recognized all over the world. I was as happy as happy can be.

Raj and I drove back to our home in Newton, and I returned to work. I told my colleagues the good news. At thirty-two years old, I had become the youngest in my department to pass the FRCPC. I was also the only doctor at BLI of Indian origin, so whenever an Indian patient delivered when I was not at the hospital, one of the staff would leave a message for me on the scheduling board with the patient's name, and I would always pay the patient a visit out of courtesy.

There were many doctors at BLI who worked at other suburban hospitals as well. One of them was Dr. W, who was very fond of me. One day he suggested that I consider changing to private practice. I took it only as a passing comment. But a few days later, Dr. W pursued the idea again, and he convinced me to at least give it some serious thought and visit the hospital.

So, in December of 1972, I visited the Leonard Morse Hospital (LMH) in Natick, a twenty-minute drive from my home in Newton.

# Photos

Chaeji's wedding surmedani, 1939

My wedding surmedani, 1964

Mosque Jali, replica

Bapaji and Bauji (in suit) with Baji's family in DI Khan, 1930's

Bapaji's father, Lalchand Bhatia,
in his police uniform

Baji, my grandmother

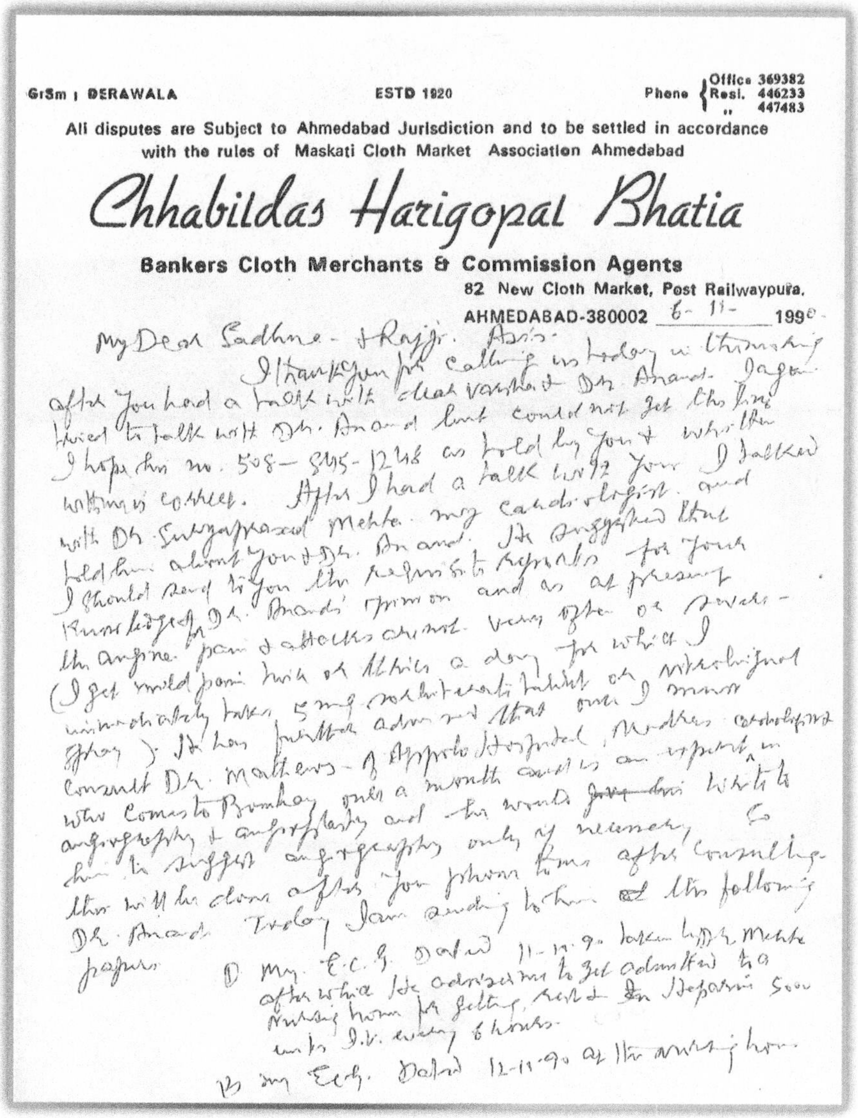

GrSm : DERAWALA ESTD 1920 Phone Office 369382 / Resi. 446233 / ,, 447483

All disputes are Subject to Ahmedabad Jurisdiction and to be settled in accordance with the rules of Maskati Cloth Market Association Ahmedabad

Chhabildas Harigopal Bhatia

Bankers Cloth Merchants & Commission Agents

82 New Cloth Market, Post Railwaypura.

AHMEDABAD-380002 6-11-1990

My Dear Sadhna & Rajji. Asis.

I thank you for calling us today in the morning after you had a talk with [illegible] Dr. Anand. Jagan tried to talk with Dr. Anand but could not get the line. I hope his no. 508-845-1248 as told by you & written is correct. After I had a talk with you I talked with Dr. Suryaprasad Mehta my cardiologist and told him about you & Dr. Anand. He suggested that I should send to you the reports for your knowledge & for Dr. Anand's opinion and as at present the angina pain & attacks are not very often or severe (I get mild pain twice or thrice a day for which I immediately take 5 mg [illegible] tablet or [illegible] spray). He has further advised that once I must consult Dr. Mathews of Apollo Hospital, Madras cardiologist who comes to Bombay once a month and is an expert in angiography & angioplasty and he would [illegible] write to him to suggest angiography only if necessary. So this will be done after your phone to me after consulting Dr. Anand. Today I am sending to him the following papers.

1) My E.C.G. dated 11-11-90 taken by Dr. Mehta after which he advised me to get admitted to a nursing home for getting rest & [illegible] Heparin 5000 units I.V. every 6 hours.

2) My E.C.G. dated 12-11-90 at the nursing home

Bapaji and Bauji's original business stationery

Bauji in business attire

Bhatia Building, in shambles today

Bauji's gift, the pink saree

Prewedding Thali dinner, January 18th 1964

Prewedding Thali dinner, January 18th 1964

Bauji and Chaeji in 1950's, happy times

Mataji and Pitaji

Mataji dressed for tennis

Shayru, the eternal baby

Mohit and Payal's wedding invitation

Mohit's surprise saree gift to me

Pagri Mohit's wedding turban

# Chapter Twelve

*When I arrived at LMH,* the chief of the Anesthesia Department, Dr. A, was waiting for me. He was a tall, athletic, handsome man in his fifties. He and his surgeon colleague, Dr. Capobianco, were the two doctors actively involved in the building of the new, state-of-the art hospital, so naturally, they were very proud of the amazing results.

My first impression of the hospital was favorable. It was a beautiful contemporary building situated on a hill surrounded by vibrant greenery. From the outside, it looked more like a five-star hotel than a hospital. The inside was, if possible, even more impressive.

The operating rooms were state-of-the-art, the hallways filled with beautiful artwork and big windows with plenty of sunlight streaming in. The architect, Tom Payette, had done a phenomenal job. (Payette even had the honor of showing the hospital to the Prince Aga Khan, the Imam of the Nizari Ismailis. The Aga Khan called the hospital "terrific" and later hired Payette.)

I had been working at old, inner-city hospitals, so I was taken aback by how advanced LMH was, even though it was only fifteen miles away from the others. I was used to narrow corridors, out-dated patients' rooms, and ancient, nearly obsolete, equipment.

What was most extraordinary to me, though, were its operating rooms, which were equipped with Anesthetic Gas Scavenging Systems. In the inner-city hospitals, we were far behind in purchasing safety systems, even though studies had already been published showing the dangers of anesthesia personnel breathing in anesthetic gases every day. These gases can even cause pregnant providers to miscarry (and other dangers of breathing in these gases were being discovered as the problem received more attention). Having this scavenging system in place at LMH was very persuasive to me, because I was now seriously planning on having a baby.

In fact, everything in LMH's operating rooms was designed with safety in mind, both for the patients and the staff. I was enticed.

Dr. A had a dynamic personality, and I enjoyed the tour. At the end of it, I had a good feeling about the hospital and about him. I went home to sleep on it.

Later on, Raj and I drove out to look at the campus together. He was impressed with it, too. Then, a few days later, I returned again for a meeting to review the job proposal. LMH definitely had an opening. There were three anesthesiologists, all white males; I would be the fourth anesthesiologist. A small part of my job would be working with the ob-gyn department, but most of it would involve all different kinds of surgical cases (except for open-heart surgery). My specific role at the hospital would be to introduce the epidural. I had been working at BLI for five years—from 1968 to 1972—and I had become subspecialized in providing ob-gyn care, so this would be an opportunity for me to continue learning and developing my skills in other areas.

The proposal also offered me a big jump in salary—from thirty-five thousand to fifty. Their procedure for night calls was also alluring: I could do them from my home, in the comfort of my own bed.

Granted, I would miss teaching residents every month, but with abortion now legalized, my work at BLI had become much more difficult mentally. Every day I was assisting a large number of abortions, all while I was hoping to get pregnant. Even though I tried to compartmentalize my feelings, I knew the situation was still draining me.

The job-proposal meeting went well, and I left seriously considering the offer. The next step, then, was to meet the other two department-head doctors. Dr. A had already given his approval, so this step was mostly a formality.

First, there was Dr. M. He was a short, happy, old-fashioned Italian. He had a sense of humor and looked like a farmer. Then there was Dr. H. He was sulky, introverted, and conceited. He was like a riptide: seemingly calm and still on the surface but dangerous underneath.

Dr. M conducted most of the interview. I was shocked by his questions: *How often every month will you call in sick? Not actually sick, but call in sick. During your menstrual periods?* How ridiculous! I replied, "Why would I call in sick regularly every month? I'd only call in sick if I were sick."

Then Dr. M repeated something Dr. A had said earlier to them: *When you call in sick, let me know when and where your wake is.*

As shocking as all this was, I was not bothered by it. I was in excellent health and never abused, or even used, any sick time. In fact, I don't recollect ever knowing of the existence of sick leave then. I knew only about vacation time.

Another question from Dr. M: *Will you take off early for your hair or nail appointments?* My answer: "I would do those on my days off."

This was 1972. Most women today could never imagine having an interview like this. Even for me, coming from an inner-city hospital, where I had a strong professional image, these questions were akin to being struck by lightning. It showed the very limited thinking and views of doctors who lived in such a small, conceited world, only twenty miles away from the big city.

Dr. H did not ask many questions; instead, he listened. He was the kind of guy who appreciated less talk and more action, a go-getter.

Meanwhile, Dr. W was urging me to accept the job. He went on and on about the excellence of LMH. But Dr. W had his own agenda for getting me on board: he was the chief of the OB department, and I would be introducing epidurals to his staff.

At the time, LMH had only one female surgeon, and she worked part-time. There was also one woman who was an internist in the office, but other than that, there were no other female doctors in the entire hospital. I was surprised by this, but ultimately, it was of no consequence to me. I never asked during my interview the ratio of female doctors to male. In my mind, we were all professionals; gender played no part.

After my second interview, they offered me the job. I had passed Dr. M and Dr. H's test, limited and superficial as it was.

While considering their offer on my drive home, I was still disturbed by their presentation and lack of professionalism. When I got home, Raj asked me how it went. I told him, in short, that there had been only one farmer-doctor at BLI, but at LMH, it felt like two out of every three doctors were farmers in the Anesthesiology Department.

This was only a guess at the time, but I later found out I was pretty spot-on: Dr. M ran a farm with pigs, goats, and many other animals. It wasn't uncommon for him to get calls at work about some runaway animal or another, and he'd have to go chasing after them.

Despite my concerns, Raj and I carefully weighed the pros and cons of accepting the position, because no job is 100 percent attractive. I knew I would enjoy giving epidurals to the patients, and I would enjoy teaching the procedure to others. I would also have the opportunity to learn beyond my subspecialty and work with state-of-the-art technology; these two pros in particular would be helpful when we returned to India, which was our ultimate goal, our big dream.

I knew the major con would be working with doctors who had very backwards views of women, but as I mentioned earlier, Dr. A was the head-honcho, and he had a dynamic, powerful personality. I knew that if I worked with him, I'd be able to bypass these trivial issues.

So, in the end, after summarizing all these points, Raj and I decided that I would accept the offer. It was a compromise I would never regret.

Even though I knew I had made the right decision, it was still with a heavy heart that I handed in my resignation at BLI. Everyone was surprised, but they generously gave me wonderful letters of recommendation. They also told me I had a standing offer to come back if my new job didn't work out. I felt strongly reassured.

It was in February 1973 that I started a new chapter in my career at LMH. My commute on the first day went smoothly. It was a mild winter, and the roads were clear; I was also going against the flow of traffic, driving out of the city while everyone else was trying to get in.

There was plenty of parking at LMH too, and when I walked into the building, I got a short orientation to the locker room, the OR, etc. Then I met the OR nurses. They were excellent—competent, helpful, and friendly. I was the only woman doctor in their domain, so perhaps they saw me as an ally; I shared their locker room.

The senior doctors, however, were a different breed. They could not comprehend a female doctor invading their man's world, and they had no hesitation in expressing their feelings.

Based on how few female doctors there were back then, I guess I cannot entirely blame them for their masculine narrow-mindedness and ignorance. The USA in 1970 was still behind in the higher education of females. It's ironic that the U.S. is considered to be the most advanced country in the world in regards to technology, medicine, and science—I mean, Neil Armstrong walked on the moon in 1969—but the U.S. was still behind third-world countries such as India in encouraging females to go into medicine. Then, medicine comprised only 20% females; now it stands at 50%.

Dr. W, who had championed me from the beginning, gladly went against the prevailing male sentiment and rolled out the welcome mat for me in the OB department. He was eager to offer his patients pain-free childbirth with the epidural, which for the most part, was still widely unavailable in the area.

The rest of the doctors, though, were in disbelief that I would be administering anesthesia to their patients on a daily basis. They had never had a female doctor on their permanent team before, and their initial impression of me was not favorable: not only was I female, I was also a foreigner. In their eyes, I might as well have been an alien.

Except for a few of the younger doctors, they were all macho men, self-anointed "Kings of the OR." Superiority was their birthright, and I was the peasant intruder. It was their way or the highway, and some of them expressed that with language which would not be permissible today.

This was going to be a tough collaboration, like trying to bring the North Pole and South Pole together. I had been living in the U.S. for five years now and had never dreamed I would find myself in a situation like this. I had done so well in my field—had trained with the best and passed the most stringent exams—that I could not imagine such a rude, condescending welcome.

But I did not let their opinion of me affect my opinion of myself. I knew that I was extremely competent, that I worked hard, and that I had integrity. I did have to recalibrate my expectations, but I was ready for the challenge.

I was lucky to have Dr. A in my corner. As chief of the anesthesia department, he was respected by all the surgeons and the OR staff. They called him "the benign dictator." He had high values, and he played a fair game. I knew that Dr. A supported me 100 percent; he was my silent strength.

But now for a description of those in the Anti-Sadhna Club. First in line was the senior surgeon, Dr. Anthony Capobianco (a difficult surname, which I mastered before my first day at LMH). In fairness, he was an incredible surgeon. He was also an old friend of my OB colleague at BLI, Dr. S. They had been classmates and stayed in touch throughout the years. This gave me a small brownie point in his eyes, but not enough to put me completely in his good favor.

Dr. Capobianco had gone to school with Dr. A as well, and together they had been the master planners during the building of LMH. They were good friends both in and out of the hospital. But even with Dr. A on my side, Dr. Capobianco still did not approve of me. At LMH, he was The Godfather. There was only one way of doings things in his OR, and he was not open to change.

He still reminds me today when we reminisce that I did not follow the leader. I was not afraid to disrupt his carefully laid-out plans, all in the interest of patient care. My good intentions, however, did not go over well in the beginning, especially since we had different opinions on what the best treatment plans were. Dr. Capobianco had set ways, and while I respected conventional values, I did not hesitate to part with them and change when change was required. We butted heads, but I remained confident, buoyed up by my upbringing of patience, persuasiveness, and competence.

As time went by, Dr. Capobianco and I forged a positive relationship. With my Indian roots and British training, I preferred to call him Dr. Capobianco, as it was formal and showed respect in our professional work, but as we became friendly, he would often tell me to call him "Tony"; everybody else on staff did, he said. For me, though, this was nigh impossible. Calling him "Tony" felt like I was addressing a kid.

After much prodding from him, I stepped outside of my comfort zone one day and called him "Anthony." He was a bit surprised. From then on, I forced myself to call him "Anthony." Then one day during an operation, I addressed him again as "Anthony" and he looked over at me and said, "Sadhna, there are only two people in the whole world that address me as 'Anthony.' One is my mother, and the other one is you." I'd had no idea. Since then, I've gone against my upbringing and called him "Tony," even up till today.

It's interesting how differently I address people based on where I am in the world. When I worked in Indian hospitals, the senior staff and faculty were strictly addressed as "sir." In the UK, I had to change my ways and call them "Mr." Now, in the U.S., I've had to change again, lowering the bar in my opinion, by addressing them by their first names—Tony, Bill, Bob, Jim.

Over time, Tony became a good friend, mentor, and our family's surgeon, all in one. I had complete confidence in him, and he in me.

Years down the road, I gave anesthesia to his mother, your typical, old-school Italian mom. She was a difficult personality. Tony once said to me that his family thinks of me fondly every Thanksgiving.

I was blessed to have The Godfather's friendship. In 1996, Bauji became very sick, and Tony offered to fly to India with me at his own expense to operate on him. What a touching, thoughtful gesture. He was a true friend.

Tony's wife, Eileen, was a nurse, and he was lucky to be married to her. She was an angel, a beautiful woman who fulfilled all of her duties with grace. She was appreciative and cared about family deeply. She was also a classy lady who wrote the nicest, heartfelt thank-you letters. I miss her and Bhen's letters. Today it's just e-mail and texting.

Eileen passed away three years ago, but I have stayed in touch with Tony, and it's a pleasure to occasionally get together for lunch.

The second most difficult surgeon at LMH was Dr. Johnston. He was the most vocal of all the doctors on staff, like a tiger that never stopped roaring. Four-letter words were a regular part of his vocabulary. He had fixed ideas, and he was loud and clear about what they were.

He was another one of the self-anointed kings who believed the surgeon was still the captain of the OR. He had a hot temper and was known among the staff for his volatile personality. According to him, he could do no wrong. He had no respect for female doctors, and he could not fathom one of them being on his team.

On the plus side, he was an excellent surgeon with good medical ethics. Still, though, it was against my nature to work with a personality like his. I tried to forge a harmonious relationship with him, but it was a losing battle. Unfortunately, he was a busy surgeon, and we worked together pretty much every day. After some time, I realized he was not going to change, and neither was he going to leave LMH. The only options left for me, then, were to either leave or be resilient and survive. I chose the latter.

The next doctor on my new team was Dr. Kim, Tony's junior partner. Dr. Kim was a younger surgeon of Korean origin with endless energy. His outside interests were gourmet food and wine. He had a sense of humor and loved to tease and pull pranks. When I ate in the doctors' dining room, I was not only the sole female but also the sole vegetarian, and Dr. Kim would often jokingly say, "Sadhna, I see a speck of meat in your salad." Times have changed, and now vegetarianism is quite common in the U.S.

Surprisingly, Dr. Kim's humor did not stop inside the OR. When I was administering spinals, Dr. Kim would frequently joke that I would be good at playing darts. One day in particular, I was giving a spinal to a patient, and I could tell that Dr. Kim was clowning around behind me. This didn't bother me, but another one of the anesthesiologists actually asked Dr. Kim to leave the OR because he was a distraction. On another occasion when I was giving a spinal, Dr. Kim secretly moved the OR clock forward by fifteen minutes and told me I was going too slow.

Actually, it was nice having a surgeon around with a sense of humor, and Dr. Kim and I enjoyed working together for many years.

Dr. Frager was another junior partner of Tony's. He was a very nice, sincere man. His hobbies outside of work were dogs and politics.

All of the surgeons, and even the staff, at my new job were at least five years older than me. And all of them except for me and one other doctor were American. (The other doctor was a surgeon from Egypt.)

Next was Dr. Shepard, an ear, nose, and throat specialist at LMH. He had very proper manners—absolutely no foul language—and carried himself with class and dignity. He was a seasoned world traveler and a great admirer of art, music, and gardening. When we met, we had an instant mutual liking and went on to become lifelong friends. I enjoyed working with him and talking to him about a wide variety of topics. Dr. Shepard did have one weakness, though: lateness.

He was consistently twenty minutes late for his 7:30 a.m. surgery appointment, the first of the day. He lived only seven minutes from the hospital, and he even shaved while driving to work, but to no avail. His tardiness had been happening for so long that it had become an accepted fact by the OR staff.

Because hospital teams work together on a daily basis, we become a sort of family, so we'd all cover for Dr. Shepard, telling the patient that Dr. Shepard had been stopped on his way to the OR by colleagues for corridor consults (this was usually true).

One particular day, he was late as usual for his first appointment. His patient was waiting in the OR suite, a six-year-old boy. When Dr. Shepard walked in and said "Hello," the boy looked him straight in the eye and said, "Shepard, you're late." You could have heard a pin drop. Here was a kid who not only knew the value of time but had confronted an adult about it. Dr. Shepard himself was dumbstruck.

Outside of his proclivity for lateness, though, Dr. Shepard was a very good doctor and went on to become a strong opponent of smoking. At the time, smoking was normal, and the hazards were both largely unknown and ignored. Some of the surgeons, in fact, even snuck a smoke inside, in the men's locker room or even in the OR, ignoring the extreme fire dangers. Bad habits are hard to break, and for a long time, accountability was not enforced.

I remember during Christmas of 1975, Raj and I went to a party at Dr. Shepard's beautiful home in Sherborn. It was a typical snowy, cold Boston winter, but there was a constant stream of traffic going in and out of Dr. Shepard's back door. Dr. Shepard and his wife, Grace, were very much ahead of their time as strong advocates against smoking. They did not allow smoking inside their house, so all the doctors had to go outside to light up—doctors going in and out explained that they wanted to be invited again. Yes, even doctors at the time ignored the hazards of smoking.

Dr. Shepard also took on the responsibility of convincing the staff and hospital administration at LMH to make the entire hospital campus non-smoking. This was no easy task—as they say, old habits die hard—but he succeeded. We were all proud of him, probably one of the first doctors to promote preventative medicine in a public place.

After six months at my new job, I was still ambivalent about it. I was getting along well with most of the surgeons—except for the truly difficult machismos—and I was comfortable with the work itself. But still, I wanted complete job satisfaction, and I was not getting it.

One day, I got a call from Dr. Weiss, my old mentor and department chair at BLI, now BWH, Brigham and Women's Hospital. He asked how my new job was going, and we set up an unofficial appointment to talk at his house.

When I arrived, he invited me in with his usual warmth, and after a while of chatting, he persuaded me to return to BWH after completing my one-year contract at LMH. He said, "Come back home. The door is always open." And he added that, with my clinical experience, I'd be able to bypass research work and be promoted within one year from instructor to assistant professor at Harvard. I was excited to return to a place where I was wanted and that felt like home.

The very next day, though, I had a meeting with Dr. A, the "benign dictator" at LMH, for my six-month evaluation. When we sat down, I launched straight into the heart of the matter and said, "So, what is your feedback? Will I be released?" He replied that staff always had complaints when a new team member was getting settled into the department, but surprisingly, Dr. A had heard very few complaints against me. Not only had the surgeons accepted me, but none of the male patients had had any objections, either. In fact, it seemed the patients were more open-minded than the surgeons. I had proven to everyone that a female doctor was neither inferior to nor less competent than a male doctor. Dr. A then offered me a permanent position on the team.

As I considered it, I thought about how I was the only female doctor at their quarterly staff meetings and the weekly grand rounds. I was not uncomfortable (in my mind, we were professionals, and that was all that mattered), but it did matter to me that at BWH, the door for female doctors was wide open, while here at LMH, the door was barely ajar.

After some thought, I decided to stay at LMH rather than accept Dr. Weiss's offer to return to BWH. Raj and I were still planning on returning to India, either the following year or after having a baby with U.S. citizenship. We thought it best, then, to favor stability and stay put at work.

As I continued on at LMH, I eventually graduated out of Dr. Johnson's proverbial boxing ring. He still did not like female doctors, but he gave me the title of "You Are Different." Every time he went off saying something negative about female doctors, I'd remind him that I was a woman; his reply was, "You are different." This was his version of a compliment. We later served on many hospital committees together, and he valued my input, even though for everyone else he valued the men's opinions above the women's. I think it helped that I was confident and never refrained from speaking my mind but also thought twice before opening my mouth. My mantra was *Speak only when you are 99 percent sure.*

One incident of speaking up I remember in particular. A nationally renowned speaker had been invited to speak at our weekly grand rounds. This speaker was an expert in his field, and I very much wanted to go, but I had a conflict in my schedule with a case I had to follow up on. Dr. Capobianco and Dr. Johnson, however, could have gone but had both decided not to because of the speaker's well-known chosen lifestyle.

While we were together performing an operation, I told Dr. Capobianco and Dr. Johnson that this speaker was addressing a very important topic and that we were lucky to learn from him. By now I had built up enough goodwill with them that they had begun listening to me with less resistance, more receptivity.

So, they agreed to attend the rounds without prejudice. And guess what? Their feedback was positive. They said that the speaker was superb, the lecture excellent, and they were glad they had gone. Change is not easy, but with small steps and compromise, it is possible.

When Christmas and New Year's rolled around at LMH, we were all rotating time off. Dr. A, the chief of our department, put together the schedule: he and I would work together; on our days off, Dr. M and Dr. H would work with two of the CRNAs (certified registered nurse anesthetists). I asked Dr. A what his reasoning was with the two groups, and he said, "The two of us are equal to the four of them." That meant a great deal to me, especially coming from Dr. A, as everyone on our staff respected him.

Outside of work at LMH, life was still moving along wonderfully. Raj and I were both coming to the realization that the U.S. was a country where our dreams really could come true. With hard work, determination, patience, and a little bit of Lady Luck, we were climbing the ladder of success. True, there were still obstacles in our way—some small, some big—but nothing we couldn't overcome. We were happy to be living in this wonderful country.

Before we knew it, spring had sprung. It was our first spring in our new house, and we were pleasantly surprised by all the beauty in our yard (and throughout our neighborhood). We had forsythias and magnolias, dogwoods, a weeping cherry, and a majestic umbrella pine. Every day it felt like we woke up to more magic, with another tree exploding in flowers. We were mesmerized.

Along with enjoying Boston's beauty, I was also taking full advantage of its shopping. My store of choice was still Filene's

Basement. It was a discount store, even though I had told myself that once I was earning good money, I'd upscale, I was too much in love with FB. I couldn't believe some of the treasures I found there. Once, I found a set of flatware for half the price that I had paid for my initial set in the UK. At first I thought it had to be a knockoff, but I examined it with a microscopic eye—it was authentic. I had also bought a designer suit while sightseeing in Austria—a Geiger skirt and sweater—and I later added another one to my collection that I found for half the price at FB. In fact, I found designer clothes at FB from pretty much all over the world—Italy, France, and elsewhere.

When I was still working at BWH in the late '60s, I wasn't yet a convert to FB, but I knew that my male colleagues always went to FB's door-buster sales to buy their suits. Sadly, all good things must come to an end; it's too bad FB got caught up in the economic downturn of the early 2000s and had to close its doors.

In the summer of 1973, Bauji and Chaeji came to visit us for the first time in our new home. Raj and I, as well as the Marshalls, were excited to see them and entertain them.

First we introduced Bauji and Chaeji to all our friends, and then we drove to Florida in our Impala for a vacation. Coming along with us was my cousin Minni and my sister Varsha. Raj was our official driver, with me as the occasional relief driver. As luck would have it, our Impala had never failed us before, but on this trip, she was practically on life support. Every day it seemed we were dealing with new wear and tear. Even with these delays, though, we still had a wonderful time. Bauji and Chaeji had visited us in London, in 1967, but we were still finding our feet financially then. On this visit, we could finally afford to indulge in some luxuries: while in Florida, we went to Cypress Gardens, Miami Beach, many dolphin shows, and much more.

The Watergate Scandal was in full swing when Bauji and Chaeji were with us. The news was disturbing, and Americans were full of uncertainty. Bauji had always been interested in world news and current events, so he was very interested in the scandal.

After returning from our Florida trip, we did some more sightseeing in New Hampshire and then Maine, where we visited the beautiful Acadia National Forest. The Marshalls also took Bauji and Chaeji to Cape Cod in their Ford Model T.

Bauji one day said, "Most of the population here is not vegetarian, yet still God has bestowed His bounty. There are lakes, mountains, plenty of food, no natural disasters—no famines or floods—no hunger, no beggars, no poverty." In India most people were vegetarian because they believed in a Hindu God, and Bauji wondered if America had a different God.

Our next stop with Bauji and Chaeji was Filene's Basement. This was their first experience at FB, and it was a memorable one. In later years whenever they came to visit, they would always go to FB, as if it were a pilgrimage site.

They went shopping at many other stores, too, and they had even become confident enough to use the subway by themselves. India's economy was still young when it came to home goods and western clothes, so their shopping list was lengthy—not so much for themselves as gifts for the relatives and friends.

With Bauji and Chaeji still visiting, Raj received a letter one day from Pitaji, saying that Mataji's health was declining and that he should visit her. So, Raj went to Delhi for two weeks, but he didn't notice anything alarming during his stay other than some unusual requests from Mataji.

For one, Mataji insisted that Raj get a safe-deposit box at the bank for my jewelry. Up to that point, my jewelry had been perfectly safe in Pitaji's closet.

Also, Mataji had somehow accumulated one thousand of her own rupees, and she insisted on gifting them to Raj. This was shocking because Mataji had never even gone shopping on her own, much less had her own pocket money. How had she saved up so much cash without Pitaji knowing about it?

When Raj returned to Boston, it was time for Bauji and Chaeji to leave. He asked them when they would be visiting again, and Chaeji replied, "When you have a baby."

Unfortunately, we weren't having any luck in that department. Raj and I had both gotten everything checked out, and all was well. The tests had come back normal; nothing needed to be done. We just needed to wait patiently, but the waiting felt like forever. We were falling behind in our ideal schedule—we had hoped to have a baby with U.S. citizenship before returning to India. We tried to continue with our normal lives, working and enjoying time with friends, yet secretly we hoped every month that I would be pregnant.

Meanwhile, there had been a few changes at LMH. A new doctor had joined our team, Dr. TB, a man in his late fifties. Of course, he was immediately accepted by the surgeons, unlike me, who'd had to work hard for it. But at least he was easy to get along with and was more cultured than his two colleagues.

Also during this time, hospital politics were in full swing. I was not interested in them, though, and consciously chose not to participate. I trusted Dr. A, our department head, and had complete confidence that he would steer us in the right direction. Unfortunately, the trustees on our board did not feel the same way.

There were about seven trustees, voted into office by town election, and some of them were very critical of our staff doctors. The local newspaper always had some controversy or another to write up.

One night I was on call and had to go to the hospital for an emergency. A patient was in shock due to a bowel obstruction. When I arrived, I discovered that the patient was one of the nastiest, most hated trustees on the hospital board. I went to work right away, resuscitating and then anesthetizing him. At one point, his blood pressure went down, and mine went through the roof, but in the end, the surgery was a success, and he pulled through.

Because I had kept my mouth shut throughout the board conflicts, this man had no idea who I was, and I had never seen him in person, either; I had only heard horror stories about him from the other doctors. But still, I was relieved and happy that the operation had gone well. The next morning, though, when I walked into the OR, I was greeted by a bunch of doctors accusing me of botching the chance of a lifetime—I had aided and abetted the enemy. They were only joking, of course, and we all shared a good laugh.

In March 1974, Mataji was still struggling with her health, so Raj and I decided to take another trip back home. We reached Delhi at lunch time and found Mataji sitting in the kitchen, attempting to making *roti*, her hands trembling with the effort. She looked sad and helpless as she struggled to complete a simple task she had done every day of her life.

I was shocked to see her in such a state and said, "Why are you doing this?" She was embarrassed and softly replied, "Division of assignment. I prepare the morning meal, and Alka does the evening." Shivers went down my spine, and my eyes filled with tears. Even the worst taskmaster would have some consideration for Mataji's condition, but not Darshan and Alka. Mataji had done nothing but care for her youngest son; now she was being forced—in sickness—to earn her keep.

Although Mataji was a woman of few words and seldom gossiped, she shared with me that Alka always spoke negatively of me and taunted her about me. So, when Alka heard I was coming to visit, she said sarcastically to Mataji, "Wait until your foreign daughter-in-law arrives." Mataji replied, "I have no complaints with her. She has always obeyed me and shared my work. We've never had a single issue." I realized then that Mataji could truly see me for who I was, and sadly, she was a hostage in her own home.

The following day, Darshan took out my wedding gift of silver glasses with a pitcher as well as Alka's matching wedding gift. Then he said, "Guess which one is yours." I was going to say the older, more tarnished set, but Mataji interrupted and said, "The heavier one is yours; the lighter one is hers." The cost of silver goes by weight, and she knew Darshan was trying to trick me into choosing the wrong one. This explained Mataji's unusual earlier request that Raj put all my jewelry into a safe deposit box at the bank; Mataji knew all too well Darshan and Alka's evil, selfish motives.

Our wedding glasses and pitcher were beautiful, so Raj suggested we bring them back to the U.S. with us, as we both enjoyed hosting dinners. Mataji's jaw dropped and she said, "If you take these, that means you will never return home." I understood Mataji's desperation, so I spontaneously replied that, of course, we were planning on moving back to India, and to reassure her, our silver would remain there.

Seeing Mataji in such a bad state, Raj and I decided to treat her to a night out. We took her to the cinema to see *Bobby*, a popular movie that had been in theaters since November 1973. Darshan and Alka had already seen it several times (since movie-going was their only vocation), but they had never once invited Mataji to come with them.

Mataji loved the movie, and Raj and I were so glad we could bring a little joy and laughter into her life. We could still sense, though, a pervading depression and loneliness in her. In a select few words, she conveyed to us how much she missed us and longed for us to return. She also expressed, in her own way, how much she appreciated me, and she even softly asked me what I thought of Alka. I replied, "She is likeable." My hope was to encourage family harmony, but later I regretted not telling her the truth. Perhaps more than anything, Mataji needed someone to share her pain and thoughts.

Unfortunately for all of us, Darshan and Alka never stopped acting despicably. They had no conscience. Darshan was all play and no work. He said that his aches and pains from playing tennis prevented him from helping Pitaji with the family business. And Alka was just as bad. Even though she was sharing everything in Mataji's home, she had no problem accepting her share of gifts and then coming up with whatever ridiculous excuse she could to nab Mataji's gifts, too. This was, in fact, Alka's forte. Many of Raj's and my belongings that we had stored at Pitaji and Mataji's would end up mysteriously disappearing. Mataji, of course, knew who the culprit was, but she kept her mouth shut.

Darshan and Alka had taken over the house, and they lived as if they were on permanent vacation. Darshan thought his big achievement in life was giving Pitaji and Mataji a grandson. He had named him "Prince"—a black prince for the self-anointed royalty.

I felt sorry for Mataji. She lived in isolation, a prisoner in her own home—no visitors, no power, no hope. Raj and I wanted to confront Darshan and Alka but were helpless under the evil circumstances. Dying in front of Mataji's eyes was her dream of having a happy family.

Munni told us she was unhappy about the situation, too, when we went to visit her. When we arrived at her house, she greeted me warmly, as we had become good friends—she had even had her silver tea service polished for our visit. She was gracious and hospitable throughout, and RG and the kids were good company, as usual. She told us how frustrated she was with Darshan and Alka; she had seen their true colors. They made her feel unwanted with their passive-aggressive ways, but like us, there was nothing she could do about it.

While we were in India, I also did some preliminary job hunting by visiting a couple of hospitals as well as my alma mater medical school (Lady Hardinge). It was encouraging to see that I had several choices.

Raj and I also made a trip to Ahmedabad. As always, everybody welcomed us eagerly and lovingly, although Bauji and Chaeji expressed their concern about my not getting pregnant. They had some suggestions, they said, which Raj and I decided wouldn't hurt to check out.

First, they invited a *pandit* to come over to perform a *puja* (prayer). Afterwards, the pandit asked Raj and me some questions, one of which involved stars and my birthstone. He believed that my birthstone, a sapphire, was unlucky for me. Raj was more believing than I was, so I removed, albeit sadly, my favorite sapphire ring and earrings and put them into storage.

Next Bauji and Chaeji made an appointment with an astrologer/mind reader, a gentleman in his fifties. When we went to his modest home, he told me that I would have a baby in December. I wanted to reply that that would mean I was already pregnant, but out of respect for his age, I bit my tongue.

In the end, no one had a good answer for us, and no one could guarantee us success. We had been trying for more than a year now, but it had felt like ten years. It was the longest year of my life.

It wasn't surprising, then, that both Raj and I were stressed. I especially felt helpless. We had been waiting and waiting, stretched to our breaking point. *What could I do differently?* I wondered. *How could I change myself?* But in reality, I knew the answer was "Nothing." So Raj and I tried to just keep on living our lives. We had each other, and that was our strength.

On a lighter note, I was able to meet up with Ragini during my visit. We had been friends for nearly three decades by now after meeting on my first day of kindergarten at the age of four.

Ragini, my childhood friend, had married young, but she was still full of life. Her husband, Skant, was an industrialist and a good person; we got along very well. While Ragini and I chatted, she gave me all the latest news on our old classmates. She had never left Ahmedabad, so she frequently ran into them—at weddings, funerals, shopping malls, grocery stores. She asked if I'd like to go shopping at a cloth market where one of our school acquaintances now worked. I declined; I had barely known him.

Ragini told me a story about the day she went to the Bhadra Kali Temple. She was in deep, silent prayer, with her head bowed and eyes closed, when she heard her name: "Ragini." She was shocked—God was speaking to her!—and she kept her eyes shut. She heard her name again: "Ragini." This was it, God Himself! She slowly opened her eyes, looked up, and saw a priest standing next to her. "Do you recognize me?" he asked. "I am Avasthi. We were classmates in college. My father was the head priest here, and after his retirement, I inherited the job."

Ragini was disappointed. Of course, she was happy to see Avasthi, but he was certainly many steps down from the Almighty.

Many of my classmates, in fact, had inherited their family's business. Some had inherited rich businesses, others not so much.

But we also had classmates who struck out on their own: engineers, doctors, lawyers. There was lots of diversity.

Ragini's job was living a life of luxury as a housewife, but she said college was still more fun (even though she'd had only minimal interest in the actual learning part; in Botany and Zoology, her lab partner had always come to her rescue). Even today, we still reminisce about our school days together.

Ragini and Skant had built a new high-end mansion in the suburbs with lots of land; the prestigious term back then was "farmhouse." She had developed a passion for gardening (by which I mean she had ten other people do the manual work while she supervised them).

Her grounds were beautifully landscaped with flowers and a large section for growing gourmet vegetables: lettuce, broccoli, celery, parsley, sage, thyme, dill, and other produce exotic to India. All of the produce from her farm was highly sought after by the restaurants inside Bombay's five-star hotels. Ragini couldn't keep up with the demand, and she loved her new role as a busy businesswoman.

Ragini and her husband also enjoyed parties. Ahmedabad, however, is a dry city, even still today, which means no beer, liquor, or wine for the locals. Foreigners, on the other hand, can request a permit. Of course, people who want to break the rules easily find a way around them. Ragini and her husband once made the local newspaper when the police raided a private party, and they had to pay a monetary penalty. Bauji saved the newspaper clipping for me. Ragini didn't mind the attention, though. She enjoyed living the good life and being in the spotlight, so it all worked out in her favor.

Then it was time for Raj and me to say our goodbyes and head back to Boston. Soon enough it was April, and life was moving along as usual, except I had missed my period. I had assumed it was late due to all my traveling and the change in climate, but two weeks passed by and still nothing. I went in to my ob-gyn to figure out the problem. He did a test and announced, "You're pregnant." *I'm pregnant?* I couldn't believe it.

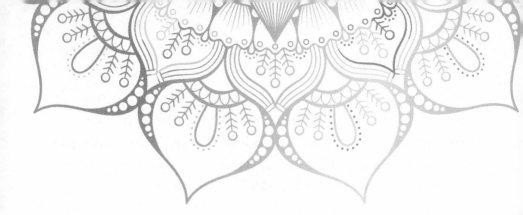

# Chapter Thirteen

*Raj's and my dream* had finally come true. We had been waiting and waiting for what felt like an eternity. We were ecstatic. Still, though, it took us some time to completely accept that it was real and not some rude joke.

My due date was December, the last week of 1974. The astrologer/mind reader had been right.

I thought back and remembered that Raj and I had only had sex once during our trip to India; it was while were staying with his family in Tilak Bazaar. We had been so busy visiting everyone, there hadn't been any other time for it.

I wondered if some greater power had played a role in my pregnancy. After all, Tilak Bazaar was the place where Bapaji had worked his first job. It was where all good things for him had begun. Had Bapaji seen my pain and misery? Had God been kind to him and allowed him to help me? Maybe the astrologer's prediction, which I had dismissed at the time, had been Bapaji's way of communicating with me, telling me that everything would be all right.

And perhaps Mataji's silent but deep love had played a role, too. Raj was her favorite son, the obedient one, and he held a special place in her heart.

There were just too many coincidences for me to ignore. Mataji's blessings combined with Bapaji's heavenly power had made the impossible possible.

Ironically, that trip to India was the last time I would visit the house in Tilak Bazaar. Even though it remained in the family, I never stayed there again. This was its parting gift to me.

After Raj and I got over our initial shock, we began planning for the future, and a month later, we announced the great news to our families. Bauji and Chaeji were beside themselves and pointed out that the astrologer had been right. From then on they had permanent, unwavering faith in the man, even though all his other predictions never came true. I believe it was because Bapaji had chosen him that one time to be his messenger.

Pitaji and Mataji were also very excited to hear the news, and they called up Bauji and Chaeji to share their happiness.

Later Raj and I heard from Munni that Darshan and Alka had assumed, and told everyone, that we had been lying about the pregnancy just to get attention. When it became clear we had not been lying, they were disappointed.

Then, a few months into my pregnancy, I received a letter from Mataji saying Darshan's daughter had had measles when we were visiting them without our realizing it. Raj and I were, of course, concerned about the possible complications with my pregnancy, but there was nothing we could do about it other than hope for the best.

In July, about halfway to my due date, I announced my pregnancy at work. Dr. A coordinated with the hospital administration to have a locum tenens (temporary anesthesiologist) lined up so that I would have three months off, from mid-December through mid-March.

In those days, the U.S. was far behind the rest of the world; the States had no maternity-leave laws. I had to use all my earned vacation, and the rest was unpaid leave of absence. There wasn't even any sick leave for me to use during my pregnancy; it was a different era for women back then. Luckily, I had a very healthy, easy pregnancy—I didn't even get morning sickness—so my work schedule and night calls stayed the same.

On the Fourth of July, we went on vacation to Montreal and Quebec with my sister Varsha and brother Pradeep. We all had a wonderful time.

Then in August, we received news that Mataji had been hospitalized for severe depression. She was basically a statue: bedridden and refusing to speak, eat, or drink. She was being force-fed through a tube.

Raj was torn between staying beside me during my pregnancy and supporting his mother. I encouraged him to go and be near her. He knew I was independent and strong, but still, this being my first pregnancy, he was understandably apprehensive.

Raj was in Delhi for one month. He stayed at the hospital with Mataji during the day and then switched with Pitaji at night.

Mataji was completely unresponsive to Raj. She did not greet or even acknowledge him. This was hard on Raj, who had been hoping his presence would lift her up.

On Raj's last day, he tried to feed Mataji one spoonful of water, but to no avail. Although she had not improved at all, he could not stay any longer; he had done his best. He said goodbye and returned to Boston with a heavy heart. I could not do much for him except offer comfort and moral support.

Finally, two weeks later, Mataji began showing signs of improvement. She was now eating, drinking, and semi-mobile, but since she'd had no physio-therapy while in bed during her deep depression, her muscles were weak, and she was confined to a wheelchair until she could build up sufficient strength. She was glad, though, to hear of my pregnancy, and we were all relieved to see her expressing interest.

My pregnancy was progressing smoothly, and every day brought new adventures. Raj and I dreamed of what it would be like to have a baby after many years of just the two of us.

# Chapter Fourteen

*In September, we began the hunt* for a nanny. An old colleague of mine called to say that his three children were now in school and that they no longer needed their nanny. The nanny, Mrs. Pinto, had been with them for three years, and she had been wonderful. What better referral could we possibly have?

So, Raj and I went to Dr. B's house in Needham to meet Mrs. Pinto. We felt lucky to have her; it was relief to have such a big part of our maternity plan in place. The only hitch was that Mrs. Pinto needed to undergo total hip surgery before coming to work for us. Luckily, the planned date of the surgery perfectly coincided with my pregnancy. She'd join us in February 1975 with her new hip in place.

Mrs. Pinto's surgery day came, and all went well. Raj and I stayed in touch with her and even visited her in the hospital.

That same month, in September 1974, Chaeji and my sister Varsha were in Delhi, attending a wedding. During their stay, they stopped by Tilak Bazaar to visit Mataji and meet Alka.

While Chaeji and Varsha were chatting with Alka, Alka said that Munna, her sister, was very lucky: she was married to a rich man who was an only child who didn't have to share with anyone. The inappropriateness of the comment was shocking. Chaeji especially was taken aback by Alka's shallow greedy and monetary values, and Mataji, who usually ignored comments like these, actually spoke up and asked Alka what the problem was with her own in-laws having siblings.

Back in Boston, I was still feeling great, even though it was December, so I was in my final month. Chaeji had said she would come out and help when delivery time came (Raj especially was holding on tight to this promise!), but there was a problem: Chachaji's daughter, Minni, was getting married on December 24. Raj and I knew the wedding was important to Chaeji, so we insisted she go to it and then come to Boston after.

Thankfully, the rest of my pregnancy progressed uneventfully, except for the last fifteen days before my maternity leave, when I started suffering from constant, severe pain in my right shoulder. It got so bad on the last day before my leave, Friday, December 15, that I could not work through my pain. But I had no sick leave I could use, so instead I had to call my colleague Dr. TB. He was on vacation but still in town, and he agreed to cover for me, and I would cover for him the following Monday. The agreement worked out great for both of us.

After that last Monday, I was officially on my self-created maternity leave. Now Raj and I were just playing the waiting game.

Chaeji arrived on December 30, after attending Minni's wedding. Raj and I went to pick her up from the Logan International Airport. As soon as she saw me, she said I looked exactly as she did when she was pregnant.

To Chaeji's delight, it snowed the next day. All her other visits had been only in the summer. She stood in the garage with the bay door open, watching the snowflakes fall and admiring the winter scene unfolding before her eyes. She had been to Jagannath, a Hindu pilgrimage site in the Himalayas, but again, only in the summer; now she could imagine what it looked like there in the winter.

Chaeji's delight, though, was rather short-lived. As the days went by, we had several more snowfalls, and with each progressive one, her excitement waned. We'd tell her that more snow was predicted and she'd reply, "Not again." Meanwhile, we were all anxiously waiting for the baby. I was overdue, but nothing was happening.

Finally, early in the morning on January 11, I went into labor. Raj and I left for the hospital, while Chaeji and Varsha stayed at home, waiting to join us later.

I checked into a room and waited for my epidural. Throughout my pregnancy, I had been checking the anatomy in my lower back, and I was confident that the procedure would be technically easy. But when my ob-gyn arrived, I got a big surprise. He examined me and then sent me for an X-ray. Turns out, my baby was breech!

Now I understood why my right shoulder was in so much pain: for the last two months, the baby's head had been pressing against my right diaphragm.

So, this meant no epidural for me. Instead, I was in line for a C-section (once all the emergency surgeries were done). January 11 was a Saturday, so staffing at the hospital was limited. I immediately called my friend, Dr. MC, at his home and asked him to give me a spinal for the surgery. He gladly agreed.

At 4:57 p.m. on January 11, 1975, our son came into this wonderful world via C-section. He was a healthy baby—eight pounds, nine ounces—and that's all that mattered. Our dream was finally in our arms.

I was watching the clock carefully to make sure we had the exact right time of birth for his *kundali* (birth horoscope). Raj was waiting outside impatiently to hear the news, since back then, we did not have ultrasounds to determine the sex of the baby.

After the C-section was complete, Raj met Mohit. Chaeji and Varsha had arrived at the hospital, and he shared the good news with them.

After seven days at the hospital, Mohit and I went home (these days, the length of stay is down to two or three days). Both Bauji and Pitaji had gotten Mohit's *kundali* written by their family *pandits* (priests) in India.

Chaeji was still staying with us, and I was doing well. I was mostly self-sufficient, but it was nice to have her company. Mohit was progressing well, too. By the time he was four to six weeks old, he was sleeping for four- to six-hour stretches. I would be returning to work full-time on March 15, when he would be nine weeks old, and it looked like the transition would go smoothly. But then, only two weeks before my scheduled return, we ran into big problems with the nanny.

Mrs. Pinto had joined us on February 15, as planned, when Mohit was a little more than one month old. We had thought one month would be sufficient for her to become comfortable in the new surroundings and for Mohit to become comfortable with her.

Mrs. Pinto was in her sixties. She was a short, somewhat stocky woman at four foot ten and one hundred forty pounds. When she joined us in February, it had been six months since her hip replacement, and she had claimed to be fully functional.

We had planned on her being a live-in nanny and had prepared a bathroom exclusively for her use, as well as our entire family room, which had a forty-inch television screen and a deluxe sound system. Raj and I were happy to adjust to this new arrangement, and we did our best to make it as comfortable for her as possible.

The day after Mrs. Pinto moved in, she gave us a grocery list and announced that she would be cooking her own meals. We agreed to this. Then, that evening, she ate her dinner at 5 p.m. and retired to her room for the rest of the night. Raj and I were shocked. She was a live-in nanny; it was not a 9-to-5 job. How were we supposed to have a trusting, comfortable relationship with the woman taking care of our son if she refused to be around us? But Mrs. Pinto was set in her ways, and this was not part of her job description.

We also quickly discovered another problem when she arrived: our house was a split-level, and she could not keep her balance on the stairs without a cane. This was particularly scary, considering that she was supposed to be caring for an infant. We'd had no idea of her true condition.

Raj and I knew we needed to get another nanny. Not only was Mrs. Pinto ill-equipped for the physical demands of the job, but she was not even a pleasant person to be around. She told us that her previous employers (my colleague Dr. B and his wife, Lynn) had been very flexible with her. "Their children drew on the walls with crayons," she said, "and they did not get upset with me so long as I was in the house physically." But this mindset fit neither our needs nor our standards.

The problem was, though, that we were running out of time. I was supposed to back at work in three short weeks.

So first, I called Mrs. Pinto's son to ask him to help relieve us of his mother's company. Unfortunately, he was not a pleasant person, either. Mrs. Pinto had planned on being with us permanently (after all, Mohit was only an infant), and together

Mrs. Pinto and her son were very difficult to deal with. It was no easy task to get rid of them, but in the end, we managed it.

Next, we placed an ad for a new nanny in the *Boston Globe*, and luckily, we soon received several promising responses.

Our second nanny was Mimi, an attractive French-speaking Algerian in her fifties. She was articulate and pleasant to be around. She was divorced and said she did not smoke or drink because her ex-husband had been a heavy smoker and drinker.

Mimi joined us in early March, but unlike Mrs. Pinto, she did not live with us. Raj and I felt good about the arrangement, as we had realized we could manage by ourselves at night. Mohit was now two months old, weighed ten pounds, and slept eight hours a night. He was happy and content. Furthermore, we had hired a separate housecleaning service, so Mimi's only responsibility was Mohit.

The schedule was: I left the house at 6:45 a.m., when Mohit was still asleep; Mimi arrived at 7:30 a.m., and Raj left for work at 8 a.m. Mimi's daily hours were flexible, depending on our needs, but she usually left at 5:30 p.m.

Compared to our first attempt at a nanny, Mimi was a joy to have around. She was pleasant and cheerful, and most importantly, Mohit liked her. Every morning, he'd greet her with a big smile. Mimi once asked me if Mohit's smiles made me jealous. I replied, "No, it gives me peace of mind."

Twice a day, Mimi would take Mohit in a fancy baby carriage that had been a gift from Chaeji for a walk around the school playground. Mohit loved it, and I couldn't have been happier about it myself. Spring was in full bloom, the weather was beautiful, and Mimi was accomplishing what we as working parents could not.

Time flew by. Raj and I were very busy between work and home, so our social activities were kept to the bare minimum. But still, life was wonderful (a feeling which was helped along by a full night's sleep every night!).

One day Raj mentioned that Mimi arrived almost every morning in a different luxury car. It was only a passing comment, and neither one of us gave it much thought.

Then in October, my old school friend from Ahmedabad, Ragini, was visiting Boston with her husband, and we were having them over for dinner. Before the meal, Raj went to the liquor cabinet to get everyone drinks, but when he opened it, he got the shock of his life: almost all of the bottles—Scotch, gin, vodka—were empty.

Raj didn't say anything in front of Ragini and her husband, but after they left, he was very upset. We had been so busy lately that we hadn't even touched the liquor cabinet in a long time, so Raj accused Mimi of drinking all of it. I defended her, reminding Raj that she didn't drink and that she had even left her husband because of *his* drinking.

I thought Raj was being paranoid for no reason, but he was sure Mimi was drinking on the job. It was a Friday night, and Mimi would be coming on Monday, so Raj marked the level of all the bottles with a pen.

The weekend passed slowly, with a great deal of anxiety. Raj and I actually both liked Mimi and were hoping nothing would come of it.

On Monday morning, Mimi arrived, her usual bubbly self. I left for my typical workday without a second thought; I still believed Raj was being paranoid.

Raj arrived home after work first, and he anxiously waited for Mimi to leave. Once she was gone, he opened the liquor cabinet.

Sure enough, the proof was in the pudding: the liquor levels were considerably lower than they had been on Friday. Mimi was drunk and taking care of our son. That's when I remembered that she was always chewing gum—I hadn't thought anything of it before.

Now the question was, *What do we do next?*

First, we called our good friends and mentors, the Marshalls. After we explained the situation to them over the phone, they drove over from Belmont right away. We often turned to them when we needed advice, and if there was ever a time for it, this would be it.

After a serious conversation, Raj and I decided to let Mimi go immediately, no second thoughts or second chances. Our trust had been broken, and it was irreparable. We were lucky that Mohit was still safe and that nothing bad had happened while Mimi was pushing his carriage around the neighborhood twice a day for two hours, intoxicated. Unfortunately, we couldn't cut ties with her immediately, as we needed her to watch Mohit one more time. As I mentioned earlier, work back then was different. I couldn't simply call in unexpectedly and take the day off. I had a full schedule of patients who needed me to administer anesthesia for their operations. An unplanned day off was only for a life-threatening emergency.

So, the next morning we left Mohit in the care of Mimi for the last time. This was a very long day for me, full of anxiety and *what ifs*. Normally I could compartmentalize my home life and work life; it wasn't common for me to be at the hospital and realize it was past 10 a.m. and had forgotten to call Mimi with my usual morning check-in. That day, though, I felt guilty, recalling all the times I had forgotten to call because I was completely focused on my patients. But I reminded myself that, at the time, I had thought Mohit was perfectly safe and settled with his nanny—I'd had no reason to worry. Of course, now the situation had changed, and I was questioning what kind of mother I was.

After a never-ending day, Raj and I finally returned home, and, as planned, we sat Mimi down to talk. We directly but politely addressed her drinking problem. To her credit, Mimi immediately confessed, expressing sorrow and promising not to drink another drop. But Raj and I had already made our decision—Mohit's safety was on the line.

After nine months of what we had thought was the perfect arrangement, we said goodbye to Mimi. Thankfully, the parting was civilized. (But if Mohit had been old enough to understand that Mimi was leaving for good, he would have been a mess. He had truly bonded with her.)

A few weeks later, Raj and I were pushing Mohit in his stroller on Mimi's old route when we ran across the school grounds-keeper. He recognized the stroller and asked where the nice lady was who usually pushed it; he hadn't seen her in a while and missed her. He said, "I used to bring her green beans." Then, a few days after that, Raj was by the tennis courts when he met another landscaper who was missing Mimi. He told Raj that he used to bring Mimi apples.

Apparently, Mimi was quite the social butterfly and led a rather colorful life. It suddenly made sense why she had arrived in a different luxury car every morning and why I'd overhear her saying to Mohit, "Mimi is not a very good lady." At the time, I had dismissed the comment as something funny to say to a baby. Now, though, knowing what we did, Raj and I were glad our relationship with Mimi had ended.

However, this meant we were yet again on the hunt for a new nanny. To hold us over, we hired a part-time, temporary replacement, Nana Burke. She was a nice lady in her seventies who lived three miles down from us, and, unlike Mimi, drove herself to work. Nana Burke was a good helper, but due to her age, she was not looking for a permanent position.

As Raj and I continued our nanny search, we did consider putting Mohit in daycare. We had many friends whose kids went to daycare, and they all seemed happy, but we decided to try again with a nanny. Our search continued.

The first lady we interviewed was no good. We asked the second lady, "Have you taken care of infants before?" Her response was "No, I have not taken care of kids, but I have taken care of cats and dogs, so what's the difference?" "No further questions," we replied. (In later years, Raj and I did develop more warmth and understanding for pets, but still, there *is* a difference between animals and humans.)

The third nanny we interviewed was a soft-spoken woman in her thirties named Laurie. She was a musician who played guitar and violin. She was looking for day work to supplement her evenings, playing in a band. We agreed to the arrangement and hired her, under the same conditions as our previous nannies: that there would be no smoking and that all her time and attention would go to Mohit.

For months, we were all satisfied, and life was stable. Then one evening, we got a call from Laurie: she was going to travel with her band, and she wouldn't be coming anymore.

Just like that. No warning, no notice, just gone.

Again we turned to Nana Burke to cover us. She had become our nanny version of a security blanket.

Yet, life continued on at the usual hectic pace, until, in the spring of 1976, our doorbell rang. It was Laurie, appearing as unexpectedly as she had disappeared. She was holding Mohit's stuffed toy Bert (from Sesame Street), which she had spotted in our bushes. Apparently, Bert had been buried in the snow all winter; he was soaking wet and had aged with the harsh weather. Mohit, though, was delighted to see his old Sesame Street toy of the character Bert, and he couldn't stop hugging and kissing his old friend even though it was soaking wet.

Laurie said she was done traveling with the band and ready to come back to work for us. She also added that she'd bring back the fifty records she had taken from our stereo cabinet.

Wait, what?

Raj and I had been so busy, we hadn't even noticed that our music collection had disappeared.

"No, thanks," we replied. And that was the end of Laurie.

Next, we hired Kathy, a younger woman in her twenties who lived in a yoga center in Newton. She was energetic and pleasant, but she also had a hearty appetite. I had to keep our pantry well-stocked, but that didn't bother me.

Kathy loved yoga, and she started teaching it to Mohit. At eighteen months old, he happily followed her directions and learned quickly. It's still entertaining to watch our home movies with Mohit enthusiastically following Kathy's instructions, showing off his moves. He was quite good; I wish he had kept up his practice.

Not surprisingly, with our history with nannies, Kathy did not last long. She was leaving, she told us, because she never stayed in one place for more than six months. But at least she gave us two weeks' notice.

Mohit was barely two years old, and we were already moving on to our fifth nanny. Raj and I started wondering if the problem was somewhere on our end. We had been careful to treat all the nannies with care and respect and fairness, but still, we couldn't keep a single one in place, either because we had misjudged them or because they'd quit on us. What were we doing wrong?

# Chapter Fifteen

*Meanwhile, changes were going on* with our family back in India, too. In the summer of 1975, Pitaji had bought a house in the suburbs, and after renovating it, they were ready to move in. The business would still be in the same building in Tilak Bazaar, but the upstairs would be empty. The new house was jointly owned between Pitaji, Darshan, and Raj.

Raj and I were very excited. We were looking forward to our future in India, and we began tentatively putting the final pieces into place, which included a visit to this new home.

So in December 1975, after Mohit's checkup and immunizations, we took him on his first trip to India. We had thought ahead three months earlier and shipped cases of disposable diapers and other necessary items that were not available over there.

Raj's and my first glimpse of the new home from the outside was encouraging. It had a beautiful lawn with plenty of flowers and trees. The house itself, although new to us, was actually very old, and unfortunately, the inside had been renovated under the nefarious direction of Darshan and Alka.

For one, Raj's and my bedroom was nothing more than a cubby hole in the remotest corner of the house. We had no air conditioning, even though other units were available in the house, and it was the only bedroom without an attached bath. To get to the bathroom, we had to travel through a maze of the living room, dining room, and Darshan's children's bedrooms.

The plan was to put an addition onto the house for Raj and me after everyone had gotten settled. Luckily, there was plenty of land in the front and back of the house.

Pitaji's bedroom had an attached bath but, like our bedroom, was in a remote corner of the house. Not surprisingly, Darshan and Alka's bedroom and their kids' bedrooms were at the center of the house, and it had two spacious attached baths.

Darshan and Alka had also taken the air conditioner we had sent to Pitaji and Mataji and installed it in their own bedroom. It was sickening to see the warm air that was blowing outside the unit so close to Pitaji's bedroom.

To get a phone line for the new house, we'd normally have to be on a wait list for several years, but since I was a physician, I had priority. I was required to regularly update my information by going to the main post office in Delhi, which I had been doing every time we had visited India. It turned out, though, that the telephone company had also sent me some follow-up forms in the mail that I was never told about. Darshan had simply forged my signature and sent them back.

Furthermore, when all the family had packed up the old house and moved into this new one, many of Raj's and my belongings, which had been moved along with everybody else's, had gone missing between there and here.

Pitaji knew of all the underhanded things going on around him, but he chose to stay quiet, and he even asked that we do the same. He said Mataji would be very disturbed hearing about all of it, and she was already feeling so helpless.

The only good news during this visit was both Pitaji's and Mataji's health was stable. Mataji was slowly but surely recovering from her bout of severe depression. She had recovered 60 percent of her physical faculties and 90 percent of her mental, and she was absolutely in seventh heaven to see Mohit. He was looking even more like Raj—a plus in her book.

Pitaji, too, was doing well. He played tennis in the morning, driving himself fifteen miles to the club. Then he went to work at 10 a.m. with his lunchbox and returned home at 7:30 p.m., six days a week. As usual, Darshan did not help. Raj was hoping to return soon and take over the business so Pitaji could retire.

We knew Pitaji and Mataji were hoping we'd be moving back to India now that they had finally moved out of Tilak Bazaar. And in fact, Raj and I were still very optimistic that we would be.

During our visit, we had a joint ceremony called *Mundan* for Mohit and Deepu, Darshan's son, the black prince. *Mundan* is the ritual first shaving of a boy's head, usually when he is between one and three years old. Alka's parents joined us, along with Bauji and Chaeji.

Darshan and Alka were not happy about Mohit's presence. It meant that their Deepu had to both share his grandparents and, more importantly, his inheritance. But, by now, we all knew that Darshan and Alka brought out the worst in each other.

After the ceremony, Alka's mother (the devil herself) said to me, "Your room is very cozy." She was mocking us for having the least desirable room in the house, more like a cubbyhole. She continued, "Why do you want to return to India? You are better off staying and enjoying the U.S." I refused to respond to her evil scheming.

Later I told Pitaji and Mataji about the conversation. Pitaji could not believe a grown adult would say that, but Mataji knew it and said, "She has no business interfering in our household matters."

With each passing day, Darshan and Alka continued their attempts to get us out of the way. It was difficult to tolerate, but Raj and I kept our mouths shut for the sake of family unity. We told ourselves that the situation was temporary and that, soon, we'd have our own house, a place on the grounds, close but separate.

We began consulting with an architect, drawing up initial plans for a simple two-bedroom house—nothing lavish. But then we ran into a problem: for some reason, the house phone was out of order, so I had to ask Darshan to drive me to the business office in Tilak Bazaar so I could call Bauji and Chaeji in Ahmedabad. Years later, we found out that Darshan had purposefully disconnected the house phone from his bedroom just to make our lives difficult.

On top of all that, Mohit got very sick during our stay, as he wasn't immune to the common sicknesses and germs in India. For the majority of our miserable flight home, Raj carried Mohit up and down the aisle, trying not to disturb the other passengers with our sick, crying infant. We sighed with relief when we finally landed in Boston; we went straight to the pediatrician, where Mohit got some antibiotics and soon recovered.

The new year, 1976, went by quickly. We were enjoying our lives in the U.S. but also mentally preparing to move back to Delhi. Raj was continuing to pursue the construction plans for our new home and was optimistic about it. Mataji, however, was slipping back into a deep depression, so we planned to visit India again in December.

But before then, in May 1976, we went on a four-day trip to Montreal. I had a conference at McGill University, and since Mohit was seventeen months old and usually well-behaved, we went as a family.

The first night of our stay, we decided not to go to the conference reception. For one, it cost a hundred dollars per person, and for another, we didn't know yet if babysitters were available at the hotel. So instead, Raj, Mohit, and I all piled into a cab and asked the driver to take us to a nice restaurant.

He ended up taking us to a very fancy place in beautiful old Montreal. For a moment, Raj and I just stood outside with Mohit, admiring the beautiful weather and majestic surroundings. Then we went inside and were seated, with Mohit in his stroller next to us. The ambience was very formal, the menu gourmet. Everything was going well, until our entrees arrived. Suddenly, our well-behaved son started crying, and horror of horrors, we had no pacifier to save the day.

Raj and I were completely embarrassed. We tried everything to quiet Mohit, but nothing worked. Finally, we ended up taking turns standing outside with him, while we each ate our gourmet meals separately.

In those days, children were not the norm in restaurants, especially in one as fancy as this. So we were amazed that none of the other diners even gave us a hint of disapproval or annoyance. Years later, we visited the restaurant again and showed Mohit the scene of his crime.

But the rest of the three days in Montreal were great. We found out that the hotel did provide babysitters, so Raj and I were able to have a night out on our own. When our sitter arrived, she had a big bag of toys. She opened the bag and began showing her treasures to Mohit, who was, of course, enthralled, but then the babysitter turned to us and asked us to leave immediately.

Montreal ended up being a great first family trip that we still remember to this day.

That fall, after placing an ad for yet another nanny, we finally found Shelly. She was twenty-two years old, heavyset, and pleasant. Although she was young, she was very experienced. She had worked in a daycare center in Marlborough for two years, thirty-two miles outside of Boston, and she had driven herself every day.

Shelly was sincere, dependable, and prompt. She also liked to whip up lasagnas big enough to feed an army. I tried to discourage her from cooking such large amounts, but in the end, I let her do as she pleased.

Mohit loved spending time with Shelly. He enjoyed listening to Donny and Marie music with her, and in the cold winter months, she'd drive him to the newly opened Chestnut Hill Mall so he could burn off some energy.

We had finally found the right nanny for us.

Soon enough, it was December and time for our second annual trip to India. When we arrived at the new house in Delhi, Mataji was isolated in a remote corner. A full-time attendant had supposedly been hired to care for her, but in reality, she was completely neglected. Alka was instead using the attendant for her own needs, keeping her busy all day. Pitaji had no idea what transpired during the day as he went to the office.

Ironically, Darshan also claimed during this trip that he was going to get a vasectomy so that he would have no more kids but could devote all his time to taking care of Mataji. Raj and I saw right through this scheme—it had nothing to do with selflessness and everything to do with making Pitaji (and his money) feel dependent on Darshan.

It was clear that Darshan did not care at all about Mataji. He even suggested she be sedated at night so that his and Alka's sleep wouldn't be disturbed. Pitaji, however, was the caretaker at night, and he strongly objected to this. He later told me that his mother had had breast cancer and had become addicted to opioids, and that's why he was so adamant.

Pitaji still went to work six days a week, even while caring for Mataji in the evenings. Darshan occasionally visited him for a few hours at the office, but, otherwise, he spent the majority of his time monitoring the help at home while watching TV and teaching his daughter, Devi, to act by watching the same films over and over.

But still Darshan constantly complained that he was the deprived son, and he was always begging for more favors. He had already cashed in Raj's insurance policy as well as some stocks that Pitaji had bought for both Darshan and Raj.

Munni, meanwhile, was fully aware of what was going on, but she had no control over the situation. When we spoke with her, she begged us to move back, even though she knew that Darshan and Alka wanted nothing to do with us. She even suggested that we dump our luggage in their living room. "What can they do?" she said. But that was not a long-term solution. Raj and I now had Mohit, a two-year-old, and it was punishment enough for him to have to run across three rooms to go to the bathroom—the only bathroom with an ice-cold black toilet seat. Mohit hated sitting on that seat. Raj and I tried to warm the seat with a blow-dryer, but it didn't always work.

Despite the bathroom issue, Mohit did have a wonderful visit with his grandparents. It was so sweet to watch him dote on Mataji. He enjoyed pushing her wheelchair, bringing her to the dining room table; when she was lying down, he'd sit by her at the head of the bed. Mataji was touched and said to him, "You have come at a time when I am unable to hold you in my arms." Tears were running down her cheeks.

During our visit, we took Mataji to the hospital for a detailed workup and to get more medical opinions on her health. When Alka found out, she said sarcastically, "Mataji must really like being in the hospital." I ignored her; by then I was used to her trying to goad me.

Raj and I also went to the American Embassy School and applied for Mohit's admission, as we were hoping to move back within a year. And we went through the futile exercise of meeting with the architect, trying to finalize the blueprint, but none of our efforts saw the light of day. As soon as we left for the States, Darshan put the plans straight into the trash.

Finally, we were back in Boston, albeit feeling disturbed and helpless. Nonetheless, we continued to pursue our plan to move back, hoping to end Darshan and Alka's cruel reign.

The first thing to do was buy a diesel Mercedes, since India's law stated that all car imports had to be one year old, and diesel was much cheaper in India than unleaded (although, even then, gas itself was three times higher than in the U.S.).

Then, in the fall of 1977, we began preparing for our third annual trip to India. Most of our preparation was just doing lots of shopping to meet Darshan and Alka's unrealistic demands.

For example, Coca-Cola was banned in India, so we had to gather all the bottled ingredients from Needham, Massachusetts, so we could mix them together with distilled water after we arrived in India. They also wanted us to bring a generator. Most people had one, as there were frequent power outages in India, but we were already bringing so much, we couldn't handle a big generator on top of everything else. Darshan complained and asked why we couldn't carry it in our arms just because they didn't want to spend their own money to buy one over there. No logic at all.

But their worst request by far was laundering money for them. Of course, our response was a resounding and absolute "No." Darshan was, not surprisingly, unhappy with us. He complained to Pitaji that money laundering was routine—relatives of his friends were all doing it for their families, so why couldn't Raj?

When Raj and I, along with Mohit, arrived at the Delhi house, we felt depressed and discouraged. Mataji was still in a downward spiral, neglected all day long by Darshan and Alka, and Pitaji was gone all day working in Tilak Bazaar. Furthermore, we weren't making any progress on our house plans; there was too much red tape. At first, our house was going to be built behind the original house, and then it was changed to the side and, finally, to the front.

As usual, Darshan was constantly scheming. He had installed an air conditioner in Raj's and my bedroom, but it was broken from the get-go. Darshan's only reply was, "Well, it was working before."

The phone was almost always out of order, too. Darshan had disconnected it so he wouldn't have to pay a bill incurred by us. He had also paid an electrician to misconnect some wires outside the house so that his neighbors paid the majority of his utility bill.

And the cherry on top was the morning when Darshan confronted me about a bottle of pills I had thrown away in my bedroom trash can. A house servant had found the pills while scavenging under Darshan's supervision; now Darshan wanted to know what they were. I was shocked at the depth of his spying. I told him the pills were expired antibiotics. He didn't believe me and replied, "If they're multivitamins, the servants could use them." I wish I would have lied and said that they were vitamins, because Darshan would have undoubtedly kept them for himself and his family, and if I had been lucky, maybe they would've taken a mega-dose. The pills were actually stool softeners, which I had brought for a friend who was no longer in town. Now the repercussions from *that* would have been funny.

Meanwhile, Mohit was yet again sick during our visit, dealing with germs here in India that his body wasn't used to. He looked like he'd been starved. Even worse, his only playmate was Darshan and Alka's five-year-old Deepu, already as conniving as his parents. Deepu was always snatching Mohit's toys away from him, so I suggested to Deepu one day that they both share their toys with each other so that everyone would be happy. He replied, "But I have no toys to share." Darshan and Alka's kid to the core.

Every day in this house was a mental struggle for me. I was surrounded by selfish, caustic people, and I could feel my own personality changing. I was becoming overly sensitive and self-conscious, and my thoughts were sliding into pettiness. And worst of all, I was constantly worried about Mohit's safety. I knew he was the most unwelcome baby, and I could never let my guard down.

Since our last visit, Pitaji had bought Darshan a slightly used Impala, because it wasn't "fair" that Raj had one and Darshan didn't. Raj, however, was banned from driving Darshan's Impala while we were there, in case he got into an accident and dinged it up. So Raj had to drive around the domestic Fiat instead.

We stopped by the American Embassy School again to update Mohit's admission—our original plans of moving back within a year had failed. Then Raj went to some auto workshops to make sure they could repair our Mercedes and have the necessary parts. Raj was taken aback by their response: they said the repairs could be done immediately, and they'd have no problem getting the parts. "We steal them from all the embassy cars." Ah, yes—this was India; bribery and corruption were endemic.

Finally, it was time for us to fly back to the States, and we sadly said goodbye to Pitaji and Mataji. We felt like we had accomplished barely anything during our stay. Our hopes for finally starting construction on our house were gloomy at best. The harsh reality was, we were ready to move back to India, but we had no place to move *to*. This was especially frustrating because Mataji was fading away a little bit more every day, and there was nothing we could do about it.

It was January 1977, and we were back in Boston. Thank goodness Shelly was waiting for us. She helped Mohit get back into the swing of regular life, and she was teaching him new things every day. Mohit was into Sesame Street at the time, so his two-year-old birthday cake was in the shape of Big Bird.

The year went by quickly, and when December came around, we were back in India for our annual visit, surviving the same old acts of deceit and torture from Darshan and Alka. We were happy to get back to the States, with Shelly waiting for us again. She gave us great peace of mind.

In January 1978, I returned to work at LMH, mentally switching gears from being on constant high alert in India to feeling secure and comfortable around my colleagues.

Winter and all its accompanying festivities were in full swing, and Boston felt magical, with its snow-covered trees, holiday lights, and merry atmosphere. The Boston Common was aglow, and the Jordan Marsh department store downtown was a big draw, too: big picture windows full of toys, and on its top floor, a grand display of Santa's village. Mohit was three years old now and delighted by it all.

But more than the merriness, this was a winter no one in the Northeast would ever forget. It was the Blizzard of '78. On Monday morning, February 6, it started snowing heavily, and it didn't stop until the evening of February 7. Boston was hit with a record-breaking 27.1 inches of snow, and the damage cost, in 2017 terms, more than $1.91 billion.

When the storm began on Monday, it took me two and a half hours to get home from the hospital—a drive that typically took me only twenty minutes. The next day, all the roads, even the highways, were shut down for the rest of the week, making this the only time I had ever called in to work for unexpected leave.

Outside our own house, we had a mountain of snow eight feet high. Mohit considered it his personal accomplishment and proudly posed at the top for a photograph, shovel in hand.

Everyone around us was finding ways to deal with the difficult situation. Our neighbors were walking two miles with pushcarts to the nearest Stop & Shop, and Dr. A was escorted by police car to deal with emergency cases at the hospital.

Then, after three chaotic days of citywide cleanup and rescue, the main roads were finally opened again, and life slowly got back to normal. Little did I know that an even bigger storm was on the horizon, one that was emotional but would have far more of an impact on me than the snowstorm.

It involved Dr. A. Out of nowhere, he started having vision problems. He went to get some testing, and the results were devastating: he had stage four glioblastoma, the most aggressive type of brain tumor. Everyone at the hospital was shocked.

My grief went especially deep and personal, as Dr. A and I had developed a warm relationship over the years. In fact, we had never once argued; he was my friend and my mentor.

Dr. A, our benign dictator, immediately underwent brain surgery, which was followed by chemotherapy. He was a strong man, a pillar of strength to us all, even with his bleak future. After he completed his chemo, he returned to work, and we all hoped it would be for a long time. Sadly, though, his remission was short-lived.

Dr. A ended up resigning from his position in order to focus on fighting the cancer. It was a professional loss for all of us on staff, and an especially personal one for me. Dr. A had been the only person in his Italian family to get a higher education—his father and brothers were all masons. Growing up, Dr. A had not been particularly good at masonry, so his father had sent him to school instead. The end result was an incredibly skilled and respected doctor.

Even while we struggled to comprehend what had happened, life still needed to move on. For one, with Dr. A's abrupt absence, we had to figure out who could possibly replace him as department chair. In reality, no one could ever fill his shoes, but I had been at LMH for a while and had staff seniority, so I was first in line to be offered the position.

I was apprehensive about it, though. It was all so sudden, and I did not feel mentally or emotionally prepared to take on the challenge. With my experience, I knew I could do a reasonably good job, but I decided to let the opportunity pass.

Next in line was Dr. TB, and he accepted. Age was in his favor, and he was a man, so the men's club didn't have anything to complain about. It was an agreeable solution and a smooth transition.

Dr. A had been the permanent department chair, but all others who stepped into his place had time limits. The position would rotate among the staff every two years, based on approval from the hospital executive committee.

I felt like an orphan without Dr. A, but my work had to continue. Along with administering anesthesia, I was also, finally, getting roped into politics. Dr. TB was close to retirement, so he wanted to just cruise along as department chair. But I had a different vision.

I wanted to maintain the department's image, to be always learning, progressing. I was concerned about the long-term health of the department, but Dr. TB was content to let the surgeons run the show while he sat back passively. Two other department doctors also agreed with him, as they were in the same age group.

Both of these doctors were in their mid-fifties. First, there was Dr. H, who looked like a Jesuit father. When I introduced him to Raj, Raj immediately thought, *He looks like a priest.* Dr. H was very gentle and had eight children, but we definitely had different views on family. When I finished my work at LMH, I always headed home straight away. Dr. H, however, never left the hospital before dark. The other doctors said he was waiting for all his kids to be in bed.

Then there was Dr. M. He was a big guy who drove a motorcycle. He frequently went on bike trips with his wife to their cabin in Martha's Vineyard. Once, a cop pulled him over for speeding. The cop was a young guy, and when he walked up to Dr. M and his wife, he was completely taken aback to see a middle-aged couple, not your average bikers. He was so surprised that he let them off with a warning.

With Dr. TB, Dr. H, Dr. M, and most of the other staff unwilling to move the department forward, I was left to single-handedly try to push us into the future. Sometimes it was difficult to always be involved. For one, I couldn't participate in the men's locker-room conversations—I had to hear them secondhand. But

I was determined to keep pursuing my goals. The next time the department chair was empty, I was ready for it.

Sadly, in April 1978, our wonderful nanny, Shelly, had to say goodbye to us. All good things must come to an end. Her mother had broken her hip, and Shelly needed to go take care of her. We wished her well and separated on good terms. I regret not staying in touch with her through the years due to our taxing schedule. We do, though, have wonderful memories of her.

Mohit had already been going to a laid-back preschool a few hours a week, and we planned to send him in the fall to a more structured program. We didn't know much about schools in the area, and we ended up choosing private school, mostly for our convenience as working parents.

We heard that Park School in Brookline was excellent. In fact, our neighbor was planning to take his son for an admission interview, and he kindly offered to take Mohit with him as well, since both Raj and I were working that day.

We later found out that Mohit was not properly dressed for the interview. Sometimes ignorance is truly bliss. Apparently, he was supposed to be wearing a dress shirt and tie, but he burst into the admission's office with his Batman cape and announced, "Here comes Batman!" The admission staff was surprised to see such an intrepid adventurer, and they admitted him to the school.

The whole process couldn't have been easier for us. At the time, we didn't realize that Park School was one of the most desirable schools in the area and was notoriously difficult to get into—more difficult to get into Harvard at the time, it was said with some substantiation.

There was one condition with Mohit's admission, though. He was too young to start kindergarten, so he would be in preschool the first two years. That was fine. Raj and I were delighted with the outcome, and Mohit was eagerly looking forward to the fall.

Meanwhile, we were soaking in another wonderful spring; the record-breaking snowstorm of two months ago was now nothing but a memory. We enjoyed looking at our garden, bursting with color, and we liked visiting the popular Boston Common with Mohit, where we took a swan boat ride and watched the real swans swimming around us. (This was twenty-five years before the famous pair of swans dubbed "Romeo and Juliet" started coming to the Common every spring. They were so nicknamed because the two never left each other's side; it was later discovered that they were both, in fact, females, i.e., Juliets, so they never had any babies.)

We also had a new nanny, Susan. We had again considered but given up on the idea of enrolling Mohit in daycare. We figured that, by now, he might not be a good fit since the other kids had undoubtedly been going for a while and were probably good friends with each other.

Susan was a great fit. She lived in the desirable neighborhood of Chestnut Hill; she was soft-spoken and low-key, and had four school-age children of her own. All was well, with no complaints from either side, until we hit the four-week mark. Then one day Susan called and told us that the next day would be her last day of work.

Raj and I were puzzled by the abrupt departure. Susan had seemed like a reasonable person, and we were reasonable people, our child was not demanding, and we'd had no disagreements with her. So I asked her over the phone what her reason was. She replied that she was seeing a shrink and that he had advised her to work outside the house for four weeks, so she had. Well, at least she was honest.

Her reply reminded me of Chaeji's own self-prescribed therapy when I was a child. Like all married couples, Bauji and Chaeji had their disagreements and personality clashes. Bauji was a perfectionist and dictatorial, while Chaeji was practical and easygoing. Usually their differences complemented each other, but sometimes they butted heads.

Whenever Chaeji was really upset with Bauji, she would threaten to move to Haridwar, the holiest Hindu city and pilgrimage site, and take *sannyasa*, the stage of renunciation in the Hindu philosophy. After announcing this, she'd walk out the door, and all we kids would be apprehensive about her abandoning us forever. But her absence was always short-lived. She'd go on a ten-minute walk and return from her little "Haridwar."

As we kids grew up, we realized that these comments were false alarms, so whenever she threatened to leave for Haridwar, we'd offer to help her with her travel plans and ask her if we could visit her in the *ashram* (Hindu monastery). To this day, we often recall these memories and laugh.

But with Susan gone now, Raj and I needed yet another nanny. We began the usual process of placing ads and conducting interviews. Luckily, we needed a nanny only for the summer, as Mohit was starting school in the fall, and since it was May, quite a few senior high school students were interested in the job. Out of the many potential candidates, we chose Linda.

She was a seventeen-year-old senior attending a private school. Her mother was an attorney, and her father was a well-known surgeon and department chair at a medical center in the greater Boston area. Linda was overweight—five feet four inches tall and two hundred eighty pounds. She lived in Needham, four miles down the road from us, and she drove a brand-new black Firebird, which had been a birthday gift from her parents.

Our neighbor was surprised to see Linda's fancy car in our driveway and even more surprised when we told him about her family. He said, "You have a rich babysitter."

Raj and I thought we were lucky to have a nice, educated nanny with a cultured background. Mohit would be attending a half-day camp for eight weeks, and, then, starting on May 10, Linda would at the house with him from 8 a.m. to 5 p.m. five days a week.

Linda's responsibilities were minimal: they included only keeping Mohit occupied and preparing his lunch. But after only one week, we knew we had to talk to her about her work habits and her hygiene, both of which were severely lacking. Unfortunately, money and class don't always go together.

I actually had *more* housework with Linda around than if we had been on our own. After getting home from the hospital, I'd have to start my second shift, cleaning up all the messes she had left behind. To her credit, Linda was punctual, but other than that, she was a living nightmare.

Raj and I were in turmoil about how to approach the situation. We knew the issues were sensitive, but they simply had to be addressed. Then on Raj's birthday, May, 20, 1978, our babysitter angst was unexpectedly put on the backburner.

At noon on Raj's birthday (9 p.m. Delhi time), we got a call from Pitaji. We had assumed he was calling to wish Raj a happy birthday, but instead we were told that Mataji had passed away at 5 p.m. their time.

Raj and I were stunned. Even though international phone calls were expensive and the connections were not always clear, Raj and I had stayed in close touch with our families. Mataji had been stable, enjoying her meals. She had been restricted in her mobility, but other than that, she had been doing well.

The story was that Darshan and Alka had given Mataji a glass of milk at 5 p.m., and after finishing it, she had immediately passed away. It was sadly coincidental (and also suspicious) that her death was not only on Raj's birthday but also on his birth *hour*.

After Mataji stopped breathing, Darshan called Pitaji at work to notify him of her passing. He had not called an ambulance or a doctor, nor had he made any attempts to revive her.

Many questions hung in the air, and they were never answered. Munni had her own theories about what had happened, and sadly, knowing Darshan and Alka, Raj and I could not disagree with her.

After we recovered from our initial shock, Raj made plans to immediately fly out to India for Mataji's last rites. (He could not make it for the cremation, as it was the next morning.) I was very sad that I could not go with him. Mohit was recovering from five days of high fever and an ear infection, and we couldn't risk taking him on such a long trip.

So, the next morning, Raj flew out by himself—we were forced to grieve separately. By now, my only memories of Mataji were fond ones. Through the years, I had gained an understanding of her emotions, and she had started caring for me, praising me and showing appreciation for the customary gift of a saree I had given her every Karva Chauth. Together we had forged a bond stronger than I could have ever imagined when I first joined her family.

Raj arrived in Delhi in time for the *chautha* ceremony, the fourth day of mourning, which is very important in the Hindu religion. Bauji and Chaeji had also come up from Ahmedabad for the ceremony. Then Raj's family, Pitaji, Darshan, and Alka, drove to Haridwar for Mataji's last rites in the holy river Ganges.

Meanwhile, I was still battling the babysitter nightmare back in Boston. Linda was a prima donna, but I couldn't do anything about it. Raj suggested that I was spoiling her, but what choice did I have? I was a working parent and needed her.

After two very long weeks, Raj returned to Boston. We were both still grieving the unexpected death. He told me that Munni said Mataji's face was glowing after passing away. After all, Mataji was only sixty-two years old and had not suffered from any chronic or severe illnesses that would have affected her looks.

We never found out what exactly had happened to Mataji, but as the years passed, we saw more and more how selfish, toxic, and extreme Darshan and Alka were. They were capable of doing the most degrading things to serve their own perverse purposes. With Pitaji at work all day, they'd had unfettered access to Mataji, and Mataji had had no power and no voice in her own home. Even though we could not comprehend how Darshan and Alka could commit such an atrocious act—and we had no autopsy to confirm our suspicions—we could not deny that, in all likelihood, they had done it.

With Mataji gone, Pitaji was now alone. He was in shock and pain, and he became even more private than ever. None of us knew what was going through his mind.

Munni did open up and discuss her instincts surrounding Mataji's death with Raj and me, but she had no more answers than we did, and she felt very uncomfortable with Darshan and Alka still being a part of her life.

As time went by, Munni told us how Darshan would declare every year on Raj's birthday that Mataji was cursing Raj because she had chosen to die on that day, that hour. We knew it was not true, but it still hurt to hear it. Mataji loved Raj dearly; he was her favorite son, the one who did no wrong. These vicious thoughts of Darshan's only supported our fears about Mataji's death. Sadly, even today, thirty-eight years later, there has still been no closure—no healing, no explanation.

Throughout the summer, Pitaji and Darshan kept reassuring Raj and me that construction on our home would start soon. Now, more than ever, we wanted to move back to India. Pitaji needed our help. So, we kept the faith that everything would eventually work out as planned. In the meantime, though, we invited Pitaji to come out and visit us. Pitaji agreed but said he first had to wait for some pending issues at work to be resolved. Since Darshan refused to help, it was all up to Pitaji to keep the business running smoothly.

Raj and I were very excited to host Pitaji; we knew it was a much-needed vacation for him, and as the weeks went by, we constantly reminded him to see it through. But unfortunately, the visit kept having to be put off because of Pitaji's work commitments and dealing with the family vultures.

In the middle of all this, Raj, who was still grieving his mother's death, caught a severe GI bug. He had a high fever and other concerning symptoms and had to be hospitalized, where he underwent multiple tests and workups. He ended up losing fifteen pounds in two weeks, and during that time, it was a challenge balancing my schedule with everyone's needs.

Finally, after being put on a heavy dose of antibiotics, Raj recovered, and we regained stability in our daily life. We still, however, had to deal with Linda, our sitter.

After talking to our neighbors, Raj and I decided to share their sitter and get rid of Linda with due notice. Raj and I were relieved to have found a solution.

So, on June 25, we paid Linda for a full eight weeks of work, even though she had worked only six of them. She wanted to work for the whole summer, but we told her that simply was not feasible for us.

Then, a few months later, Raj and I got a certified letter in the mail. We had no idea what it could be, and we opened it apprehensively. To our rude surprise, it was a letter from the law office of Linda's mother, who was an attorney.

In the letter, she basically told us that we were foreigners and ignorant of the U.S. labor laws. Since Linda had been paid for eight weeks' worth of work, she was entitled to Social Security benefits, and she demanded we deposit the money immediately.

Now we saw why Linda's money had not given her any class. This letter was proof of her upbringing—these were the values she had been raised with. We wrote a short letter in response, saying we sent a check with the requested amount to the Social Security Office. We didn't question the legality of such a meager payment; it wasn't worth rolling around in the dirt to find out. More than anything, the situation was a disturbing nuisance, and we simply wanted to move on with our lives.

Years later, in 2002, I ran across an obituary in the newspaper for a woman named Linda Gomez. She was forty-three years old and had died of breast cancer. Her father had been a physician, her mother an attorney (who also recently passed away). Linda had one son. I was shocked at randomly running across her obituary, and for a split second, I had the nerve to think she had deserved it, but then I scolded myself for thinking such a thing. I especially felt very sad for the little boy, who now had no mother. After seeing that obituary, I found my own inner peace with Linda and our troublesome past, and I never thought ill of her again.

# Chapter Sixteen

*In July 1978, karma smiled* down on us. After placing another ad for a nanny, we found Connie. She was a big Irish woman in her sixties, very proper, well-mannered. Her husband had died when she was young, so she alone had raised their two daughters, who were now in their forties. One of her daughters lived in Connecticut, and her husband worked for IBM.

Connie also had several grandchildren. Her grandson was studying at Yale Law School, and one of her granddaughters was working in the business office of Buckingham Browne & Nichols School (known as BB&N).

Connie had nannied two other children for eight years, but they were now eight and thirteen and attending school, so she was no longer needed. Her references spoke very highly of her.

Connie was not looking for a job because she needed the money but because she liked to have a purpose. Her own family was all settled, and she enjoyed being independent and having outside responsibilities.

She lived in Newton and drove herself to our place. Her work hours were extremely flexible, including evenings and weekends. She was punctual to a T and maintained a familiar, comfortable routine for Mohit. On a typical day, she would greet Mohit after school at 3 p.m., the kitchen table set with a placemat, napkin, glass of milk, and some cookies for a snack. Also, when she fed Mohit lunch, she always used the proper silverware, and she even taught him how to set the table. This eventually became Mohit's job at home, and he does it perfectly to this day (unlike his father, who is still learning).

Mohit's only concern with Connie was her left arm, which was almost double the size of her right. For a young child, this was a little alarming. Connie had had breast cancer and undergone surgery, and back in those days, all the lymph nodes were removed; hence, there was no drainage. Once we explained this to Mohit, he was perfectly comfortable with the situation.

We could not have been more thankful to have Connie. After years of revolving nannies, we had finally found a keeper. Mohit bonded with Connie very quickly. On the days I got home early from work, I would go to my room and take a nap; this was a win-win for everybody because I got to recharge my batteries for a happy, rested evening with the family, and Mohit got to enjoy his time with Connie.

Connie would also sometimes watch the news with Mohit, and she would share with him her opinion of the anchors. As Mohit got older, he would tell us about these conversations, and it was interesting to hear the dialogue between a child and a senior.

Raj and I also found out that Connie had once dated the actor Jack Lemmon. When the relationship hadn't worked out, Connie later tried to get her daughters to date Jack Lemmon's son, but that didn't happen, either.

When fall came around, Mohit started at Park School, and he easily adjusted to his new schedule. The campus itself was impressive, with lots of greenery and state-of-the-art buildings. Our schedule was familiar and comfortable: I left for work at 7 a.m.; Raj would drop off Mohit at school at 8 a.m. (sometimes carrying Mohit out to the car half asleep); at noon, a private bus would bring Mohit home, where Connie would be waiting for him. My rule was that, as soon as he got home, he needed to call me at the OR and let me know of his safe arrival. Some days, though, he wouldn't get home until 3 p.m., so if I was busy in the OR, our wonderful secretary, JE, would tell Mohit, "Your mom said, 'Eat cookies, drink milk, and watch TV.'" Mohit knew JE was only joking; she was a wonderful friend—and like Wonder Woman in the workplace. We were lucky to have her in our lives.

In October, Mohit's new school hosted the Harvest Fest. It was an annual event, but this would be our first time attending. The weather was perfect, and there was so much to do—kids' rides, food, drinks, games. Mohit had an Indian friend at school, Rohit, and his mom and I set up a stall selling homemade Indian snacks. They were a big hit. And the favorite game among the students at Harvest Fest was dunking the headmaster by throwing balls at a target. Luckily, the headmaster was a good sport about it.

The parents were also helping fundraise by auctioning off donations. There were many fantastic offers, like vacations at summer homes and rides on private planes. There was even the surprising offer of a truckload of horse manure. Raj and I auctioned a wine-and-dine for four at our place, which did well. By this time, I was a good cook and enjoyed doing it (when work permitted).

Sadly, around this time, Dr. A passed away from the brain tumor. Even though his death was expected, it was still difficult. No matter who you are, doctor or not, you still hold on to the tiniest hope that a miracle will happen.

It was also sad that Pitaji still hadn't visited, and his letters indicated that construction on our house was still being delayed. Darshan was using every weapon in his arsenal.

The New Year came around; it was now 1979, a time of healing and hope after losing Mataji and Dr. A.

Mohit was in his second year at Park School. He was in a new nursery class with new classmates, and he could not have been happier. He also loved celebrating all the festivals that year, especially Halloween. He dressed up as Spiderman and went trick-or-treating in our neighborhood as well as at the Marshalls'. We celebrated both Diwali and Christmas, and we even put up a tree with lights. Mohit loved opening his Diwali gifts and his presents from Santa Claus.

In December 1979, we went again to India; this was our first trip since Mataji's passing, and a lot had changed, especially Pitaji. This man, who had once been so strong, was now silent and subdued; he had been reduced to a puppet, his strings pulled by Darshan and Alka. Pitaji kept promising us, "Soon you can plan your return," but we knew that was not true. Either he was unaware of all the problems, or he knew about them but felt helpless and was in denial.

Meanwhile, Munni and RG were constantly urging Raj and me to move back immediately. I told them we would, but we didn't have anywhere to live. Typical Munni, aggressive and stubborn, always replied, "Dump all your bags in their living room." Raj and I, however, knew that that was not a sustainable solution.

Munni was fully aware of Darshan and Alka's greedy ways and inflammatory comments, as they were constantly trying to undermine her. And, of course, Darshan and Alka did not hide their dislike for Raj and me. They were emotionally abusive and constantly stealing from us, but we put up with it to fulfill our duty to the family. Raj had equal ownership in the house, and we needed to help Pitaji. Sadly, this trip to India was far from a vacation.

One of the only bright spots was a visit to Ahmedabad. We also attended a wonderful Punjabi wedding in Morinda, where we got VIP treatment. It was the wedding of Anil, Bhen's son. Bhen and her family were delighted to see us, and Bauji, Chaeji, Chachaji, and Auntyji had also come from Ahmedabad.

The *baraat* (groom's party) came by car, a four-hour drive from Morinda to Jalandhar. Anil arrived at the wedding on a strong, healthy mare decorated for the procession. On the mare with Anil were two boy guards who had knives attached to their waistbands. In the front of Anil was Asha's son, and behind was Mohit. All three of them were dressed up in suits and *pagadis* (ceremonial headgear).

This was Mohit's first experience with an Indian wedding, and he loved it. When we got back to Boston, he told his story in detail to his classmates during show-and-tell.

We also drove to Chandigarh, one hour away, for a day trip of sightseeing. Chandigarh is a very modern city; construction for it began in 1951 and was completed in 1965. The city was designed by the famous Swiss-French architect Le Corbusier. This was the only urban project Le Corbusier ever did, and many of his sculptures dot the city as well. (Le Corbusier designed the Carpenter Center for the Visual Arts at Harvard as well. It was the only building he designed in the U.S. He also designed the Mill Owners' Association Building in Ahmedabad.)

Our visit in Chandigarh was enjoyable. The roads were wide and had excellent flow of traffic, and the entire place was clean and had many beautiful gardens. Nowadays, however, the city has not been maintained, and it isn't what it once was.

Despite the wedding and sightseeing, Raj's and my overall feeling while in India was of unhappiness and worry. Life for Pitaji, Raj, and me had only gotten worse after Mataji's passing. We returned to Boston very concerned.

In March 1980, it was election time for all department chiefs at LMH. Dr. TB had completed his two-year term as department chair, so all nominated individuals were presented to and reviewed by the executive committee. This time, I was ready to take on the role—provided I was accepted by the committee. Department chair would be a huge step for not only me but also for the whole hospital: I was only thirty-nine years old, and I would be their first female department chair.

When I heard the committee had elected me, I was elated. I was on to another adventure. With my new job came new opportunities and responsibilities. I had a monumental task in front of me; I was stepping into uncharted territory. As the first female chief (and a foreigner at that), everyone would be watching my every move—I would have to be a touch above the men in order to be treated as an equal.

Luckily, Bapaji had prepared me for this challenge since my childhood. His strength was my backbone, and his confidence my momentum.

I knew I had it in me to make positive, sustainable changes in the department, but I also knew I needed to be careful not to push too much. So, I carefully prepared a detailed two-year plan that would cover everything: high-quality patient care, safety, efficiency, improved hospital resources, and, of course, clearing out all the political gridlock.

I had my flaws like everyone else, but by relying on wise friends and colleagues, I minimized them as much as possible. Every day I reached out to learn more from the surgeons, OR staff, and hospital administration, and I tried to always put myself in their shoes. It was truly a team effort. I am so grateful to them for supporting me during my time as chief, helping me achieve a healthy, respected department. By the end of my two years, we all had a deep bond.

From the get-go, I knew my time as chief would be difficult, no matter how prepared I was, but I was determined to succeed. The OR surgeons had given me their full support and respect, and I could not fail them. The work was both deeply meaningful and humbling; I used a combination of my judgement, intuition, and advice from others to make decisions. Not everyone agreed with me all the time, but after thoroughly researching my options, I proceeded unapologetically. I viewed roadblocks as learning opportunities to prepare me for the future.

Every day during my two years as department chair was a defining moment for me. I worked hard, constantly feeding my fire to excel. In the end, I believe that most of the changes I made were successful and good.

Besides overseeing the OR, I had other responsibilities as chair, such as setting the department's annual budget and working with the many hospital committees, which included the executive committee, the OR committee, the blood-bank committee, the ICU committee, the quality-assurance committee, and the patient-care-review committee. Some of the committees were more challenging to deal with than others; in particular, the patient-care-review committee was the most stressful, because I had to monitor colleagues and, when necessary, report them to the executive committee.

Reporting required sensitivity in finding the balance between dealing amicably with the individual (not personally judging him or her) while still giving due diligence to the process.

One particular situation stands out in my memory. A senior surgeon had yelled at a circulating nurse and thrown a surgical instrument at her during an operation. Such abuse is unheard of today, but this was the '80s.

The surgeon was a big guy and belonged to the old-school of thinking that believed a surgeon could do no wrong. Maybe he had done things like this in the past and had never been reprimanded, but not anymore.

The nurse, rightfully, asked him to apologize. She warned him that if he refused, she'd lodge a complaint with the Medical Board of Registration. He refused.

So, I met with the patient-care-review committee to discuss the ugly task of reporting him to the executive committee. During the meeting, I swallowed my fear and suggested that they give him a second chance to apologize. They all looked at me like I was a crazy person, and one of them asked who would volunteer to approach him and suggest such a thing. I said I would.

I gave myself a big pep talk, and then I invited the surgeon to my office for a consult. Even though he was big and loud, I knew I was strong on the inside. When he arrived, I firmly but gently suggested that he seriously consider apologizing. If he did not, the repercussions would be severe.

I looked calm as I sat and waited for his response, but inside my heart was pounding. I honestly believed the meeting would come to naught, but then he replied, "Oh, what the hell." And he went and apologized. This was like the sun rising in the west!

Thankfully, the nurse accepted his apology and withdrew her complaint. It was an incredibly proud moment for me as department chair. I had helped the hospital dodge a landmine, and the CEO of LMH was very appreciative.

Years later I reminded the surgeon of our confrontation and my amazement at his reaction. That was probably the first time he had ever apologized at work, and I wouldn't be surprised if it was also his last.

My average day as department chair consisted of running four surgical operating-room theaters while supervising the administration of anesthesia as well as administering anesthesia to my own patients for many different surgical procedures, and, of course, dealing with administrative work.

I interacted with at least fifty people every day, which included the administration staff, patients and their families, housekeeping, and doctors and nurses in pre-op, intra-op, post-op, ER, and OB. Each interaction was important in its own way. I also learned that it was often times more important to focus on *how* something was said rather than *what* was said. So, I set up some ground rules for myself, and they worked most of the time.

My first rule was *Start the day off right.* I left for work at 6:45 a.m. Every morning was the same: I'd say, "Good morning" to Raj; then I would eat breakfast in silence. Then I'd say, "Have a nice day." Nothing else. I needed to concentrate on my day's work and my patients. All home issues were discussed in the evenings.

My second rule was *Don't argue when reason, persuasion, and patience will give me the edge.*

Third rule was *Never compromise my values.*

And fourth, *In difficult patient situations, decide as if the patient were family, and then accept the results for what they are.* This one was an important reminder for me that even doctors an; sometimes the patient outcome was distressing, but I had done the very best I could.

During my time as department chair, the OR culture had slowly evolved. The newer surgeons were younger, and the place became less of an oligarchy. Even the new CEO of the hospital was a young woman in her forties.

Occasionally, I would have an unplanned hospital call, and Mohit would have to come with me. He'd bring along his backpack with books, crayons, and toys, and he'd stay either in my office or the nurse's lounge next to the OR. On the plus side, he got to know my workplace and many of my colleagues, and no one at the hospital minded.

Besides working, I had also signed up for a cooking class. This made Raj happy, as he had always had a passion for good food. At home, Connie's job had also expanded with Mohit's needs. She now drove him to appointments, such as the dentist and hair salon, and she even occasionally watched some of his friends as well, who were allowed to come over on the weekends.

In the spring, Bauji and Chaeji visited us. Bauji had always been particular, and rather compulsive, about his medical care—he wanted only the best. (Chaeji, on the other hand, was the exact opposite with her health, very *laissez faire*.) So, Bauji had waited to get eye surgery until he was in the U.S. and could go to the Massachusetts Eye and Ear Infirmary. He had done extensive research while in India on which doctors he wanted to see, and nothing could change his mind, so that meant that, in addition to my work and home responsibilities, I was now also in charge of Bauji's medical checkups.

Thankfully, the surgery went well, and Connie, who was by now my personal angel, drove Bauji to his follow-up appointment.

Overall, life was good. Raj and I had good jobs and a good family, and we were in good health. We couldn't have asked for more. But we still had one mission to accomplish: moving back to India. We were still constantly, relentlessly, trying to make it happen.

Although we knew moving back to India would require us to adjust and that the situation might be rough for a while, it was still our top priority. It was so important to Raj to step in for Pitaji, who deserved to retire after working long hours for years. It was also important to both Raj and me that Mohit be with his grandfather and have time to bond with him. I was lucky to have had such a special relationship and companionship with Bapaji, and I wanted Mohit to have the same with his grandfathers. We still had time to make it happen: despite Pitaji's age, he was still healthy and active, playing tennis at the country club six days a week.

At the very least, Mohit was able to be with Bauji in the summers. Their time together was short but precious. Bauji had never taken care of any of his kids except for me, so he was completely under Mohit's thumb. One day Bauji ventured to give Mohit a bath, but, of course, Bauji had to abide by Mohit's rules, the number one rule being "No water on my head."

They also read together, during which Mohit occasionally disagreed with Bauji on his word choice. Bauji had never been boldly confronted by his own children. Mohit would say, "I will check with my mother when she comes home. We don't speak your kind of English. We speak American English."

They also had differing opinions on skin color. In India, fair complexion is considered superior, a sign of upper class. Bauji was so fair he could have been mistaken for a Caucasian. Meanwhile, Mohit was very tan from summer camp, and he was equally proud of his complexion. Mohit said to Bauji, "Look how brown I am." Bauji countered, "No, Mohit, you are white." Back and forth they went, until finally Mohit won. Mohit told Bauji, "Why don't you go sit in the sun and be brown like me." These were my evening updates after getting home from work.

Mohit had Chaeji wrapped around his little finger, too. On this particular visit, Mohit was still very attached to his security blanket, even though it needed to be retired and had tears all along the seam of its border. Mohit called these tears "pockets," and he asked Chaeji to sew them up. Lucky for him, Chaeji was a good tailor and agreed to it. Every day Mohit found a new "pocket," and every day Chaeji happily repaired it. Now, if it had been me as a child with this bedraggled blanket, it would have been thrown in the trash!

During their visit, Chaeji and Bauji also took a trip to New York, bringing along Mohit and my sister Varsha. Chaeji was hoping to find a new blanket for Mohit, so Varsha suggested Bergdorf Goodman. They were overjoyed to find Mohit's exact same blanket. So, Mohit came home with a new security blanket, but unfortunately for Chaeji, he was not at all attached to it. The blanket stayed in mint condition, untouched. But at least Chaeji did not have to fix any more "pockets."

On the day Connie drove Bauji to his post-surgery eye appointment, Chaeji stayed home with Mohit, so she was in charge of fixing him lunch. Mohit requested French toast, but Chaeji was a vegan and had absolutely no idea what Mohit was talking about—she had never even touched an egg in her life.

Mohit told her the recipe, but Chaeji was confused: mixing milk with an egg made no sense to her. To confirm, Mohit dialed the neighbor's phone number, and Chaeji spoke with them. After that, Chaeji followed the rest of Mohit's instructions.

By the end of their little adventure, Mohit had French toast for lunch, cooked by Chaeji for the first, and last, time. It's amazing what grandparents will do for their grandchildren.

Mohit had a fun relationship with Bauji and Chaeji. Our house rule for him and his friends was that they were allowed to do whatever they wanted in his bedroom and downstairs in the playroom, even jumping on the playroom's sofa, but playing in the living room was an absolute no. Mohit took this rule very seriously, and he told Bauji and Chaeji, "No sitting in the living room." Bauji and Chaeji, as always, took his orders in good spirit.

Even though Mohit's time with his grandparents was limited, we still felt so lucky that he was able to create wonderful, treasured memories like these.

Bauji and Chaeji usually visited in the summer and they would return to Ahmedabad refreshed and in good health, with bags full from shopping (more for family and friends than themselves).

In September 1980, my sister Veena, who lived in India, had moved to Bombay with her husband, Ashok, and she was now pregnant. After some discussion, everyone in the family agreed, including Veena, that she should come to Boston to ensure the safest labor and delivery. Unfortunately, Ashok could not come with her, but Raj and I were more than capable.

I scheduled Veena to deliver at my old hospital, Brigham and Women's Hospital, and chose Dr. S to be her ob-gyn. Dr. S was one of my favorite colleagues at BWH; in addition to being a skilled doctor, he was also known for his excellent bedside manner.

Despite all my planning and medical connections, I was still stressed about everything going smoothly for Veena while she was under my roof. But I needn't have worried.

When Veena went into labor, one of my ex-colleagues gave her a wonderful epidural, and the rest of her delivery went by the book. Everyone in the family was glad she had come to us to have her baby.

After the delivery, life moved ever faster. With Halloween came the start of the holiday season, and as usual, Mohit was beyond excited, running around in his Batman cape. Next came Diwali, celebrated at our home with the Marshalls, and then another gift-giving occasion in Christmas. We put up a Christmas tree in our living room, and, much to Mohit's delight, Santa Claus delivered the requests on his wish list. Next was Mohit's birthday in January 1981, when we invited his entire class, more than twenty kids, for a party. Then finally, February came. Time for a break—or so I thought.

Mohit's school had its annual parent-faculty dinner scheduled for February 15, and the parent committee approached me with the idea of an Indian dinner. They would all be my helpers, but I would have to orchestrate the event. The meal would be prepared from scratch in the school's kitchen and would have to feed three hundred people. By now I was a reputable chef at home, but I had never attempted such a major cooking project before. After some serious thought, I decided to take on the challenge.

My helpers were the other mothers at the school, most of whom lived in affluent suburbs—Beacon Hill, Brookline, Chestnut Hill, Newton, and Wellesley. They were eager to pitch in, but I had to teach them the basics of Indian cooking. At the time, real Indian food was pretty much nonexistent in Boston, with only a couple of substandard restaurants.

So, between work and this dinner project, I was feeling the strain of multi-tasking, compounded with the stress of not knowing whether I'd be able to pull off the meal. Since I had never done anything like this before, I simply multiplied my original recipe for thirty people by ten and hoped it would work.

The night of the dinner came. All preparations were complete, and the meal was ready to go. With a sigh of relief, it went off without a hitch. Everyone loved it. It also ended up being a memorable night for more reasons than just the food. One of the parents, Dr. John Collins, who was the chief of Cardiac Surgery at BWH, arrived late because that very evening he had successfully completed a major heart operation. Dr. Collins' son, John, was Mohit's friend, and Dr. Collins' wife, Mary, was also a doctor; she was the nicest person and very involved at the school.

During the evening, I was called out as the mastermind behind the meal and received a standing ovation, which embarrassed me. Not bad for someone who used to hate cooking as a child.

I also met many mothers throughout the evening who recognized me as the anesthesiologist who had given them their epidural. Most anesthesiologists work in an operating room and aren't recognized by their patient, even if they go visit the patient the day after surgery. But L&D anesthesiologists work closely with their patients, trying to make them as comfortable as possible. Sometimes, despite our best efforts, we can't take the pain away, leaving both the patient and anesthesiologist frustrated. Whenever one of the moms recognized me, I silently hoped she had happy memories of her labor under my care.

The day after the dinner, I received a touching thank-you letter from the school principal as well as another thank-you from the parents committee. All the time, effort, and worry had paid off.

Summer rolled around, and we were all enjoying it. Connie, wonderful as ever, was staying busy with Mohit's schedule; he was now getting swimming lessons as well as playing tennis at camp.

In June, Raj was between jobs, so he planned a two-month visit to India to finalize our long-awaited move. His heart was set on helping Pitaji retire. It would be difficult for me to get along without Raj for so long, but I supported him 100 percent. We both knew we'd need to sacrifice in order to achieve our goal.

When Raj arrived in Delhi, it was 110 degrees Fahrenheit. But the welcome he received from Darshan and Alka was frigid. Both of them treated Raj's stay (in a home he jointly owned) as an unbearable intrusion. Their attitude, though, did not bother Raj; he was determined to see his plans through.

Not surprisingly, the air conditioner in Raj's room was still broken—the one Darshan claimed had once worked. This illustrated our biggest hurdle in moving back to India: we had no place to stay! But Raj was determined to find a solution.

A new apartment complex had been built across the street, and it was almost ready to rent out. So, until our house was built, we could live in a two-bedroom apartment. This was the most rational solution to the house delay, and we were more than prepared to compromise with temporary modest quarters; Pitaji, however, would not hear of it. It was insulting to him to even hear of his son living in a rented unit. We were back at square one with the stalled house plans.

We couldn't get past all of Darshan and Alka's red tape. They objected to building our house in front of the main house, as it would eat up the beautiful lawn. And they objected to building it behind the main house, as it would sacrifice the vegetable garden. We had nowhere else to go. Their message was clear.

Meanwhile, Pitaji had no voice at all. His job was to pay the bills; beyond that, he was under Darshan and Alka's thumb, total subservience—even his words were rationed. No doubt they had threatened him in some way. What's more, whenever Raj was out of earshot (or out of the country), Darshan and Alka would tell Pitaji the most grotesque lies about him.

When Raj was visiting, he wanted to go to work with Pitaji, but the demonic king and queen replied that his help was "not required." So, while Pitaji was at the office for long hours every day by himself, Darshan's work consisted of playing tennis, eating breakfast and lunch, supervising the gardener, and watching TV with the rest of his family. This was clearly parental abuse— something you hear about, but until you witness it, you have no idea how truly horrific it is.

Also per tradition, Darshan had programmed the house phones to malfunction whenever Raj tried to use them (even though, ironically, Darshan had forged my signature to get a second telephone line, since I had priority in India as a doctor). In order to talk to me, Raj had to ride the servant's bike and use the phone at the post office; for all other communication, we had to rely on handwritten letters and recorded audio tapes.

Raj tried his best to ignore Darshan and Alka's daily attempts to sabotage him and instead focused on continuing to find ways to achieve his plans. His only ground support during his whole stay was Munni and her family, but they lived two hours away and could only occasionally visit.

Munni had stayed in touch with Darshan and Alka for Pitaji's sake, but Munni knew she was neither welcome nor loved by any of them except Pitaji. Like Raj, she, too, felt helpless in this disturbing situation.

Munni warned Raj that he was putting his life on the line by staying with Darshan and Alka, as Raj was a big threat to their possessions, lifestyle, and inheritance, and none of us knew what they would attempt next. They had severed all ties to human decency in service of their god, Money.

Every day of the two months Raj was visiting, Darshan would call Munni and ask her when Raj was leaving. Munni's reply was always, "Ask him yourself." Darshan bragged that his kids had mastered the art of breaking into Raj's room and sifting through his belongings.

Munni passed on all this information to Raj, and she constantly reminded him to eat only what they ate and never to take the first bite. None of us had ever gotten answers as to what had actually happened to Mataji.

Darshan and Alka's world revolved around food, food, and more food. They were all obese, including their daughter and prince of a son, who now resembled a baby elephant. They were all candidates for bariatric surgery.

But besides food, they had no other standard of living. Their house was not a home; it was sparsely furnished, not warm or welcoming, especially to Raj, whose privileges were beyond limited.

Raj was flabbergasted by Darshan and Alka's deplorable ad hominem attacks. If he tried to ignore them, they only shot out more shrapnel. His misery was both their target and their entertainment; Darshan and Alka had an unquenchable thirst for schadenfreude. To them, this was war, and they'd do anything to win it.

Raj, meanwhile, felt like a prisoner of war. Pitaji could see Darshan and Alka's blistering attacks against Raj, but for whatever reason, he did nothing. We can only assume he was afraid for his own safety.

It was difficult for Raj to handle the daily attacks, but it was far more painful for him to watch Pitaji suffer. He was truly a hostage in his own home, trapped and at the mercy of Darshan and Alka.

I could feel Raj's pain when we spoke, and I grieved with him. We tried to carry on with our plans, helping each other keep our spirits up through words of encouragement, but after two months of no progress, we had to face reality: the longer Raj stayed, the longer he risked his safety. He needed to leave.

Darshan and Alka had refused to compromise in even the smallest way. Their evil schemes were relentless, their greed bottomless. Family and unity meant nothing to them. Still, I have withheld the ugliest details of our interactions with them. On a scale of one to ten, the stories I have shared thus far are a one.

# Chapter Seventeen

*In August 1981,* Raj flew back to Boston. When I met him at the airport, I was struck by his appearance. He seemed to be both deflated yet overflowing with sadness. All his efforts had failed. He was discouraged, disturbed, and in pain. We had both suffered during our separation, but Raj far more than me.

The light at the end of the tunnel was Mohit, who was beside himself with excitement when he saw Raj. He had missed his dad tremendously. To finally be together again was heavenly; our joy was boundless.

Mohit was finishing up summer camp, and soon after, he came down with chickenpox. Thank goodness karma was on our side with Raj back, as I could not have handled my work and Mohit's sickness on my own. Raj was a huge help, and even the chickenpox itself was kind to us—it gave us an excuse to relax. We all needed a break anyway, so we planned a trip to Mount Washington.

The weather was not the best, but the adventurers Raj and Mohit still wanted to go. I was apprehensive but was outvoted two to one. Luckily, nothing went awry, and we came back down with a bumper sticker on our Audi: *This car climbed Mt. Washington.* Both father and son were very proud of their accomplishment.

After a while, Raj's jet lag wore off, the clouds of depression lifted, and we decompressed. Now it was time to start objectively analyzing our options for the future.

Raj's solo trip to India was the straw that had broken the camel's back. We knew we'd never be welcome in our own home with Darshan and Alka around, and more than that, we'd never be safe. We simply could not move back. That door was shut forever, and to keep knocking at it would do no good.

Still, though, it was painful for Raj to accept; it was as if a dark cloud hung over him, with no silver lining. I reminded him that, although we had failed to achieve our goal, at least we had not compromised our values. We had turned the other cheek, maintaining our dignity and integrity. Even now, as we decided to abandon our plans, we did so without any caustic exchange with Darshan and Alka. So while they may have won the battle, we had won the war: Raj and I walked away with a clear conscience.

I also tried to ease Raj's pain by reminding him of the song "Que Sera Sera": "Whatever will be, will be/The future's not ours to see/Que sera sera." Our entire future was now open to us. We were no longer at a crossroads—we were on a one-way street, and it pointed us to the US. We had been tangled in an ugly web for so long that our hopes and dreams were nearly dead. We needed to rally, to take our pain and turn it into momentum. We were starting out anew, and we had our sights set on a bright horizon.

We began our American odyssey with undivided enthusiasm. The past was the past; we did not allow ourselves to get bogged down in regret. Instead, we threw ourselves into the present possibilities. I felt strong, confident, and energetic, in spite of all the emotional upheaval. I attribute my resilience to Bapaji and my upbringing. His teachings have always been my guiding light and my anchor during life's storms. Although Raj and I would never completely heal from these emotional scars, we did not let them hold us back. We actually felt lucky that we had walked away from the situation without any bodily harm; Raj had come home without even a virus this time. We were on to greener pastures.

As our decision set in to stay in the U.S., we realized that the elaborate 220-volt stereo system and tape recorders we had imported from Hong Kong for our move to India were now useless. We also had to reconcile ourselves to the fact that, from here on out, we would be only visitors to India. We would still go every year in the winter during Mohit's school break to see Pitaji, Bauji, and Chaeji, but we would only be guests, not residents (and even "guests" was a stretch at Darshan and Alka's).

Although it was not always convenient or emotionally easy to visit every year, we were determined to. Pitaji was only getting frailer and frailer with each passing year, and we needed to support him in whatever small ways we could.

With this momentous decision behind us, Raj and I enjoyed the rest of the summer. Although we both still occasionally felt waves of disturbance and disappointment, we knew we were doing the right thing.

In September 1981, Mohit started at Park School again, and we hired a housekeeper/kitchen helper, Devi. She was a soft-spoken, fifty-year-old woman from India. Back when Raj and I were still planning on moving back to India, we had hired her to be my night-call support while Raj made frequent trips there. Of course, our plans had changed drastically, but we thought it would still be nice to have the extra help. Plus, as an added bonus, Mohit enjoyed speaking to Devi in Hindi. (And the extra help was especially needed in 1983, when our house was full to capacity with family and friends. Devi was a lifesaver. Taking care of all the guests worked out well for her, too, as she got lonely during the day without company.)

Connie was still the backbone of our household, but Devi filled an important role, too, and luckily, they got along. While Devi did not speak a word of English and neither did Connie any Hindi, they found ways of communicating with each other, and both had a clear understanding of whose job was whose.

I remember one day Connie got a flat tire and was late, but she didn't have a cell phone and had no way of calling the house. So, when Mohit hopped off the school bus, he was expecting to be greeted as usual by Connie (who was punctual to the minute), but instead he found himself locked out of the house. He rang the doorbell and pounded and pounded on the door until finally Devi opened it. She had been taking a siesta and was ignoring the knocking because that was Connie's job. At least Devi and Connie did not step on each other's toes.

Another day when I got home from work, Devi was waiting to tell me another exciting story. That afternoon, Devi had offered to make Connie lunch. Connie had agreed, and Devi had proudly whipped up her very own recipe for a jalapeño omelet. But when poor Connie took a bite, her bland Irish taste buds went ballistic. She started screaming that her mouth was on fire; she said over and over, "Water! Water! Water!" Devi, panicked, did not understand. Eventually Devi figured it out, and Connie recovered. That day Devi learned two English words: *fire* and *water*. Devi and Connie were strange but funny comrades from two different worlds.

In December, it was time for our annual pilgrimage to India, but this year, only Mohit and I were going; Raj was staying home. In the past, I had been the one left alone, both when I was pregnant and when Mohit was a baby. But Raj wouldn't be completely on his own—he had Devi to cook and clean, which was a good thing because his skills in the kitchen were limited to making toast, coffee, and eggs.

First Mohit and I went to Delhi, and we stayed as unwelcome guests in our own home. This visit was more out of family duty, although thankfully, Mohit had at least reached an age where he enjoyed spending time with his cousins. It was a short stay, and then we were off to Ahmedabad.

As always, we received a warm welcome from everyone in my family. Unji Ben was still in command as housekeeper, twenty-five years and running; she was getting old, but she was as sharp as ever and kept everything on an even keel. She also loved to pamper Mohit.

Bauji and Chaeji had adopted a niece of Chaeji's, Ujwala. She was about seven years old and was treated like a member of the immediate family. She did, though, question Bauji more than we would have had the guts to as children, but maybe that was simply a change in the times.

While staying at Bauji and Chaeji's, Mohit liked to go next door to Chachaji's to get spoiled by my cousins. We were in town during the Uttarayan Kite Festival on January 14, and Chachaji went all out with the celebration, setting up a tent on the terrace, with Mohit as his proud assistant. Chachaji gave Mohit a gift of money during the festival, and when Chaeji heard about this, she told Mohit that she would give him double. Mohit replied, "I don't want your money. Just get the lizards off the walls." With the tropical climate, lizards were everywhere, and Mohit was not fond of them.

We had a lot of fun during our stay in Ahmedabad. Mohit enjoyed playing around with Chaeji's harmonium (which he called "the open piano"). Chaeji also arranged for a street peddler to come to the house and do tricks with his monkey, and, the following day, a snake charmer came with his huge snake dancing to music.

My sister Veena was settled in Bombay, so before heading back to Boston, Mohit and I stopped by for some sightseeing. Even though it was December, Bombay stays hot all year round, so it was sunny and in the eighties. We visited Victoria Gardens (which brought back some memories for me) and Mohit got so hot that he took his shirt off and complained loudly, "Why did God have to give the biggest sun to India?" None of us had an answer.

Then our trip was over, and we were back in Boston with Raj. In May, my two-year term was up as department chair of the anesthesiology department. Dr. TB approached me and expressed that he would like to take over as chief again. I responded, "Sure," but suggested he first unofficially get the approval of the men's locker-room club before sending our recommendation to the executive committee. I knew my time as chair had changed the culture in the department, but Dr. TB had yet to realize that for himself.

When Dr. TB did not get the approval he was seeking from the locker room, he decided to withdraw his name. This meant that I had the complete backing of the hospital staff for a second nomination as chair. I had, in short, won over the enemy.

Dr. Johnson still did not like female doctors, but I was, as he put it, "different." I had also passed Dr. Capobianco's social test. As much as it was unnatural for me, I now called him "Tony." We had become friends, and he had even entrusted me to give anesthesia to his mother, his lovely wife, his sister, and many more family and friends. I had slowly but steadily proven myself to these two formidable surgeons and everyone else at LMH.

My achievement felt surreal. I was not invisible. I had a voice, and I could shape the world I was living in. As chairwoman, I had instigated a paradigm shift—a change of heart—in a department that had previously fed off male dominance. They had even learned to accept my differences as a foreigner, such as when I confused my v's and w's.

Although these men would always be driven and were still vociferous with their opinions, we had found a way to peacefully work together.

As always when I celebrated success, my heart turned to Bapaji in gratitude. I know now how incredibly lucky I was to have grown up with a grandfather who had made time for me. His teachings were my rock. Because of him, I knew that, if I wanted something badly enough and was willing to work hard for it, I could make it happen. I also know, though, that no man or woman is an island. If it hadn't been for the support of my colleagues at work and the sacrifices of Raj at home, I could not have achieved what I did. I admire them for their open-mindedness and willingness to change. If it had not been for their efforts, all of mine would have been for naught.

I was also lucky to be in America, in a country where changes like these *could* take place and were encouraged to. Yes, I had encountered obstacles along the way, but in the end, I had reached my destination, because I was living in a place where independence was valued and opportunities were infinite. The sky was the limit for me, and I was ready to go for it.

Being re-elected as department chair meant it could very well become a permanent position for me. I had set the bar high, but I was ready for the challenge. I pushed myself in every facet of my life: I attended leadership seminars to improve my interpersonal skills; I went to the annual meeting for the American Society of Anesthesiologists to keep up with the latest innovations; and I implemented new practices in my ever-changing field, viewing it as an opportunity for intellectual exploration. I also handled complicated relationships and searched for sustainable, long-term solutions. I was working hard because I knew the value of the outcome. Of course, at times, I stumbled and felt uncertain, but I did not let that stop me from pushing forward professionally. With each challenge I overcame, I grew in endurance and confidence.

In the end, my years as department chair were filled with gratifying, extraordinary experiences.

The summer of 1982 went by quickly. Mohit was going to his yearly camp, and Raj was getting ready to start his own business. Then, before we knew it, we were into the holiday season. By now, Mohit knew that Santa Claus was not real, and Raj and I felt that the gift situation was getting a little out of control with Diwali in late fall, then Christmas in December, and Mohit's birthday in January. So we chatted with Mohit, telling him that he would continue getting birthday gifts but that he needed to choose between getting Christmas presents and Diwali presents. Even though we were Hindu, we did not pressure him. In the end, he chose Diwali; we asked him why, and he said, "Because Diwali comes earlier." The spirit of Christmas was still celebrated every year, but without the gifts. The holiday season became much more feasible and less stressful.

In October 1982, I had my annual meeting for the American Society of Anesthesiologists. This year, it was being held in San Francisco, so Raj, Mohit, and I all boarded a plane, excited to spend time together and see the West Coast. Halfway through our flight, though, things got a little too exciting when the plane had engine trouble. The pilots had to land the plane with only two working engines; those were some anxiety-filled moments.

We were supposed to arrive in San Francisco at eleven in the evening, but with the plane problems, we didn't get in until three in the morning. By the time we got to our hotel, we were all exhausted and ready to collapse into bed, Mohit especially. But since we had arrived so late, the nice lady at the registration desk suggested that we wait to check in until 6 a.m., or else we'd have to pay for a full night, which would cost us one hundred fifty dollars. Raj and I decided to save the money and wait in the lobby for two hours.

Mohit was not happy with our decision. I told Raj that twenty years from now, Mohit would have forgotten all the luxuries and remember only our penny-pinching. By then, one hundred fifty dollars would seem like nothing.

Years down the road, Raj and I were reminiscing with Mohit, who was now grown, about this incident, and we asked him if he thought we'd made the right decision. He said, "Yes."

Despite our unexpected plane adventure, we enjoyed our stay in San Francisco very much. The city reminded us of Beacon Hill in Boston. Raj and I both agreed that San Francisco was the only other U.S. city we could have happily settled in; Boston still won out, though, because we loved its four seasons.

The year of 1983 was both busy and challenging. Bauji and Chaeji were visiting us in May, and Bauji had scheduled his usual plethora of medical appointments. This time it was prostate surgery. It was stressful dealing with a patient as informed as Bauji. We didn't have Google back then, but Bauji's bedside reading was the previous year's edition of my 2,500-page PDR (*Physicians' Desk Reference*). With Bauji's vast knowledge and

Type A personality, he was difficult to convince of anything without first presenting him with exhaustive research.

Even with the upcoming surgery, Bauji was still in good health and as active as ever in his business, his social life, and his philanthropic endeavors. He was a trustee at the school he had founded; he was also a bank trustee and president of the textile mill owner's association. He was very recognized and respected throughout Ahmedabad. When I visited him, I'd tease him that I'd have to make an appointment just to spend time with him. It was only a joke, though—he always made time for his children, and we were lucky to have him as a father.

Thankfully, Bauji's surgery was uneventful, and I was very lucky to have Devi and Connie to help out. With Chaeji's direction, Devi made all the meals. This worked out for everybody, as Devi did not like being alone all day and was more than happy to take care of guests: she dutifully provided them with tea in bed (a British tradition), breakfast with juice at eleven in the morning, followed by lunch, evening tea, and dinner. Although they ate frequently, Devi made the servings small, so weight wasn't an issue. Everyone was happy. Then, we got an unexpected and distressing surprise.

My cousin Minni, Chachaji's daughter, who had been living in New Jersey with her husband, Rohit, and their two-year-old son, had recently moved to Delhi for Rohit's two-year job assignment. While there, Minni had been diagnosed with a benign brain tumor.

She was only twenty-eight years old and needed critical care, so she had called me for advice. I told her that the best options would be here in Boston.

Both Minni and I had been raised on the importance of family trust and unity, so without second thought, Minni immediately planned for her and her family to come stay with us in Boston.

Bauji and Chaeji were still with us, and Auntyji, Minni's mother, would also be coming. Our house had only three bedrooms, which included a basement with a playroom and an additional tiny room, but even though our place was small, it had a big heart.

When Minni arrived, I reached out to my circle of friends in the medical community and scheduled all of her many specialty appointments, from the internist to the endocrinologist to the most important one of all—the neurosurgeon. These were the days before CT scans of the brain, so the surgeon had to work blindly, without any video monitoring. It was a very delicate and difficult procedure.

With the help of friends, I was able to get Minni in with Dr. Nicholas Zarvas at Massachusetts General Hospital. He was the most experienced in his field, and people came from all over the world to have their surgeries performed by him.

Leading up to the surgery, I grew more and more distraught. Being a doctor myself, I was fully aware of the seriousness of the surgery and its potential complications. I would lie awake at night worrying about Minni's vision being compromised—the thought sent shivers down my spine—and I wondered constantly if I had made the right call advising her to come to Boston. I worked on patients every day, but when they're family and friends, it's impossible to remain objective. I knew we were lucky to be in the mecca of medical care, but still, what if something went wrong during the surgery? I would feel responsible. Sometimes ignorance really is bliss.

The day of the operation came, and with all of Minni's good karma, the removal of the tumor was a success. But when Bauji and I went to visit her in the hospital afterward, she told us she couldn't walk straight because she could not see. Oh, my goodness. I held my breath, afraid that all my nightmares had come true. Then Bauji said, "Put on your eyeglasses." And that was it. She had forgotten to put on her glasses! What a relief! Minni was tumor-free and suffered no complications. Many, many heartfelt thanks go out to all my doctor friends who put in the extra effort to care for Minni.

Minni stayed at our house for a month to recover, and Connie, my sanity-saver, drove Minni to her follow-up appointments. Meanwhile, at home, Devi expertly handled all the day-to-day needs of our many guests, which now included my sister Veena and her son, who were visiting us from Bombay. Veena said to me, "You have a housekeeper and a chauffeur who are both dependable. We don't get that kind of service in India."

My life was pretty hectic that year, between work and maintaining the house and grocery shopping, but Raj was my big support. Yes, our house was crowded for a while, but with tolerance and a dedication to harmonious living, we all enjoyed our time together.

Throughout the years, we regularly hosted visitors from India; some gave due notice, and others were a last-minute surprise. It was always nice to catch up with them, either out at a restaurant or at our table. Even after long absences, we'd easily reconnect like two magnets.

After that summer, though, we had reached a time when we no longer needed Devi's services, so we planned for her to return to India with Bauji and Chaeji. Before Chaeji left, she told me, "Sadhna, in the entire two months I've stayed with you, I have not opened your refrigerator once due to Devi's attendance to our needs." (Chaeji had always spoken very sincerely and transparently; she was not one to worry about diplomacy.) Since I was not around during the day, I was a little surprised by this, but Devi was such a hard worker, I believed it.

After a hectic but productive summer as hosts, Raj, Mohit, and I needed a vacation, so we went to Hyannis Hotel Resort for some R&R. In those days, Mohit enjoyed getting Happy Meals from McDonald's, and he felt sorry for me because I was a vegetarian. One day I heard him pray, "God, please let my mom eat a McDonald's Happy Meal." He thought that my being vegetarian was some kind of punishment and that God could forgive me. Later he realized this was my choice, not a curse.

At the end of 1983, we planned another trip to India. My little brother, Pradeep, was getting married in Ahmedabad, and he had set the wedding for December 24, so we could all attend. Everyone was excited for the lavish event and to see family gathered from all over the world.

December is the best time of year in Ahmedabad, perfect weather. Pradeep arrived at the wedding in an imported convertible alongside his procession—no pony ride for him—and then it was three days of dining and festivities. Bauji had put his heart and soul into every detail of the affair. In later years, he told me that the two weddings he was most excited about planning with absolute excellence was Pradeep's and mine. My hat was off to him; he had left no stone unturned.

Of course, Raj, Mohit, and I also visited Pitaji in Delhi. Darshan was upset with us because we had not brought a generator (how we could have fit it into our plane luggage was beyond me). Darshan and Alka claimed to want the generator for Pitaji's sake, as India had frequent power outages, but we knew these parasites were scavenging and hoarding everything for themselves, waiting to live in luxury after Pitaji passed away. Our lips were sealed regarding why they didn't just buy one over there—we weren't looking forward to the eruption of that volcano.

We faced Darshan and Alka's routine derogatory remarks and despicable deeds. Pitaji was still being deprived and silenced, but apparently he had suffered such constant doses of their poison that he had built up a small resistance to it. One day he announced he was taking us all out for a fancy dinner. By then, Delhi was full of five-star restaurants, and we went to the Taj. Mohit immediately went to check on the state of the restrooms—he gave them five stars.

Pitaji had also realized that Darshan's family was obese. During the dinner, he said to Mohit, "You are not eating. Take some more." Then he turned to Deepu, Darshan's son, and said, "Hold back now." This became a familiar phrase of Pitaji's the few times we went out with him.

After we had all finished eating, Darshan and Deepu disappeared. We were waiting for them in the lobby when they finally showed up; apparently they had crashed a wedding reception at the hotel to indulge in more food. Raj and I were shocked, but Deepu mentioned that this free-food indulgence was a regular trick of theirs.

We obviously had very different values than Darshan and his family; ours were chiseled in granite, indestructible, while theirs fluctuated according to the situation and their wants. It was difficult for me to comprehend how Raj and Darshan could even share the same DNA—perhaps Darshan was a mutation. Restraint was Raj's and my motto while around them. We kept our emotions in check. We refused to sink to their level.

We said our goodbyes and returned to Boston. These trips to Delhi only reinforced our decision that we could never return and live there. We had come to accept it. As Stephen Colbert said, "Acceptance is not defeat. Acceptance is just awareness."

# Chapter Eighteen

*In January 1984* we started our next big adventure. Our first home was too small; we needed either to renovate or to move. We had been putting off the decision for so long because we had thought we'd be going back to India, but now our future had changed.

Although we had shared many happy memories in this house in Newton, we wanted to move to a bigger house in the Boston suburbs. We started looking in Weston because it was centrally located and within twenty minutes of my work—a must. We had a few absolutes in the type of house we were looking for, but we also had some flexible wants so that we could fit the price into our budget. I was especially interested in finding a place in which I could pursue my passion for interior decorating.

As we continued to house-hunt, life moved along. Raj and Mohit were both Celtic fans and enjoyed going to games together at the old Boston Garden. We were also fans of the TV shows *Dallas* and *Dynasty*, which we liked to watch on Friday nights to relax and unwind at the end of the week.

In the summer of 1984, Raj and I thought it would be fun to visit Kashmir and show Mohit the beautiful valley. Mohit and I left first, with Raj planning on joining us later. At first Mohit was very unhappy. He was a loyal Celtics fan, and because of our trip, he couldn't cheer them on in the playoffs. He received daily updates from Raj on the team's progress, and when the Celtics lost, Mohit felt responsible. He said his presence at the game might have brought them good luck. But the trip to Kashmir was still wonderful, a real treat for everyone. Raj, Mohit, and I were able to tour some saffron fields, because one of Pitaji's business associates was a saffron dealer and welcomed us to visit. We also did the classic outings of horseback riding and hiking around beautiful gardens and waterfalls. Seeing all of the beautiful sights rekindled some sweet memories for Raj and me. At the hotel, Mohit was excited to watch the Wimbledon Tennis Tournament on TV, Jimmy Connors versus John McEnroe.

When we returned to Boston, Raj and I were refreshed and ready to continue our search for a home that, unlike the one in Delhi, would not be hemmed in by petty thinking and caustic deeds. At times we still got roped into the convoluted happenings in Delhi, but overall, we knew were on the right path. We believed in our new vision, and we had the tenacity to roll with the punches. I often thought during this time of Bapaji and his life journey, overcoming so many obstacles at such a young age without even a mentor. He was and always has been my inspiration.

Unfortunately, our house-hunting was not progressing, but at least in the meantime, we were all busy, working hard, leading balanced but fun lives. Mohit was becoming more and more independent, and Connie drove him to swim lessons and tennis camp. Work was keeping me busy as well, but I still found the time to pursue my hobbies of gourmet cooking and interior designing; I was reading many magazines on architecture and home decorating. We also went and watched some Indian artists from Bollywood perform at the Kresge Auditorium in Cambridge.

I enjoyed spending time with my wonderful group of Indian origin female friends. We had formed an exclusive group of twelve, and we met the second Wednesday of every month at a restaurant. No men or kids. Just an evening of us chatting and relaxing. I'd bet it was as good as any therapy session.

Our group started small rituals to remember and reinforce our cultural heritage. Further back than 1974, I and one other lady in the group held a potluck to kick off the fast of Karva Chauth. Eventually more of us in the group were participating in the after-fast potluck. We also started holding a potluck with friends in the '70s to celebrate Diwali.

At the time, we twelve ladies needed each other in order to remind ourselves of our upbringing and beliefs. Nowadays, though, the population of Indian professionals in the U.S. has grown tremendously and, with it, the availability of Indian programs and celebrations. The need for a group of one's own, such as I had, isn't as important, but I'd still argue that the potlucks alone made the get-togethers worth it. It's nice to enjoy authentic, homemade food, surrounded by friends.

Most of us in the group were professionals; some were homemakers. We developed a deep bond, and, while some are no longer part of the group, the rest of us still keep up the commitment after many years.

In September 1984, Mohit began the fourth grade. In October, I had my annual meeting in San Francisco. This time, we had a smooth flight, thank goodness. After arriving, we watched our weekly allotment of *Dallas* and *Dynasty*, and then Mohit suggested we visit one of the many grand wineries in California.

So between my meetings, Raj, Mohit, and I drove over the mesmerizing Golden Gate Bridge to wine country. Once we chose a winery, however, Mohit changed his mind; he said they had looked much more impressive on TV. But Raj and I told him it had been his idea and that were going to follow through with a tour. On TV, Mohit had only seen the wineries' beautiful surroundings; the real tour, which consisted of walking around barrels inside, was boring for his age.

At the end of the tour, while we were standing in the reception area, our tour guide pointed to a huge barrel with a picture of a God figure on it. He asked the group if we could guess who it was. Before anybody else could answer, Mohit excitedly said, "It's Bacchus, the Greek god of wine." Everybody—including Raj and I—were surprised! Apparently, Mohit had gone on a school field trip to the Boston Museum of Fine and Arts and thus was knowledgeable on the subject of Greek Mythology. Goes to show that even kids can teach us something new; in fact, they can be our best teachers if we let them. As William Wordsworth said, "Child is the father of man." By ending the forced tour on a personal success, Mohit felt much better about the whole escapade.

We returned to Boston and resumed our house-hunting. Finally, after much looking, Raj and I decided to build our own house on a nice plot of land in Weston. One of my colleagues, Dr. Shepard (the anti-smoking advocate), had a neighbor named Terry, who was an architect. Terry was knowledgeable and friendly, and, by coincidence, I had given his wife anesthesia during her labor and delivery. Terry seemed to be a good fit for our goals, and he was amicable to our input.

In 1985, our house plans got underway. Building our own home became both Raj's and my passion. We had regular meetups with Terry to discuss the progress; he was a big believer in conserving trees, so we kept as many of them as we could during construction. By winter, the foundation was complete.

The only potential negative with our new home in Weston was the fact that Mohit would have to change schools. He was not at all happy about this. He would much rather have kept his little bedroom and continue going to a school he'd been going to for eight years and was like a second home to him, with all his friends and happy memories. Raj and I completely understood his feelings and were concerned, but we hoped that, over time, he'd adapt. To pacify Mohit, Connie agreed to his request to drive him to Park School from Weston, but this was not practical. We needed to find a new school for him when it was time to transfer.

The public schools in Weston were excellent, and private schools were expensive, so it was a difficult decision, but, in the end, we chose another private school. With how difficult the transition already was for Mohit, we thought it might be easier for him to switch to a school that had a familiar feeling and methodology to it. Many of the private elementary/middle schools in the area went only through seventh grade, so we decided on Buckingham, Browne & Nichols School (BBN) in Cambridge, because it went from pre-K through twelfth grade, which meant avoiding another transfer for Mohit.

Mohit and I went to BBN for an interview. This time Mohit was wearing a navy blazer and tie, no Batman cape. We both passed our written exams, he was admitted, and Connie agreed to pick him up from school every day. (Whenever she had to get surgery, Raj and I prayed to the gods for her speedy recovery. Thank goodness our prayers were answered and her absences were short. Our household wouldn't have been able to function without her.)

Soon enough, 1986 rolled around, and construction on our house was progressing smoothly. Mohit was not happy about this, but Raj and I were excited. Our weekends were filled with planning the interior-design details. A friend gave me a book that said building a house was the perfect recipe for divorce, but, thankfully, Raj and I did not have any major disagreements.

In the summer, Bauji and Chaeji visited again. When they arrived, Bauji said, "Are you missing Devi?" I replied, "Not till you came." With no Devi, Chaeji assumed kitchen responsibilities, so, unlike her last visit, she did have to open the refrigerator. I wished I could've made their stay more comfortable. Connie, though, was a big help and drove them to their shopping spots, including the usual pilgrimage to Filene's Basement as well as other department stores.

In September 1986, Mohit started school at BBN. The plan was that Raj would drive Mohit to BBN in the mornings, and Connie would bring him home in the evenings, driving along Route 2 and 128 South for about fifteen miles. Connie had just bought a new Toyota and was still getting familiar with the controls; Mohit was her tutor. One day, while on Route 128, other drivers were honking at her. Connie asked Mohit why, and he replied, "Because you are driving below the minimum speed limit." Every so often Connie and Mohit would have their interesting exchanges that would make us chuckle.

We were all apprehensive about how Mohit would fare at BBN, but to our pleasant surprise, within three days, he had acclimated to his new campus and had already made three new friends, who were also new students, and Mohit is still in touch with them years later. In fact, Mohit became so comfortable at this new school that he even was elected to his class student council.

Next on the list was to put our Newton house up for sale. It was a bittersweet moment; we had spent eleven memorable, happy years in that house. We were hoping to move into our new house in November, as most of the construction would be complete by then, and the rest could be finished up while we were living in it.

For the remainder of September and October, we were busy running to and from Weston. Before Bauji and Chaeji returned to India, we invited friends and family over for a small *puja* (prayer service) in our semi-completed house. We also introduced ourselves to our new neighbors. We were pleasantly surprised to found out that our neighbor's neighbor was Dr. Bill, an old colleague of mine from Brigham and Women's Hospital.

Our Newton house sold in October, which was lucky because the real estate market was not hot at the time. We had to be moved out by November, coinciding perfectly with our original plan.

Our big move happened one week before Thanksgiving, so we were able to celebrate our favorite holiday in our dream home. The first morning we woke up in this new house, surrounded by woods, it felt like we had landed in the middle of a resort: it had snowed the previous week, and the trees were covered in their first layer of sparkling white.

Our new neighbors had arranged for their yard-maintenance guy to take care of our snow removal as well; he was a nice Italian man but very territorial—no other competitor was allowed to stomp on his work domain.

We were so lucky to be surrounded by wonderful new neighbors. Mohit's earlier complaints about moving vanished into thin air when he met all the new kids in the neighborhood. Mohit was the youngest of the lot, and he got spoiled. So, Mohit was happy at his new home and happy at his new school. A big sigh of relief.

January 1987 was filled with birthday plans for Mohit. He had mentioned once that it'd be fun to have a surprise birthday party, so Raj and I thought this year would be perfect. On January 11, we surprised him by inviting over all his new friends from BBN and all his old friends from Park School. It worked out great, and everyone had a wonderful time.

Raj and I got a surprise of our own around this time. We received news from Delhi that Munni and RG's son, Anil, was getting married on January 19! It was the first wedding of the next generation, and we absolutely had to go. Pitaji especially was excited about it.

First, we had to coordinate Mohit's absence with his teacher. She gave Mohit his homework for the week and asked him to keep a journal so he could share his trip with the rest of the class. I also mentioned the trip to Dr. Shepard's wife, Grace, and invited her to come along; she excitedly accepted.

We bought our plane tickets for January 15, four days after Mohit's twelfth birthday. If we had left before January 11, we could have paid half price for Mohit's ticket, a savings of eight hundred dollars. It was a big temptation, but we didn't want Mohit to miss too much school.

Munni greeted us when we arrived. She was doing wonderfully; business was booming for RG and Anil, and they now lived in a modern, nine-bedroom home.

The weather was perfect for the wedding, and the atmosphere was one of jubilant celebration. Mohit was pampered the entire visit and treated with special attention by all his relatives. He was honored to sit in front of Anil on a majestic white mare for the wedding procession, accompanied by a live band. Mohit was thrilled by all of it, his excitement endless.

The wedding was the perfect opportunity to reunite with family members whom we hadn't seen in years—uncles, aunts, nieces, nephews, cousins. Raj had a wonderful time reliving old memories with them.

During the wedding reception, Mohit was on a mission to meet as many of his cousins as possible; every few minutes, he would run back to give me an update on his numbers. He was so proud of his big family. His final count was thirty-five cousins. Besides family, Mohit also loved meeting Munni and RG's little dog and Pitaji's handsome Pomeranian.

Our guest, Grace, was also having a wonderful trip, warmly welcomed by everyone and soaking in the splendors of the Orient. Before leaving, I had prepared her for some possible rough times, and she replied that she was an adventurer and a good camper. When we returned to the States and Grace's husband, Dr. Shepard, asked her to rate her trip on a scale of one to ten, she gave it a ten.

After the three-day wedding gala, we stayed at Pitaji's place for two days. Despite being in the presence of monsters, Pitaji did his best to give us small indulgences and palliative care. We then divided into two cars and drove to the pink city of Jaipur, six hours away, for a short day trip. Raj drove one of the cars, and Grace got a taste of his safe but aggressive driving.

In Raj's defense, he had to be an aggressive driver to be safe. The highway was crowded with motorcycles, bicycles, cows, water buffaloes, camels, donkeys, stray dogs, pedestrians with large loads on their backs and heads, even elephants. There were no such things as divided highways or traffic lights. Drivers abided by their own rules, and everybody had the right of way, everyone had to be strong of heart, with their car horn like an additional appendage, constantly beeping, making themselves heard above the racket. This was an ordinary day in Indian traffic, and we made it to Jaipur without event. In fact, this was Raj's last time driving in India. He retired with an A+ rating from Grace.

We visited Jaipur's city palace in the old part of the city. It had beautiful gardens and courtyards and was full of tourists. Next we stopped by the Hawa Mahal, or "Palace of Winds." Constructed with red and pink sandstone, Hawa Mahal has nine hundred fifty-three small windows and looks like the honeycomb of a beehive. This screen-like structure was built so that the women of the royal household could watch street festivals without being seen by the public, since they had to observe strict seclusion of women from public observation.

After Jaipur, Grace and I went to Ahmedabad for two days to see my family, while Raj, Mohit, and the rest of his family went back to Delhi. While in Ahmedabad, Grace got to see more sights, including the Gandhi Ashram, with Bauji as her tour guide.

Then it was time to head back to Boston. Grace had had a wonderful time, and she was looking forward to returning again when she and Dr. Shepard went on a guided trip the following year, put on by Boston's Museum of Fine Arts.

Raj and I got back into the swing of everyday life back in Boston, but Mohit was having a harder time of it. He was lonely and missed all the great company and adventures he'd had in India. All of a sudden, he announced he wanted to move to India. He was ready to give everything up in Boston to be with his family over there.

Every day Mohit was fine-tuning his moving plans, but Raj and I knew it was absolutely not possible. Just thinking about living with Darshan and Alka made our blood curdle. Mohit, however, was completely unaware of the very real animosity and danger involved; he was young, and Raj and I did not want to share such an ugly reality with him, so we simply crossed our fingers and hoped the desire would pass.

Spring came around. The crocuses and forsythia were beautiful and blooming, but Mohit was still out of sorts. Then Raj and I got an idea. We had been batting around the thought of getting a puppy for some time; Raj had always been a dog-lover, and with Mohit so lonely, now seemed like the perfect time. We visited some breeders, kennels, and pet shops, and we unanimously agreed that we wanted a small dog. We fell in love with the breed the Shetland sheepdog, or Sheltie.

On March 30, I mentioned to my mentor, Dr. Capobianco, that we wanted a Sheltie, and he said to leave the rest up to him. Only a few days later, on April 2, Dr. Capobianco and I were working together in the OR when he received a call from a friend of his, Dr. Zullo. Dr. Zullo was a well-known vet in Natick, and he had some Sheltie puppies ready to find homes. I was pleasantly surprised but completely unprepared both physically and mentally to take a puppy home after work!

I had actually already met Dr. Zullo, because he had been my patient a few times when he needed surgery. His animal clinic was only two miles from LMH, so I drove straight there after work. When I arrived, I was thrilled to see an adorable five-pound Sheltie puppy running around. I instantly knew that Mohit would love to be his owner. Dr. Zullo gave me a crash course in puppy care and a basic list of necessary items to pick up from a pet store. He didn't want to wait any longer to hand off the puppy, because he was concerned about it catching an infection, so I rushed to the pet store, picked up the basics, and then returned to the clinic.

I had, of course, also called Raj to tell him the good news, and he kept the secret from Mohit as a surprise.

When Mohit walked in, he heard some soft barks from the puppy, and a look of complete joy spread across his face. He could not believe the puppy was his. I'll never forget how his eyes glittered.

Dr. Zullo mentioned that the puppy had a brother who was more subdued, calmer, but, knowing we had a twelve-year-old boy, Dr. Zullo had chosen the more energetic one. Mohit was already in love with this puppy, it was already his prized possession, but he was still curious to meet the brother.

Between the two puppies, there was no comparison. Ours was slightly smaller but more active and handsome. Raj, Mohit, and I returned home completely satisfied with the newest addition to our family.

After some thought, Mohit named the puppy Shayru, or "baby tiger." Shayru quickly became the pride, joy, and entertainment of our entire family; Shayru had this magnetic force to draw attention and bring out love. I'm sure even Bapaji, who had not liked dogs, would had have been converted by Shayru.

And just like that, Mohit's plans to return to India vanished into thin air. Shayru was his cure.

We gave Shayru his own private room in the downstairs bathroom, complete with a bed and toys. He also had a second bed in the kitchen for napping and spending time with us, and he had full access to the rest of the house, except for the bedrooms upstairs and the living room. He had his own favorite nooks around the house from which he could watch the people on the street and the wildlife in the yard.

Shayru was a smart pup and followed the rules, most of the time. Sometimes his curiosity got the better of him. We tried to keep the house Shayru-proof: no temptations of food left on the counter or open trash cans.

Our schedules and priorities changed as well with Shayru's arrival. Raj was in charge of Shayru's breakfast and morning walk; Connie would watch him as needed. Even though Connie had dogs of her own and was comfortable handling Shayru, Mohit had strict instructions for her on the do's and do not's of Shayru's care. In the afternoons, I tried to return home right after work to let Shayru out and give him his dinner. All errands were put on the back burner until Shayru was taken care of. The evening walks were shared by Mohit and Raj. Shayru was so handsome that people on the street would call him a "her."

Time passed quickly, and Shayru grew from a five-pound puppy to a twenty-pound adult. He was handsome, intelligent, and temperamental. He was also not shy and would confidently bark his likes and dislikes. He had a particularly strong opinion of our coffee percolator. No matter where Shayru was in the house, Raj could not get that percolator going without Shayru charging in at full bark. This behavior was a no-no, so Raj would let Shayru outside (although Shayru could do no wrong in Mohit's eyes), but even then, if Raj dared turn the percolator back on, Shayru would run back to the house, fast as a bullet, reprimanding Raj with more barking, as if to say, "I told you not to do it!"

The only times Shayru was submissive and obedient was during his checkups with Dr. Zullo. Then he transformed into a little angel. Dr. Zullo passed away in September 2016, at the age of ninety-four. His obituary was touching and reflected his lifetime of accomplishments; to us, though, he was simply Shayru's vet and my patient.

Shayru's strong opinions were amusing to us; we gradually adapted to him, and him to us. Mohit researched Shayru's ancestry and discovered that he had been born on February 2 and was a pedigreed dog from Montana. His father was Tiny Tim and his mother Magic Mindy. Every year, we celebrated Shayru's birthday on February 2 as well as his homecoming on April 2. We had twelve joyous, memory-filled years together—many celebrations of Thanksgiving, Diwali, and Christmas. Then on November 28, 1999, tragedy struck when Shayru suddenly and unexpectedly passed away.

After Shayru's passing, Mohit, then twenty-four years old, said that although he'd been in love with Shayru the instant they'd met, he'd had mixed feelings about bringing the puppy home. Mohit had known even then that a dog's life was typically ten to fifteen years and that, someday, he'd have to face the pain of Shayru's death. Mohit had never expressed this submerged feeling before, and I was amazed to hear of a twelve-year-old thinking about and fearing death for his loved ones in the future.

Back to the summer of 1987. We were busy furnishing the new house as well as managing challenges at work and enjoying our social lives. Life was well balanced. Connie was still driving Mohit to tennis camp and his other activities, and she also stayed at the house when Raj and I went out in the evenings. One day Mohit said he could now stay home alone, as he had Shayru for company. Raj and I didn't agree. We asked Mohit what would happen if he got hurt and had to go to the hospital; who would drive him? Mohit replied without hesitation, "I could even tell Shayru where to go and he'd do a good job, driving carefully below the speed limit." Well, we declined his creative suggestion. Besides, Connie loved her job with us, and we loved having her around.

Around this time, a Hindu temple opened in Ashland. There were many Hindu temples already in New York and Texas, but this was the first large Hindu temple in Massachusetts. The plans for the temple began back in 1978, and it took twelve years and the dedication of many people for it to finally be completed. The building itself was impressive with its carvings and many statues of gods. Since then, we've visited the temple two to three times every year.

In January 1988, Mohit celebrated his thirteenth birthday. Then, during winter break, Connie called to say she would not be able to drive Mohit once school started up again. She needed surgery, and one of her daughters would be coming up from Texas to help her. Raj had to move around his schedule a bit in order to pick up Mohit.

We stayed in touch with Connie throughout her absence. She had a lot of desire and determination to continue living independently, and her health was always a concern in the back of our minds—she had become a staple in the family.

In February I got a call from Connie's daughter. She said Connie would be undergoing major surgery the next day. Then, at ten the following morning, her daughter called us again: Connie had passed away in her bed, only an hour before she was to leave for the hospital.

Raj and I were incredibly sad to hear this news. We had become close to Connie over the years; we had respected her, admired her, and treated her as if she were family. She had been a pillar of strength.

Mohit had a big school exam coming up, so we decided to withhold the news for a few days. Raj and I went to Connie's wake and spoke with her two daughters, both of whom were kind, good people. They enjoyed telling us how Connie tried to get them to date Jack Lemmon's son, and Connie had once dated Jack Lemmon himself. Raj and I were also surprised to hear

Connie's age, which she hadn't shared with anyone. There had even been an error in her obituary in the *Boston Globe* saying she was seventy-eight, when actually she was eighty-seven. Her two daughters said, "Mother must be happy in heaven being seventy-eight instead of eighty-seven."

When the weekend came and Mohit had completed his test, we told him the sad news. This was his first time losing anyone close to him, and he was full of questions. Some of them we could answer logically, while others we simply had to admit we did not know for sure. Mohit grieved Connie's death, but with time and the comfort of Shayru, he found healing. We will always remember Connie; she was truly a remarkable lady.

The next month, March 1988, Mohit had spring break, so we took a short trip to Delhi and Ahmedabad. Pitaji was now eighty years old, but he was still active and healthy, keeping up with his tennis pals and driving himself everywhere. Raj inherited his father's driving skills—seasoned and defensive and sometimes very scary! Both of them knew how I felt, and one day Pitaji commented while driving, "I am going slow to keep Sadhna calm and happy."

Pitaji was still working full-time, feeding the vultures, and he was still maintaining silence on his prison-like sentence; we didn't know if he was being threatened or what, but we knew something was going on underneath the calm façade. From Munni's reports, Darshan and Alka's deceptive ways were only getting worse, and the tension during our visit was evident. Still, though, it was nice to see Munni, and Mohit enjoyed playing with his cousins. Then we left for Ahmedabad, where the atmosphere was, thankfully, much lighter.

Bauji, Chaeji, Chachaji, and Auntyji lived together harmoniously. Chaeji and Auntyji had their occasional disagreements, but they all cared for and trusted one other. No malice, no deception. They all enjoyed each other's company, they shared in one another's joys and sorrows, and they supported each other through the good times and the bad. The disparity between this house and the one in Delhi was striking and painful.

We returned to Boston with spring in full color. The trees were showing off their bright green new leaves, and the flowers in Boston Common were glorious. In our own wooded yard, the air was fresh and invigorating, infused with the aromas of maple, oak, and pine. This was in sharp contrast to the suffocating crowds in Delhi and its smell of smog and pollution.

Down the street from our house was eighty acres of conservation land. It had many trails, a reservoir, and even a waterfall. Walking through it, the scenery was so captivating I felt like I was at a beautiful resort.

These woods were also a dog lover's paradise, but we never brought Shayru on walks here to explore the different trails; Mohit was overprotective about ticks and his getting hurt, so we never exposed him to the trails. On any given day, we'd see upwards of fifty mostly well-behaved dogs running around and playing fetch with their owners.

We also had frequent animal visitors in our backyard: deer, turkey, the occasional fox or coyote, and the usual gang of rabbits and squirrels trying to steal from Raj's carefully installed birdfeeder. Raj tried many different tricks to keep them away, but they always outwitted him.

That summer an international anesthesiology meeting was being hosted in Nice, France, so Raj, Mohit, and I decided to combine it with a European vacation. Along with southern France, we visited Monaco, Monte Carlo, and the Alps in Switzerland. We took a cable car to the top of Mont Blanc; it was a sight to behold on such a beautiful sunny day. We enjoyed watching the skiers as well as the paragliding daredevils.

We returned to Boston and dove back into our usual routines. Friends from all over the world visited us, many of whom had children who were graduating from colleges in the surrounding Boston area, and we all had fun dusting off our old memories and catching up on everything new. Then we unexpectedly hosted Bauji and Chaeji.

# Chapter Nineteen

*B* *ack in '83,* Bauji had had eye surgery due to cataracts, and he needed another surgery on his other eye. He decided to have the surgery done in Ahmedabad, as medical care had improved since his first surgery. Unfortunately, the surgery turned into a nightmare. During his recovery, Bauji had severe pain and was completely blind in that eye. It was definitely a case of malpractice by the surgeon, but the doctor was still trying to convince Bauji that he would fully recover. When it was clear he wouldn't, the surgeon then extracted himself from the situation. No accountability.

So, Bauji came to Boston for a cornea transplant. We made an appointment for him once again at the Massachusetts Eye and Ear Infirmary with a specialist in the field, Dr. S. Boruchoff. Sadly, Dr. Boruchoff could not reverse Bauji's blindess—it was permanent—but he was able to minimize the pain. I felt helpless for Bauji; there was nothing more we could do.

During our appointments with Dr. Boruchoff, he surprisingly educated us on a branch of Hinduism I had never heard of:

Swaminarayan. Dr. Boruchoff had had a surgery patient from India who was a priest of the high order of Swaminarayan. The priest had had appointments with Dr. Boruchoff, during which he was hospitalized for a month, and during that time, he requested a special compliance clause that did not allow any woman to be in front of him. All the doctors, nurses, residents, even the housekeepers, had to be male. Well, money has power, and the hospital complied.

The Hindu religion is very diverse; some people claim Hinduism is a way of living life rather than simply a religion. I am not an expert on the subject, though. I am Hindu because I was born to Hindu parents.

While Bauji and Chaeji were staying with us, they met Shayru. Chaeji adored him, but Bauji had never been keen on dogs, and he had high standards for clean hands. He did tolerate Shayru being around, but he would not pet him. Shayru, being the intelligent dog he was, immediately picked up on the situation. He would ignore Bauji, walking right by him, and go to Chaeji for a pat. Because Shayru was so disciplined, Bauji had no complaints; there was total harmony in the house.

Meanwhile, work at the hospital was still clipping along. We were constantly adapting to new state-of-the-art technology and less-invasive surgical procedures. The other surgeons were completely comfortable around me and did not hesitate to use four-letter words in my presence during stressful situations. I had been accepted into their inner male circle (although there was still no female surgeon).

All of my colleagues had strong work ethics, and our department received high marks for satisfaction from patients, administrators, and surgeons. Quite a few of the surgeons were Vietnam War vets, with interesting and intense experiences. One of them stood out in particular: Dr. H.

To anyone who first met him, he came across as lighthearted and full of laughter, but he had jumped out of airplanes in Vietnam and was an intense daredevil. He lived in his own permanent combat zone, always on high alert, unconditionally helping anyone in need. Wherever he was—at a football game or driving along the highway—he would find someone to take care of. Once he was late to work because he had stopped to help a motorcyclist who had been in an accident. In fact, motorcycle gangs frequently came to the hospital for his help, and he gave them free surgical care.

Dr. H was an excellent surgeon, but he had no sense or value of time. He ran on his own clock. It wasn't unusual for him to make rounds on his patients at midnight.

Because Dr. H was always offering help, he had connections everywhere. He could get his hands on things most people had to wait for. Somehow he got an early copy from Hong Kong of the new hugely awaited Star Wars movie *The Empire Strikes Back*, and he gave it to me for Mohit. This made Dr. H Mohit's hero.

The OR staff at LMH was like family, and Dr. H was the naughty kid. His vocabulary subsisted on four-letter words, and he often broke the rules, smoking in the doctors' OR lounge. But being family, he was excused most of the time; we knew he had a good heart and meant the best.

Dr. H had the heart of a race-car driver. He owned a BMW sports car and was intent on using it to its full capacity. One day he offered a joyride to one of our colleagues who was known for being a slow, careful driver. Our co-worker returned to the hospital, sweating and thanking God that they hadn't been in an accident.

Dr. H had two children, a son Mohit's age and a daughter one year younger. Dr. H was a very loving, albeit strange, father.

We'd see his kids accompanying him on his midnight rounds to patients' rooms. He'd dry their wet socks in the oven at home, and he'd spoil them silly with pizza for breakfast, lunch, and dinner. When their mother would come to pick up the kids, they'd hide in a closet or under a bed; they didn't want to leave their carefree hospital life where there were no rules and no discipline.

When Dr. H would take his kids on vacation, instead of trying to find someplace new every time, he'd simply take them to the same hotel but drive a different route so they'd *think* they had gone somewhere new.

Even though Dr. H was a dad, he was still Dr. H. He once told me that he and his wife had taken their kids to a fancy restaurant for Thanksgiving dinner, and his wife had dressed up their four-year-old daughter in a beautiful outfit, complete with a bow, a purse, and matching jewelry and shoes. She looked like a perfect doll, and the couple at the table next to them were admiring her. Suddenly, the girl noticed them staring and said loudly to the gentleman, "You asshole, why are you staring at me?" Dr. H was so embarrassed. I said to him, "Well, who do you think she learned that from?"

Patients tend to see doctors from a clinical perspective—they exist only in the hospital setting in their minds—but doctors are human beings, too, with their own lives, unique personalities, likes and dislikes, and strengths and weaknesses.

Sadly, Dr. H died young in an accident; he was only in his forties. The hospital lost an excellent surgeon, but more importantly, two little children lost a wonderful father. I still feel the family's grief today and hope they've found peace.

After the shock of losing a friend and colleague, I often thought of Dr. H, especially when I was working in his old OR.

I wonder if he could have changed and become more disciplined if he'd been given the time.

In the summer of 1990, Bauji had been suffering from chest pains in India. Because of the eye surgery catastrophe, he did not want to take any more risks, so he and Chaeji flew to Boston for his coronary angiography.

With their arrival, my days became even busier. After working at the hospital, I'd come home, rest for an hour, and then start my second shift in the kitchen, preparing dinner and cleaning up. Raj was no help with the dishes, as Indian custom set the son-in-law on a pedestal. But at least I had Mohit. Mohit said to Bauji and Chaeji that he was replacing their boy servants in Ahmedabad: "I am the Rama, and I am the Bheema." (Common names of servants in those days.) That was good for a laugh.

During their stay, Bauji and Chaeji went for short walks around the neighborhood, enjoying the greenery. Bauji was still busy, though, corresponding with Chachaji back in India on business issues. Meanwhile, Chaeji was getting very attached to Shayru, and Shayru reciprocated her affection.

Finally, the angiography results came back: he did not need heart surgery, only meds. We were all relieved. To celebrate, we persuaded Bauji to sip some champagne. He had never had alcohol before in his life, and it helped him relax a little. Then we said our goodbyes, and Bauji and Chaeji flew back to India.

In September, school started again for Mohit. He was doing well and had many extracurricular activities: crew, tennis, and—reluctantly—the violin. He was in the school orchestra, but with as minimal input as possible. What he was most excited about that year was getting his driver's permit on his birthday, January 11, 1991. We had purchased a Jeep Cherokee for him to drive around.

On the evening of Mohit's birthday, I decided to take Shayru out on a walk before it got dark, as Raj and Mohit were delayed getting Mohit's driver's permit and signing him up for Driver's Ed.

As Shayru and I walked down a neighborhood sidewalk, a car stopped behind us, and then, suddenly, an eighty-pound dog attacked Shayru from the back. I tried to separate Shayru by pulling on his leash, but it didn't work. Shayru, smart as ever, managed to wriggle out of his collar and he ran back to the house, waiting for me in front of the garage.

He had multiple wounds from the attack, and I had abrasions on the fingers of my right hand. My helpful intentions to get Shayru outside before Mohit's birthday celebrations had backfired. Mohit was upset and concerned about Shayru's suffering. My injuries were of secondary importance. The next day, we brought Shayru to Dr. Zullo. Luckily, Shayru recovered uneventfully. My scars were visible for many years, but I saw them as Shayru's gift to remember him by.

In July 1991, Mohit passed his driver's test and got his license. He was on top of the world, lapping up his new independence. Raj could now retire as chauffeur.

Raj and I were both happy but anxious for Mohit, especially when he came home late at night. We knew, though, that he was a safe driver.

Two months later, in August 1991, we planned a last-minute trip to Australia via Hawaii. We decided to skip New Zealand because Mohit was keen on attending the wedding of our wonderful neighbor John.

The trip was great, and we were in awe of the Great Barrier Reef. While we were in Sydney, we heard the news that Hurricane Bob had swept through the northeastern States. We were worried about how well our house had held up and tried to call our neighbors (it wasn't as easy back then as it is with cell phones today). Finally, we got in touch with our friend and neighbor Carmen, who had kindly already checked on our house, and all was well. What a relief! Carmen said that her family's summer home in Falmouth had made national television. The hurricane winds had flipped over their twenty-six-foot powerboat and landed it in their pool. Mother Nature is not someone you want to mess with.

We arrived back in Boston safely, attended John's wedding, and we were just getting settled when we got a call from Bauji. He'd had more chest pains and had gotten another angiography in Bombay. The results were that he needed open-heart surgery.

After much discussion and soul-searching, we jointly agreed that Bauji needed to come to Boston, the mecca of medicine. My sister Varsha, who lived in New York, went to Ahemdabad and brought them as their escort, accompanying Bauji and Chaeji to Boston.

I had been through many stressful medical situations with Bauji in the past, but this was by far the most serious and riskiest. His left main coronary artery was completely blocked. Surgery was his only option, and it was imperative he get it done as soon as possible.

I revved into high gear, contacting doctors and making appointments. Bauji was set on seeing Dr. Buckley at Massachusetts General Hospital, as Dr. Buckley had operated before on my brother-in-law and was an excellent surgeon, but he was not available. We were lucky, though, to be surrounded by many incredible doctors and medical facilities.

Thankfully, good friends of mine came to the rescue. We were able to schedule the bypass for November 1 with Dr. Akins, a man of few words but outstanding surgical skills, and Bauji got his preliminary workup without delay. But not too long after, Bauji announced he would not have surgery on November 1, as it was Diwali. I knew how lucky we were to have his surgery scheduled so soon, and to change it would not be easy. Fortunately, we were able to convince Bauji of this, and he reluctantly agreed to keep the date.

Emotions were running high for all of us, even me. On the surface I was calm and composed, but underneath, I was running out of steam, worrying about the future and all its unknowns. After thirty years of caring for patients, some of whom were very sick, I was now applying my medical knowledge with the mindset of a daughter who loved her father very much. Still, though, I forced myself to remain positive. Everyone in the family was frightened, and they needed me to be their leader. We faced every day hand-in-hand, a united front, with hope strong in our hearts.

As the day of Bauji's surgery approached, all his children who lived in the U.S., from as far and wide as New York, New Jersey, Connecticut, Indiana, and New Hampshire, gathered in Boston. On Thursday, October 31, Bauji was admitted to the hospital, with his surgery scheduled for noon the next day.

The next morning, we surrounded Bauji in his private room; the atmosphere was tense, as each of us were stranded on our own inner island of apprehension. The rest of Bauji's hospital floor was occupied by the Saudi royal family and their guards. We thought we were a crowd with ten of us, but they were practically an army, and it was clear what they were able to buy with their bottomless wealth. I was lucky not to have to cross an ocean to access the best medical care in the world.

At eleven in the morning, only an hour before Bauji's scheduled surgery, we received a surprise visit from his surgeon, Dr. Akins. Dr. Akins apologized and said the surgery would have to be postponed until Monday; the ICU was full because a helicopter had arrived with several critical patients.

No one had expected this, and now our long wait had become even longer. But there was one silver lining to this situation: we all got to spend Diwali together in our home, just as Bauji had wished. He often reminded me of this afterward, saying it was destiny and good fortune.

On Sunday we returned to the hospital, and Bauji underwent open-heart surgery on Monday. The operation was uneventful (the best news in medicine), and we all heaved a great sigh of relief. I especially felt a weight lift off my shoulders. If there had been any complications, I would have felt responsible. But everything had gone well, and my agony had turned into ecstasy.

To see Bauji awake and healthy was indescribably wonderful; it felt like we were stepping into a new dawn, victorious. All my frantic efforts had been rewarded tenfold.

After five days at Massachusetts General Hospital, Bauji returned to our house to recuperate (with me recovering mentally as well). We were all in high spirits.

On November 15, we got a call from Munni, Raj's sistser. Her younger daughter, Sonia (whom I had delivered), was getting married. I convinced Raj to go on ahead while I figured out what to do with Mohit and myself. I was torn because my parents were still at our house, but since Bauji was doing fine and the wedding was during Thanksgiving break, Mohit and I decided to fly to India as well for an ultra-short trip of five days.

Bauji and Chaeji went up to Varsha's place in New York, and Mohit and I enjoyed four days in India, celebrating and indulging.

The last two days of our visit were spent in Delhi at Pitaji's. It was both pathetic and pitiful to see how Darshan and Alka treated Pitaji. They were constantly lying to him, especially in regards to Raj and me, and it seemed Pitaji could no longer delineate between fact and fiction; he was imprisoned mentally by their ugly wall of deceit. Raj and I, however, were not interested in playing Darshan and Alka's manipulative games, and we chose not to defend ourselves. After twenty-seven years of trying to unite the family, we had accepted that we would never be able to realize our dream. Instead, we focused our efforts on remaining positive and maintaining whatever harmony we could.

This particular visit with Pitaji was one to remember. One evening we said, "Let's take a look at family pictures together." He was so excited that we were interested in his past. He pulled out his photo album, which he loved dearly but was now in tatters due to neglect, and he glowed as he shared all his happy memories with us. Some of the pictures made us smile, like Mataji in the prime of her youth, wearing a saree, jewelry, dress shoes, and holding a tennis racket while posing in front of their old convertible Packard that had an outside horn. Many of the photos also had interesting backstories attached to them, and they all had a lot of family history. It was an evening to cherish.

Raj and I offered to bring the album back with us to the States and have the pictures put into a new album, and we'd return it to him on our next visit. Pitaji loved the idea and gladly gave us the album. Sadly, none of us knew at the time that this would be our last visit together and that this album would become Pitaji's parting gift to us.

We returned to Boston after our short trip, and in January 1992, Bauji and Chaeji also came back to stay with us after visiting Varsha in New York. Bauji was excited to experience his first Boston winter, but even though it was already January, we still had no snow. It reminded me of Raj's and my honeymoon, when we went to the Himalayas to see snow fall but had no luck (although the honeymoon was still wonderful). Raj and I had now lived for so long in Boston that we had forgotten what it was like not to have four beautiful seasons. Our solution was to take Bauji up to the ski slopes on Wachusett Mountain, and, there, he was able to take in the wonder of mounds and mounds of snow.

That January was also Bauji's seventy-fifth birthday, and we pulled off a great surprise party at our place with friends and family. It was a wonderful celebration after the stress of open-heart surgery (even the weather cooperated). There was food, champagne, singing, and we roasted Bauji a little, too. Our friends here in Boston had become family to us, and over the years, Bauji and Chaeji had looked forward to spending time with them. We have many sweet memories from that evening together, and then it was time for Bauji and Chaeji to return to Ahmedabad.

In March 1992, we started getting surprise calls from Pitaji while he was at his office in Delhi; it was the middle of the day for him but one in the morning for us. He'd simply say that he felt like chatting, and we were happy to hear from him. In the past, we were almost always the ones to contact him, as he was mentally imprisoned by Darshan and Alka. Since Darshan refused to help Pitaji at work, it was the only place Pitaji had privacy to talk without fear or restraint.

During these late-night chats, Pitaji was urging us to visit him. It seemed he was suffering from debilitating stress and repeatedly telling us it was time for us to come home. Raj and I surmised that his conscience had finally reached a breaking point and had pressured him into finally opening up and reaching out.

Munni also saw the changes in Pitaji. He was calling her during his workday as well, telling her his feelings on the family situation, which he had been jarringly silent about before.

If Raj and I had known what the future held, we would have dropped everything to hop on a plane and visit Pitaji. As it was, though, we had only just recently visited him, and with life and work going at full speed, it wasn't practical to go again so soon. Still, we kept in close touch with Pitaji over the phone, and he opened up to us as he never had before. Perhaps he knew the end was near, and he felt liberated by it.

On the morning of April 15, 1992, we received a call from Darshan. Pitaji had passed away in the midst of a family wedding. He'd had a heart attack while enjoying a wonderful evening, surrounded by family and friends. When the ambulance was being called, everybody at the party watched Alka empty out Pitaji's pockets. There was no attempt at CPR, and Pitaji was pronounced dead at the hospital.

Raj and I immediately booked the next flight to Delhi. We couldn't make it in time for the funeral, but we could at least be there for *chautha*, the very important fourth day of mourning in Hinduism.

Mohit said he could manage by himself for a few days with Shayru. His only potential problem was that he had inherited my sleeping genes—he liked to sleep in late, and he was a hard sleeper; alarm clocks stood no chance against him. It was embarrassing for him to ask the neighbors to wake him up, so Aunty Varsha came to the rescue. Every morning at six sharp, she called Mohit from New York; then she placed a follow-up call fifteen minutes later to make sure he had actually gotten up, as he needed to take care of Shayru before going to school. Everything went according to plan, and I had further peace of mind knowing that our neighbors were more than willing to help if any problems were to crop up.

When Raj and I landed in Delhi, no one was at the airport to get us. This was the beginning of a long, sad, and frustrating trip. Finally, at three in the morning, my cousin's husband came to get us, and we went back to their house for a few hours before taking a cab to our co-owned house with Darshan and Alka.

When we walked into the house, the reception was far from warm; in fact, they were all quite unhappy that we had come. Darshan and Alka's two obese children looked at us indifferently; there was no sadness on their faces. It was as if they had been waiting a long time for their grandfather to die.

The *chautha* ceremony was in the evening on the beautiful front lawn. Sometimes tragedy brings a family together, helping them let go of the past and move forward with unity, but in our family, it was the opposite.

I had said to Raj earlier, "Pitaji is gone. Out of respect for him and Mataji, let's keep harmony and fairness among the family." Darshan and Alka, however, had very different intentions. They had no respect for Pitaji or for his wishes. As soon as he was gone, they destroyed his will and immediately implemented their own selfish scheme to take everything for themselves by whatever means necessary. They did not even try to hide their deviousness, and they felt no guilt about stealing, cheating, and lying. The atmosphere turned from terrible to terrifying. We had become used to their behavior in the past, but now their animosity and contentiousness had reached a dangerous level. They did a masterful job of cannibalizing all of the family's assets; they left no stone unturned, no egregious act undone.

Unfortunately, I had to leave Raj in this situation and get back to work at the hospital. He was very disheartened. My parting words to him were, "Let it go, and make whatever concessions you need to for peace of mind and family values."

Raj returned to Boston a few days after me with paperwork to sort through. He was in very low spirits. Giving away one's belongings brings feelings of happiness and satisfaction, but to have those same things taken from you through deception and robbery brings nothing but distress. We would have gladly gifted our share of ownership to Darshan and Alka if they had been handicapped, deprived, poor, or otherwise compromised. Instead, their only goal was to work less and play more, basking in the luxury of things that did not belong to them. Our entire world in India, all our dreams, had been shattered and soiled by their insatiable greed.

This was the end of the beginning for Raj and me in permanently blocking Darshan and Alka from our lives. Sometimes it is difficult to break off a relationship, but that was not the case here. Although I'd had a change of heart after getting to know Pitaji, Mataji, and Munni, my relationship with Darshan and Alka could not be saved. If it had been only a matter of their lying and stealing, I could have forgiven them, but our physical safety was at risk, and Raj and I were prepared to enforce whatever boundaries were necessary.

Raj and I never once regretted our decision; it was a relief to escape Darshan and Alka's abuse. We had kept the relationship going in the first place only for the sake of Pitaji. When he was alive, our determination to continue visiting did not waver, even while being lambasted by cruel words and deceitful actions. We tried to maintain harmony and never struck back, verbally or otherwise. It was a difficult, dangerous situation, but we tolerated it because Pitaji needed us.

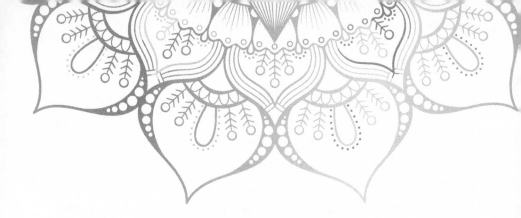

# Chapter Twenty

*Giving up on our dream* to move back to India had been a long, sad road, starting back in 1984, but we were glad to be done with it. Now we wanted nothing more than to move on, focus on new opportunities, and leave behind the pain and heartache. It would do us no good to wallow in what we had lost—to poke, prod, and dissect the spewed insults and illicit deeds. We were emotionally hurt, and we'd always have the scars to show for it, but we could at least prevent the wounds from festering.

It took some time, though, for the waters to calm. For one, Raj had to follow up with some legal formalities and paperwork, enduring one last horrible trip in June, but thereafter, we were officially done visiting that family and that house forever.

Occasionally the ugliness of the past would resurface in our minds, but Raj and I were able to help each other find humor in it and move on. We had the satisfaction of knowing we were finally safe and out of their reach. Life was peaceful, and our future was promising.

I was staying busy at the hospital. I enjoyed facing new challenges, both clinical and administrative, as well as meeting new people every day; the work kept me focused and content.

Mohit was having a wonderful summer, too, staying busy driving himself to his various social activities. Summers always go by so quickly, and before we knew it, he was starting his senior year of high school. We started visiting colleges with him. Mohit was goal-oriented and had very high academic standards for himself. At the advice of his school counselor (who was an absolute God-given gift), Mohit applied to multiple colleges. In those days, college applications were all hard copies sent via FedEx or U.S. mail, so Raj was running around, overloaded with Mohit's last-minute applications that needed to be stamped on a certain day, but, of course, Raj was the most faithful father and never complained.

In 1993 Mohit was only a few months away from graduation, and he was looking forward to the future. After visiting many campuses, including Harvard and Dartmouth, his first choice was Brown. Now it was the waiting game, checking the mail constantly for admission letters. By April, Mohit's apprehension was palpable; in fact, the entire family felt the stress of his unknown future. Then the good news started rolling in day after day: Mohit was accepted to every school he had applied to; the choice was his.

He was torn between Dartmouth and Brown—two very different colleges. We thought he'd be more suited to Dartmouth, but we did not pressure him, and in the end, he chose Brown. We all celebrated his decision; we were especially glad that he'd be within close driving distance.

On May 3, Mohit graduated from high school cum laude, and, in June, we threw a great graduation party in our backyard with friends and family. Raj and I were so happy for Mohit and counted our blessings as parents.

The summer before Mohit left for college, we went on a family trip to Europe. Whenever we left home, we usually dropped off Shayru at a kennel. Shayru hated it. When he saw us packing the doggy bag, his internal alarms went wild. He would whine the whole way to the kennel and refuse his doggy treat when it was time to say goodbye. When we'd pick him up afterward, he would moan all the way home, as if to say, "How could you do that to me?!"

For this trip, though, one of our neighbors had said they'd like to take care of Shayru and enjoy his company. They were a nice family with kids, always admiring Shayru on his walks (it's amazing how many friends you make while walking your dog). We happily agreed to the arrangement, thinking it would save Shayru the misery of the kennel.

We dropped Shayru off and flew to the south of France and from there on to Chamonix, the site of the Winter Olympics. We then drove to Switzerland and took another cable-car ride to the top of Mont Blanc. It was a sunny day, the scenery was spectacular, and we enjoyed watching all the daredevils paragliding, skiing, and parachuting.

When we stopped at our neighbors to pick up Shayru, we learned that they'd had a good time taking care of him, but a few times when they had opened the front door, Shayru had bolted out and run down the backroads and through the woods until he reached our house. They knew where he had gone and found him waiting on our back patio, but still, we were glad nothing had happened to Shayru during his great escapes. We didn't want to risk it again, so from here on out, it was only the kennel for Shayru.

August rolled around, and it was time for Mohit to get ready for college. We were all excited but also admittedly nervous. Raj and I were not used to Mohit being away, and I knew I was going to miss seeing him and being part of his daily life. While we packed, I reflected on my own past when I had headed out into the great unknown for medical school. My journey had been much more complex than Mohit's.

The day of orientation arrived, and we drove to Brown with Mohit and his bags. We met his roommate. He was a nice guy, but sharing was not one of Mohit's virtues; being an only child, he had not had to deal with it much. Communal bathrooms was another new concept for Mohit, and he was taken aback by the girls sporting all different-colored hair—red, green, purple.

There was no internet or cell phones back then, so Raj had a phone installed in the dorm room for Mohit to share with his roommate. Then, after settling him in, we said goodbye. It was an emotional parting—a milestone all parents reach at some point.

Unfortunately, Mohit was extremely unhappy at Brown. He was homesick and ready to quit. Raj and I were lonely and missing him, too, of course, but we had to conceal our emotions so as not to exacerbate his misery. We were planning on bringing Mohit a small refrigerator in his Jeep when he called us and said, "Don't bother. I'm coming home and will go to Boston University next year." His biggest issue was living in the dorm. On another day, he called us and said he had come up with a solution: "I can be a day student and commute. Please explain to the school counselor that, according to our religion, I have to visit the Hindu Temple in Ashland every day." This grand scheme of his made Raj and me laugh, but we were still very concerned for him.

When we visited Mohit the next week, Raj brought a twenty-foot cord, so that Mohit could have his own phone—no need to share with his roommate. I also reminded Mohit of my own first year in medical school, where the conditions had been much more compromising and taxing. I asked him to give it a try for one full semester, and, then, if he still wanted to come home, we would not question him.

Suddenly, the tide turned. He made some good friends, found his place at Brown, and was happy and settled. His misery was in the past. What a relief! Raj and I stilled missed him terribly, but knowing he was happy made all the difference. It's amazing how stressed we as parents become when we know our children are unhappy and we feel helpless to do anything about it. We were relieved when life began moving forward again.

One day Mohit called and said his roommate had to leave for an emergency appendectomy, and Mohit was excited to have the entire room to himself for the rest of the semester. Well, that was wishful thinking. We had to break it to him that his roommate would probably be back within two weeks. We wished his roommate an uneventful recovery and told Mohit to be nice to him. Thankfully, Mohit and his roommate had no problems with each other.

Meanwhile at home, our eternal baby, Shayru, missed Mohit, and he acted out to show his grief, doing everything he wasn't supposed to, including trespassing onto the sofa. To keep order, we had to put up multiple gates throughout the house when we were out.

Whenever Shayru broke a rule, we'd question him about it, and he'd immediately send himself downstairs for a time-out in his room. It was his way of saying, "I'm sorry." After a few minutes, he'd come back upstairs, ready for a fresh start. No more mention of his misdeed was allowed, or he'd grind his teeth, as if to say, "Now let's move on."

Thanksgiving came, and Mohit was home. Needless to say, Shayru was beside himself with joy; Mohit was his buddy, his colleague, his brother, his hero. And for Mohit, an only child, Shayru fulfilled his needs for a companion, too. They shared a mutual admiration and respect for each other. Mohit spoiled Shayru, and Shayru spoiled Mohit.

Shayru was an expert at recognizing our cars and could read time better than Raj's Rolex watch. For example, Raj usually came home from work at 5:30 p.m., and if I was already home, Shayru would stand at the top of the stairs to give Raj a welcome bark, simultaneously notifying me of Raj's arrival. And, of course, Shayru knew the sound of Mohit's Jeep. No matter how late Mohit came home, Shayru was always there to greet him. And whenever strange cars drove up to the house, Shayru made sure to inform us by barking loudly at full strength.

Shayru had unlimited energy, too. His favorite pastime was playing fetch in the backyard with Mohit. If Mohit dared go outside to shoot hoops by himself, Shayru would bark and bark until he was let out to participate with his ball.

By now, we had all learned Shayru's language and the different meanings of his barks. If Raj and I were away and Mohit was in charge of Shayru's morning walk, Shayru knew it would be delayed by two hours while Mohit slept in. Shayru would wait patiently, until his bladder couldn't take it anymore. Then he'd climb only the first two steps up to the second floor (as he wasn't allowed up there), and he'd give a friendly bark, telling Mohit, "Please come down, or I'll have an accident."

Usually in the evenings, after his walk, Shayru would get a snack of a slice of cheese, and then we'd all say goodnight. But with Mohit home for Thanksgiving, we had our traditional, mouthwatering pecan pie. Shayru walked around with his nose stuck up in the air, sniffing and waiting impatiently for his small bites. His other favorite dessert was the Indian treat *besan ladoo.* We'd warm the ladoo in the microwave, and Shayru would not move from his post in front of it until he got his tiny share. These were priceless memories and reflected a family bond that would last forever.

Soon enough the holiday was over, and it was time for Mohit to return to campus. We all missed him and impatiently waited for his winter break.

In January 1994, we were all together again as a family, although Mohit was also going on a road trip with his friends to visit New York, New Jersey, and Washington, DC. This was his first long trip without us, and we hoped they would drive safely. Parents always worry about their children's safety; it's second nature and never goes away. Thankfully, Mohit returned home just fine and in time to celebrate his birthday on January 11. We had a quiet celebration with his favorite dinner, many gifts, and a decadent chocolate cake. We all enjoyed the cake, Shayru especially, who kept licking his chops, asking for more, but his pleas were no use; Mohit had always been careful about Shayru's weight.

The next morning, I was the first one to go down to the kitchen, and when I walked in, I got quite the surprise: Shayru was on top of the kitchen counter, cautiously pacing back and forth. He had helped himself to a slice of cake that had accidentally been left out on the counter last night, and the problem was, he didn't know how to get down. He had managed to get up on the counter by hopping on to a kitchen chair and then jumping from the chair to the counter. Now, though, he realized that the reverse process was much steeper and riskier.

I was so taken aback that I just stood there for ten seconds and watched him as he tried to figure out a solution. Shayru knew

I was there, and, perhaps, that gave him the moral support to make the jump, which he did without a hitch. (Today, I could have taken a video on my phone, but this was 1994.)

When Mohit came downstairs and heard about what had happened, his immediate response was, "How could you do let Shayru do that? What if he had fractured his leg? You should have lifted him and brought him down." Of course, Mohit was right, but it had all happened so quickly that I hadn't had time to properly think it through.

The next few nights, I repeatedly dreamt that Shayru had jumped onto the kitchen counter and gotten his head stuck in the microwave, and I was trying to rescue him. Children grow up, but Shayru would always be a baby, and Mohit would always be protecting him. Whenever Raj tried to reprimand Shayru, Mohit would step in and defend him. I told Mohit many times, "I hope you're home if Shayru ever has health issues, or you'll hold us responsible." Luckily, nothing like that ever did happen.

After winter break, Mohit returned to school, and life moved on pleasantly and uneventfully.

In December 1994, I returned from Ahmedabad after attending my cousin Naina's (Chachaji's daughter) wedding. The wedding had been a very lavish affair, with plenty of space for the party between Bauji's and Chachaji's grounds. Bhen and her family attended as well, and it was a big, wonderful family reunion. While I was away, Raj and Mohit enjoyed some time together.

When I returned to Boston, however, I became very sick. At first, I thought it was the usual traveler's sickness and would be gone before long, but it only got worse. My symptoms, among others, included a high fever, gastrointestinal upset, loss of appetite, and weight loss. I had never missed a day of work before, even during my pregnancy, but this was serious. I had lots of lab work and tests done, but no diagnosis. The infectious-disease specialist at LMH, a friend of mine, made a house call and wanted me to be admitted to the hospital. I didn't say "No," but I did request to wait a few days.

At the very least, I was sick at home in the U.S. and not in India, but I was concerned that I had contracted a very serious illness, like dengue fever or something strange that might affect my brain. I truly believed I was close to death.

Even though I was very sick, I was still mentally competent, and I spent a great deal of time while bedridden reflecting on my life. What were my regrets? What would I do differently if I had the chance? What had I missed out on? And what else would I miss out on if I were to die now?

I'd had a privileged upbringing and was spoiled—no question. Bapaji, Baji, and Bhen had protected and supported me. I had taken my family's love for granted as well as the privilege of having us all living under one roof; I'd had no idea how some other people in the world lived. Over the years, I've developed an unparalleled sense of family responsibility. Nothing in this world matters more than family. Because of my family's positive force in my life, especially Bapaji's, I was able to achieve a fulfilling and successful life. And because of their unconditional love, I never had to worry about being anyone but myself.

I had my first taste of the outside world when I attended college in Ahmedabad at age fifteen, but I was still with my parents. I enjoyed two wonderful years as a rather self-absorbed teenager, and then the real adventure began when I left for medical school in Delhi. All my dreams and expectations were shattered as soon as I arrived on campus. I had to adjust and mature quickly. I was learning every day to appreciate my own privileged life and to have sympathy for those who had not been so blessed. I learned to replace my judgment with understanding and develop more empathy and sympathy as circumstances developed.

I enjoyed my five years at medical school; I got good grades but still found the time to indulge and have fun with friends. Then right before graduation, I found myself engaged, by my own choosing. I completed my internship, graduated, and got married. Thus far, I had been a good daughter, but now I needed to be a good wife, a good daughter-in-law, and a good sister-in-law. I was ready for it, because I always had Bapaji's presence guiding me, preparing me for these responsibilities. I did, though, have to face some rude surprises, including derisive relatives and a very stressful new home environment. But I dug deep and tolerated the intolerable. With Bapaji's teachings as my backbone, I was able to extricate myself from many perverse situations with my head still held high and my values unsullied.

Then I found a second life here in Boston. I achieved a good graduate education, secured a good job, worked with good colleagues, and enjoyed a good social life with good friends. With Raj's support, I was able to lead a fairly well-balanced life. We were not extravagant but enjoyed life within our means—nice food, vacations, and entertainment. I always saw my glass as half full, as Bapaji had taught me to be thankful to have more than most rather than be envious of the few who had more. I was lucky to be here in the U.S. and have the chance to recreate myself (even managing to become a gourmet cook!).

Despite difficulties with certain relatives, I still had a wonderful family, and I was grateful for their love and generosity. I was at the receiving end of many gifts from Baji, Bapaji, Chaeji, Mataji, Pitaji, and Raj; Mohit even gave me token gifts to teach him appreciation and kindness. But otherwise, I enjoyed being at the giving end rather than the receiving. Whenever possible, I did favors with no strings attached.

I was also honored to be the chair of my department at LMH, an achievement Bapaji would have been proud of; he had always known what I was capable of. LMH was my home-at-work; it was here that I grew up and matured in my skills. And in my new role as leader, I dedicated myself to excellence. I developed the fortitude and self-confidence to be decisive in my actions; I learned how to appreciate other perspectives and smooth over potentially explosive situations; I challenged precedent when necessary without being disrespectful; I overcame cultural barriers and racial myths; I carefully cultivated relationships with everyone on staff to create a supportive atmosphere in which exceptional patient care was the ultimate goal.

Sometimes the obstacles I faced were overwhelming, and I struggled with crises of faith, but I still painted a picture of cheerfulness on the outside. Overall, I was resolute, I reassessed when required, and I successfully navigated many formidable situations. In the end, my efforts were rewarded.

My dedication to the hospital, however, did require me to compromise and forgo some of my own personal wishes and dreams, but I could not complain, because I reaped a great deal of inward satisfaction and outward appreciation from my work. It gave me a higher purpose in life, allowing me to contribute to important, life-and-death issues. It also allowed me to grow as a human being. My work was both humbling and profoundly meaningful, and I learned that, if I was unable to change a situation, I needed to change myself (a realization I have Bapaji to thank for).

In short, most of my thoughts while I was sick revolved around all the good that had happened to me. My life had been a tremendous, rewarding journey of learning, jumpstarted by Bapaji and my halcyon childhood. I had few unfinished dreams; I had meaningful relationships and credibility among my family, friends, and co-workers; I had been fair and just in my dealings; I had lived my life fully and truthfully; I had embraced Bapaji's simple yet profound teachings, and I had a life of happiness and abundance to show for it.

I still had imperfections, of course. I would never come close to Bapaji's paragon of virtue and Bhen's patience. My character had advanced slowly through the years, and I still occasionally misjudged. But with each challenge I faced, I came out stronger and better for it.

Would I have done anything differently? I would have reached out to more people in need, shown more kindness, offered more community service. I was guilty of spanking Mohit—completely unforgiveable—and I should have cooked for Shayru rather than giving him packaged food.

But overall, I could die without too many regrets; I was at peace. Life had been kind to me, and if I were given a second chance, I doubt I could reproduce it, as I had been blessed and supported in so many ways outside of my influence.

Finally, after two weeks of being severely ill, I recovered. My brain had not been damaged by the high fever, and I had no other permanent disabilities. We never were able to pinpoint a diagnosis, but I viewed my recovery as a second chance at life.

Life returned to normal in 1995. Mohit was cruising along at Brown and was now home for winter break. Shayru was jubilant, as always, to have his buddy back. They played fetch and then hide-and-seek, with Shayru the winner; Shayru's confidence was boundless. Of course, Mohit also had to inspect Shayru from head to toe, making sure he was completely healthy, and Mohit made an appointment with Dr. Zullo for Shayru to have his teeth cleaned; then Mohit returned to Brown.

I left for a short weekend trip to Dallas to see my aunt, which left Raj, the ever-loyal dad, in charge of taking Shayru to Dr. Zullo. For the teeth cleaning, Shayru couldn't have any breakfast beforehand because he had to go under general anesthesia. Raj dropped Shayru off at the clinic, picked him up and brought him home after the cleaning, and they went on Shayru's usual afternoon walk. Big innocent mistake.

On coming up the driveway, Shayru collapsed. He was starved and dehydrated, not having eaten anything all day, and the walk uphill had been too much for him. Raj, panicked, picked up Shayru and carried him inside. Right then, the phone rang. It was Mohit calling to check up on Shayru after his appointment. Raj told him what had happened, and that was it—no more conversation; Mohit needed to drive over himself and check on Shayru.

Suddenly, just after Raj hung up the phone, Shayru miraculously regained his strength and climbed up the stairs. Raj was ecstatic and relieved. He called Mohit back and told him Shayru was fine, but Mohit still needed his own reassurance. Late that night, Mohit arrived home and was satisfied to see that Shayru was well.

The next morning, I called Raj from Dallas and was surprised to hear that Mohit was home. Not only that, but AAA was also at the house, recharging Mohit's car battery. In Mohit's anxiousness to see Shayru, he had left his headlights on.

I heard the story of Shayru collapsing from both father and son, and I understood their worry: Shayru was very special to Mohit; their adoration was mutual and their bond unbreakable. In fact, during my recent illness, when I thought I was on my death bed, Mohit was taking his finals and so did not visit me.

But when it came to Shayru, Mohit could not trust anyone, in case even the smallest error had been overlooked. Mohit left that morning for Brown, fully satisfied that Shayru was okay.

Later that year, Raj and I went to visit Varsha in New York, and since Mohit now had his own apartment, we dropped off Shayru at his place. Mohit thought Shayru would enjoy a nice vacation. Not so. Shayru missed his own house; he did not like being displaced. Mohit took him for a walk in the city, but Shayru was obviously bored (we had all learned the emotions and meanings behind his different barks, growls, and whines).

When Raj and I picked up Shayru after our trip, he was delighted to return home, where he had his freedom in a big yard with lots of wildlife to explore. And Raj and I loved having Shayru home, too. After a hard day's work, it was nice to be greeted with his welcoming bark and him running around in excited circles. (If only we had cameras around our yard, we could have enjoyed some rather amusing movies of Shayru's antics, but instead we had to wait until we got home from work to surmise, based on the evidence, what he had been up to.)

In August 1995, we bought a small beautiful summer house in Falmouth that was on the water and had a dock. We all loved the place, except for Shayru. He felt insecure at this place that he saw only once in a while. His territorial nature found happiness only on our grounds in Weston.

Some neighbors from Weston as well as my mentor, Dr. Capobianco, also owned houses in the Falmouth neighborhood, so we felt right at home. Many owned big boats as well, and Dr. Capobianco took us out on his boat to see his house and ours from the river. It was an exciting adventure for Raj and Mohit, and they immediately started educating themselves on boats and looking into one.

Around this time, big changes were in the air at LMH. There were talks of merging us with another, bigger hospital, Framingham Union Hospital. We were only seven miles apart physically, but our work cultures were worlds apart. The tentative plan was to combine the two hospitals under one name, MetroWest Medical Center, but keep the two campuses.

Many, many meetings ensued. The two administrations wanted the merger; the doctors did not. At LMH, we were one big family, and the surgeons were our friends, but at Framingham, they had deep, internal fissures between the anesthesiologists and the surgeons, and for some strange reason, they had two chiefs in their anesthesiology department. They were like a house of cards about to collapse.

The lack of cooperation and enmity between the Framingham surgeons and the administration was so blatant that the chief of surgery ordered an independent audit be done on both campuses before the merger. The audit included an in-depth survey of each campus's competency, strength, attitude, professionalism, and interdepartmental relations. Framingham passed in competency only. Their hubris was their downfall. My department at LMH, however, scored an A+ in all categories. This made me very proud, a compliment to my hard work as department chair.

The administration's long-term plan was to combine all the departments and services of the two hospitals, with some specialties available at only one of the campuses. This created an atmosphere of competition and survival; rivalries instantly erupted between departments of the two hospitals. The insecurity, discomfort, and outright panic were palpable; fissures between the cross-campus anesthesiologists and surgeons were open at times.

Over time, though, everyone absorbed the initial shock and started to accept the reality of the situation. In my department at LMH, our stress was minimal, and we continued to focus on our work. Although fear of the unknown was always floating around in the air, we knew we had each other's backs. We had our disagreements, of course, but we had also built up a bank of trust. We supported each other, we had become family, and, most important of all, we were unified in our goal of excellence in patient care.

One day I received a call from the CEO of LMH to discuss my future after the merger. He complimented me on my department's ranking on the audit, and without my bringing it up, he extended me an offer to stay indefinitely. He was not very keen on merging. Although Framingham was twice our size and had twice the number of patients, merging would still be a step down for us. They were focused on quantity; we cared about quality.

The surgeons were still up in arms about the merger, but all of us in the anesthesia department were united. We had our thoughts together, and everyone supported me. It was my responsibility, then, to propel the department in the right direction. In the end, I decided that it would be best for me to step down as department chair and hand over the baton to someone else, in order to ensure the smoothest merger and encourage unity and respect between the two anesthesia departments.

I had had fifteen memorable years as chairwoman. I had started as an outsider and earned my way into the inner circle. Still, though, I did not simply try to appease everyone. I was authentic in my work. I made difficult decisions and followed a trajectory of long-term success, even when the short-term choice would have been more popular. I thought deeply about my role and shepherded in many changes for the betterment of the department, despite pushback from others due to ideological differences.

With Bapaji's presence as my strength, I resisted pressure, remained optimistic, and did not shy away when the spotlight turned harsh. I developed business acumen and relied on cutting-edge resources. And the results were worth it: I had an untarnished reputation and a sterling record; I passed every annual review; I experienced far more ecstasies than agonies; and I found a deep meaningfulness to my work that enhanced every other part of my life. In short, I was content and humbled to have led my department for fifteen years, and in January 1996, I handed off the baton to someone else.

Now it was time for the next chapter of my professional life. As the merger moved forward, we navigated a winding political road, joining with our colleagues at Framingham's anesthesia department. To cultivate goodwill, we all had to compromise and adjust our paradigms, sometimes significantly. I, for one, turned down some leadership offers in order to maintain the peace. For example, although I would remain on the hospital's executive committee, I chose to have fewer responsibilities, giving them to others. This was actually a blessing. Less work meant more time with my family.

As much as I remained optimistic, the merger was still stressful, especially learning to work at two different campuses. LMH was state-of-the-art, designed by a modern architect. It had excellent traffic flow and felt like a five-star hotel; even Aga Khan, the Imam, greatly admired it.

Framingham, on the other hand, was tiny. The hospital had multiple additions built on throughout the years and the place felt like a maze, creating a feeling of disconnection and disorientation. Our colleagues from Framingham had no problem adjusting to their new work environment at LMH, but the same could not be said for us at LMH going to Framingham. Still, though, the merger of the anesthesia departments was the smoothest of all the departments between the two hospitals. We had a superb reputation, and, over time, we restored our trust with the surgeons and nurses in the OR and L&D. We worked at both hospitals on an equal schedule, but coming to LMH was an extra treat for me; it was like coming home.

In the end, I had no regrets about the merger. Life moved on, and I was happy.

In the summer of 1996, I was on the planning committee for the annual American Association of the Physicians of Indian Origin. It was going to be in Boston for the first time, and it would be a huge three-day gala during the Fourth of July. There would be educational lectures as well as entertainment and a shopping bazaar, all at the Hynes and Prudential Convention Centers.

Raj and I were excited, as Bauji and Chaeji were going to be visiting us. They were still in good health and were all for social events.

The week of the conference came, and it was a huge success. Bauji and Chaeji enjoyed everything, including meeting our friends and colleagues of many years. The grand finale of the conference was the Fourth of July fireworks. The evening started with great entertainment, delicious food, and an inviting ambience. Then, when dinner finished and night fell, the weather was, luckily, cooperative—clear, dark skies. We watched the fireworks from the top floor inside the Prudential building. The colors were spectacular, but we were surprised by the silence. Apparently the windows in the building were soundproof, so we could see the fireworks but not hear them. This was a bit of a letdown, but we still had a wonderful time.

We also showed Bauji and Chaeji our house in Falmouth. Raj and Mohit had purchased their dream twenty-five-foot boat, and we all had fun exploring the river on it with friends and family. The summer flew by, and we were so glad we could spend it with Bauji and Chaeji.

Soon it was time to say goodbye. Bauji and Chaeji always enjoyed visiting us, especially as they were getting older and were losing their friends and relatives. Some they lost suddenly, some after suffering.

Despite their social circle shrinking, Bauji remained active in his business and social engagements. He had a morning walking group, which was actually more talking than walking, and he was interested in the Laughing Club movement, which encouraged people to come together and laugh every day to strengthen their immune systems. The movement was started by a doctor in Bombay in 1995 and was gaining momentum all over India. Bauji was also involved with his philanthropic causes, and he stayed abreast of the local and world news, keeping Raj and me informed. Both Bauji and Chaeji led purposeful and fulfilling lives. Sometimes I would joke with Bauji that he was so busy I needed an appointment to see him, but I knew that was what kept him healthy and active.

As the summer came to a close, Mohit went back to Brown. He had decided that, this year, he'd like to have a better apartment, close to campus, so Raj and I came to help him move. Afterward, we were planning on driving to the Cape in two cars, so we had brought along Shayru, who was waiting in Raj's Acura. I had been gone for only ten minutes when I returned to the Acura and was shocked to find the window shattered and glass all over the seats. Fortunately Shayru had not been hurt, but he was obviously disturbed. Nothing had been stolen from

Raj's car except for his car phone. It was the size of a regular house phone—the predecessor of the first big cell phones—and this basic model had cost five hundred dollars.

Raj and Mohit had already taken off for the Cape in the other car, and I had no way of reaching them, so I drove to the Cape with a broken window. The next day, Raj drove back and filed a police report in person.

Four days later, I was driving in my own car when my car phone rang. It was the police, and they had found Raj's car phone! I was amazed. During a raid, they had discovered more than a hundred stolen phones in the trunk of a car. After searching through Raj's phone contacts to figure out who the owner was, they had found my number. They asked me a few security questions for verification, and then Raj was able to pick up his precious and expensive phone at the station.

Since it was a car phone, we had no way of protecting it better, but thankfully, it was never stolen again.

Life moved on. Work at the newly merged MetroWest was improving as the atmosphere became more palatable. Everyone was learning how to be more accommodating, and the professionalism of our department, in particular, was recognized and appreciated.

The New Year, 1997, rolled in, and along with it came new personal goals, most of them short-lived. In March, we were attending the wedding of Raj's nephew, who lived in the UK but was getting married in India. We were also going to visit my sister Varsha, who was living in Chennai, India, on a two-year work assignment. Altogether, it was going to be a big trip, and Raj and I were busy completing our usual shopping for presents.

This time around, the demand was for edible gifts, so we bought a variety of cheeses as well as lots of nuts and chocolates.

I also made sure to include the kids and bought a bag full of Kit Kats and Reese's Pieces, which I packed in my suitcase in the playroom downstairs.

One day I came home from work and went downstairs, only to find multiple empty Kit Kat wrappers strewn about the floor, along with a few Reese's Pieces opened but uneaten. It was my fault; I had left the zipper on the suitcase slightly open. Naughty Shayru had discovered my mistake and gleefully invaded the goodies. No doubt he was in a state of complete chocolate euphoria, and luckily, he did not suffer any consequences for it. In the future, I learned to be more careful. (It was interesting, though, that Shayru had selective taste. He had disliked the Reese's Pieces!)

The day of our departure came and Shayru needed to be dropped off at the kennel. As usual, his alarm bells went off as soon as we started packing the car. He sulked all the way to the kennel and refused his biscuit treat when we arrived. It broke my heart, but we needed to go. We left him with his backpack full of his favorite toys as well as slices of cheese for dessert every night. I hoped he knew that his stay was only temporary and that he'd be back home soon.

# Chapter Twenty-One

*W hile at Brown,* Mohit made a surplus of Indian friends for the first time in his life; he had had very little exposure to other Indian children growing up due to Raj's and my busy work schedules. Back then around 5 percent of Brown students were of Indian origin; nowadays it's around 20 percent.

Because of these newfound friends, Mohit finally became interested in Hindi. On his own accord, he enrolled himself in an additional course at Brown to learn how to speak it. Raj and I had been trying, futilely, to teach Mohit since he was a child, but he had never been interested. It was like he had been reincarnated, and Raj and I jokingly called him the born-again Indian.

Some of Mohit's new friends came from India, while others lived in the US as well as many other countries. His friends from India mostly belonged to the rich and famous, since they could afford to send their children across the world to an Ivy League school. These students were expert braggers, going on and on about their celebrity connections in Bollywood. Mohit had no connections to any Indian elites, so naturally he felt he had been deprived. He wanted to rectify this huge oversight of ours by staying two nights at the Leela Kempinski Hotel in Bombay (now the Leela Mumbai) for his twenty-first birthday; Mohit had heard from his friends that the hotel's nightclub, Bling, was very exclusive and a frequent haunt of Bollywood celebrities.

Raj and I agreed to the trip, but before we left, I called my old Boston friend and colleague, Dr. Dagli, who had returned to India and become an anesthesiologist in Bombay, administering epidurals to the families of the rich and famous. He was loved and admired by all his patients and their husbands. I told Dr. Dagli about Mohit's star-struck birthday wish and Dr. Dagli, as humble as ever, said he would try for Mohit's sake to rally together one or two celebrities. We had hope! Dr. Dagli then told me to call him the day before we arrived in Bombay from Ahmedabad and update him on our schedule.

We reached Ahmedabad the first week of January. The weather was fantastic, we were completely spoiled by family, and Mohit and Raj indulged themselves by getting custom-made suits. When it was time to head to Bombay, we gave Dr. Dagli a call and arranged to meet him at our five-star Leela Hotel.

Dr. Dagli was the same as ever—down to earth and kind. He began our celebrity tour by taking us to the house of a famous film producer. An escort walked us through the home, which was the epitome of a luxury mansion. Dr. Dagli made a point of telling Mohit that this producer and his mansion were an exception; even the richest people in Bombay could not afford anything close to this place.

Next Dr. Dagli took us to Juhu Beach where we watched the film *Aflatoon* being shot. We also had the chance to briefly meet the actor Akshay Kumar and take pictures with him. Kumar was surrounded by security guards and most of the public could only watch him from a distance. We also got to say hello to the heroine in the movie, Urmila Matondkar.

Next stop on our celebrity tour was Madh Mansion, a few miles down the Juhu Beach; it has since become a favorite film locale and we recognize it now whenever it pops up in a movie. When we arrived, an important shooting was in full swing and Kumar was there again, starring in another movie. One of his co-stars, Saif Ali Khan, became very excited when he spotted Dr. Dagli. He ditched the scene he was shooting and ran over to ask why the good doctor had stopped by. Dr. Dagli introduced us to Khan, and Khan was extremely gracious and posed in some pictures with Mohit.

Next we headed to Dr. Dagli's house for lunch and to meet his family. We were excited to see his wife, Shiela, after so many years. We also met their daughter, Aditi, for the first time; she was currently in medical school. We enjoyed a nice lunch together and a wonderful afternoon talking about our morning adventures. Aditi said, "My dad has never taken me to any film shootings!"

It had been a busy, hot day, and I was ready to get back to our hotel, but Dr. Dagli, who was an exceptional host, made Mohit an offer he could not refuse: he had made an appointment for Mohit to meet a very famous film star, Suniel Shetty, at his in-laws' house.

Mohit was beyond excited—he had seen Shetty in many action movies—so of course we agreed to go (me half-heartedly). We were meeting at Suniel's in-laws' because Suniel's wife had had a baby girl four weeks ago, and Dr. Dagli had administered her epidural. Both the wife and Shetty were very grateful to Dr. Dagli.

Once we arrived at the in-laws' house, I was glad I had gone. It was a beautiful seaside mansion that looked like it had walked straight out of *Architectural Digest*. The father of Shetty's wife was, in fact, a famous architect in Bombay and had built this mansion for him and his wife; even the smallest details had been gorgeously carried out (and it helped that their backyard was the Atlantic Ocean). I was keenly interested in interior design and was thrilled to have the opportunity to be inside a place like this.

Shetty and his family were very hospitable, chatting with Mohit, offering him snacks and a Coke. Mohit was in shock; could this possibly be real? He whispered to me, "I don't believe it."

After a full day of adventuring, including a wonderful evening hanging out with mega stars, Dr. Dagli dropped us off at our hotel and said he had plans for us to meet some more celebrities the next day. We thanked him for his complete commitment to Mohit's birthday wish, then we returned to our room, exhausted. Mohit was supposed to go downstairs that evening to Bling, the hotel's nightclub, but he was tired and had met enough stars that day—his wildest dreams had already come true.

To cap off Mohit's birthday, Dr. Dagli joined us the next morning in the hotel lobby where we met some older film stars. The trip had been beyond successful, the best twenty-first birthday Mohit could have asked for. (Ironically, jumping forward to the present-day, this visit with the stars has been relegated to the back of Mohit's memories, dusted off and relived only occasionally. It's funny how we go through different phases and desires in life.)

Before returning to the States, Mohit had one more birthday wish: he wanted to see village life in the Punjab province of northern India. Raj and I had been hoping we could hop a one-hour flight from Bombay to Goa and relax at one of its popular beach resorts, but it was Mohit's birthday and we honored his wish.

We decided that a visit to Punjab would be the perfect opportunity to see Bhen, Jijaji, and their family in Morinda. When we called, they were overjoyed to hear about our plans.

The first leg of our trip was a two-hour flight from Bombay to Delhi, then we hopped on a fast luxury train from Delhi to the famous city of Chandigarh; my cousin met us there and drove us the remaining hour to Morinda. Along the way we looked out the window at the beautiful farm land, passing by bright yellow mustard fields intermingled with sugarcane fields.

Mohit had had the idea that Punjabi men were all tall, big, muscular, and macho. Looking out into the fields, though, he was disappointed to see that they were all mostly average.

Bhen and Jijaji gave us a wonderfully warm welcome, and the entire family was delighted with our visit. I hadn't seen many of my extended family in years and they had all grown up so quickly. Due to our tight schedule, it was only a twenty-four hour visit, but it was memorable and we were glad we had done it (no regrets about not going to Goa). A few months later, Jijaji unexpectedly died from a heart attack. Raj, Mohit, and I were so grateful we had had the opportunity to spend some last moments with him. Jijaji was a kind person and he holds a special place in my heart.

After our visit to Morinda, Raj, Mohit, and I returned to Delhi, where Mohit went into high-gear shopping mode. He was indulging himself, and we were letting him splurge while on his dream vacation. As he took a cab from store to store, he could easily speak to the drivers in Hindi, albeit with an American accent.

Mohit commented that I was not doing any shopping for myself. I waved away his remark, saying that the breakneck pace was too fast for me to do any indulging. But when he mentioned it again, I casually said that we had to have some semblance of a budget, and since it was his big birthday bash, he got to do the shopping; I'd postpone my indulging for the next trip.

A few months later, on Mother's Day in May, I got the surprise of my life. Mohit presented me with a gorgeous handwoven silk saree with gold threads. Very expensive. During his birthday shopping in January, he had snuck off one day to a boutique we had visited together the day before. He had even kept the gift a secret from Raj the entire four months.

I was so touched. Even Chaeji, Bauji, and Varsha, who were visiting at the time, were astounded. Varsha made a comment about the cost and Mohit said, "Gifts don't come with price tags." But then in the same breath Mohit turned to Raj and said, "Daddy, this is an expensive gift; let's share the bill."

I still treasure this memory and the saree, which has taken its place alongside my other favorite saree from Bauji. Sometimes I jokingly ask Mohit, "When are you going to buy me another saree?" But I don't really need another saree; I wear them less and less these days, and besides, I already have a collection worthy of a world-class fashion designer.

# Chapter Twenty-Two

Our trip started with the wedding celebration in Delhi. It was a very emotional reunion with Raj's cousins; we enjoyed walking down memory lane after so many years apart. After the wedding, we went to Ahmedabad. Bauji and Chaeji as well as Chachaji and Auntyji had sold their houses and were downsizing in the suburbs. Bauji and Chaeji were moving from the twelve-thousand-square-foot Chhabil Villa to a four-thousand-square-foot custom-built home.

Bauji's only concern with the new home was lack of space if all the children visited at the same time, but that was unlikely to happen. He was also keenly interested in the progress of the new house, and Raj and I went with him to see it for ourselves. I was amazed at Bauji's interest, enthusiasm, and oversight of the construction. He had even brought his own chair to watch the work, as he had always had very high hygienic standards and was afraid of contamination from the dust and pollution. He was putting in so much effort and passion into the project that I silently prayed that both he and Chaeji would be able to enjoy their new house for many years to come.

Chachaji's house would once again be next door to Bauji's, and Bauji explained to Raj and me how the two houses shared the same floor plan but differed in the details. Their brotherly love and family bond was still going strong.

The new homes would be ready by June, but Chaeji was reluctant to move, as she had strong emotional ties to Chhabil Villa. She and Bauji had lived at the villa for thirty-nine years, from 1958 to 1997, and it held many happy memories.

To top it off, along with the stress of moving, Chaeji was not feeling well. We brought her to the hospital for some tests, and her EKG came back abnormal. I knew Chaeji was much more reckless about her health than Bauji, so I followed up on the EKG with an echo of her heart.

Raj and I both accompanied Bauji and Chaeji to a private hospital. It was in an affluent suburb, and, from the outside, the building looked up to date, but as soon as we stepped inside, the place sent a shiver down my spine. It had shockingly low standards of cleanliness—I wouldn't have brought a stray cat in if I'd had the choice—but unfortunately for us, we had no choice.

Chaeji's echo also came back abnormal: her ejection fraction (the amount of blood leaving her heart each time it contracted) was 30 percent. This was a serious and urgent situation.

Chaeji's best option was to go to Chennai for more workups. Chennai, a city in southern India, was more than eight hundred miles from Ahmedabad. It had recently gone through a citywide facelift and now drew in many computer and biotech companies as well as state-of-the-art medical facilities. Luckily, Varsha was already settled there for her two-year work assignment, so the decision was made for Bauji to accompany Chaeji to Chennai as soon as they moved into their new house.

Raj and I said our goodbyes in Ahmedabad and then left for Chennai ourselves to visit Varsha and travel for ten days around a few other cities in southern India.

We started our road trip in Mysore (Mysuru), a city full of beautiful gardens and old palaces. We especially enjoyed visiting the Brindavan Gardens, considered one of the best gardens in India, with its musical fountains and dancing water shows. We had seen Brindavan in movies, but to see it in person was spectacular.

Next stop was Bangalore, ninety miles down the road. This was another city full of palaces and gardens, but it had also become a technology hub and had changed its name to Bengaluru. From here we decided to visit the Venkateswara Temple, dedicated to the Hindu god Vishnu. The temple was in the hills of Tirumala, a four-hour drive away, and was believed to have been constructed in the fourth century. It is supposedly one of the richest temples in the world, bringing in more than a million dollars a day, mostly from visitors' donations.

We stayed the night in Tirumala and began the next day at 4 a.m. with the *puja* ceremony, and then we stood in a very long line. The Venkateswara Temple is the most visited holy place in the world, with about fifty thousand to one hundred thousand visitors every day. It is also highly commercialized—the more you donate, the easier the access.

Many devotees make a pilgrimage to the temple every year, but once was all Raj and I could manage. It was an experience of a lifetime; the grounds and the ambience were unforgettable.

Raj, Varsha, and I returned to Chennai, where we stayed with Varsha and did some sightseeing. We also met up with an old friend of mine, a fellow anesthesiologist from Boston, and we went on a day trip to Mahabalipuram, a coastal city forty miles south of Chennai.

Mahabalipuram is a historic city and a UNESCO World Heritage Site. We visited its Shore Temple, which is a complex of three temples built in 700–728 AD; they're one of the oldest stone temples of the many in South India. The rock carvings on the temples were breathtaking.

We stopped for lunch at the Taj Beach Hotel Resort at Fisherman's Cove, where the sand was a startling white and the ocean a clear blue. If distance were not a factor, Raj and I would have been frequent fliers here. Then we returned to Chennai and wrapped up our whirlwind of a vacation in India. It had been a fun, memorable trip, although we were still worried about Chaeji; Varsha promised to update us as soon as she could.

We picked up Shayru from the kennel, and he whined non-stop the entire twelve miles back home. He didn't want to leave any doubt in our minds as to how he felt about the situation. As soon as we opened the front door, he ran downstairs to make sure that everything was in order in his room, and then he ran back upstairs to check on the rest of the house.

It was now the end of March, and we were looking forward to Boston in the spring. Little did we know a gigantic storm was headed our way.

On March 31–April 1, a giant ice storm hit the Northeast. Since it was April Fool's Day, people didn't take the storm warnings as seriously as they perhaps would have otherwise. Trees were down everywhere; the power was out; motorists were stranded (a thousand of them had to sleep in their cars overnight), and hotels were booked to full capacity.

I was prepared to go to work if the police could escort me, but the snowplows couldn't even clear the roads because of all the fallen trees. To get to the main road would have meant walking through twenty inches of ice and snow.

There was no heat in our house, so our very nice neighbor brought us some firewood in his four-wheel drive. We were lucky we could still cook, since our stove used gas. Our friends walked more than half a mile to join us for a cup of coffee and toast. It was a sight to see them trudging through the snow, the husband first and the wife walking in his footsteps. Another of our neighbors drove to his son's house and brought a chainsaw to remove all the fallen trees along the way.

That evening, Raj and I decided to sleep in Mohit's waterbed, which was a very smart decision—it was toasty warm. But as the temperature outside continued to drop throughout the night, our house got colder and colder. We felt like human icicles. We couldn't even check into a hotel, which had generators keeping the heat on, because in those days, most hotels were not dog-friendly, and we couldn't leave Shayru alone.

Fortunately, the governor of Massachusetts had declared a state of emergency, so electric companies from as far as Canada came to the rescue.

By the next morning, our street had been plowed, and I was able to drive to work. When I returned home at five that evening, I was thrilled to see multiple heavy-duty Canadian vehicles working on the power lines. An hour later, we had light and heat! All our friends were calling each other in the neighborhood, sharing the good news; we were relieved to be out of our unexpected three-day Siberian experience. We felt great appreciation for things we too often take for granted.

The storm was the talk of all the TV shows and newspapers (once the papers could actually be delivered, that is). It was a storm none of us would ever forget.

Soon enough, life returned to normal. In June, Mohit graduated from Brown, and Raj and I drove to the campus for a two-day celebration. It rained on graduation day, but that didn't dampen the spirit of the occasion. Mohit had not wanted a personal graduation party, and we respected his wishes.

Over in India, Bauji and Chaeji had moved into their new house and were planning to visit Chennai for Chaeji's medical follow-ups. Bauji had also been having some mild chest discomfort at night, probably angina. Chaeji had no complaints and seemed to be fine, but, then again, she was diabetic, and so her angina would be silent and her discomfort not as acute.

In July 1997, after having lived through that record-setting ice storm, I was about to face an emotional storm of epic proportions that would drain all my mental reserves. The storm in April was minuscule compared to this one.

It all started when Bauji and Chaeji visited Varsha in Chennai. Chaeji underwent a coronary angioplasty, because with her condition, she was at high risk for open-heart surgery. The angioplasty was uneventful, and she was recovering nicely, but then Bauji went in for a cardiac consult, too, and was advised to undergo angioplasty immediately as well due to his symptoms.

Varsha called, asking me to come and help with this sudden, urgent situation. I was the doctor in the family, and my support and standby were crucial. The problem was that my work did not allow me to come and go at the drop of a hat. After great difficultly, I was able to rearrange my schedule at MetroWest to get a week off.

I flew into Delhi and first spent the night at Munni and RJ's. Sadly, Munni was bedridden and disoriented, and RJ, who had always had a strong, happy disposition, was deeply depressed. With tears in his eyes, RJ told me their situation. They had become very wealthy, and their three children, all of whom were now married and out of the house, were well-off but treated Munni poorly and had no desire to spend time with her. The children led busy social lives and dropped by for short visits only once a week.

Over the years, I had become fond of Munni. I felt so sorry for her and sick to my stomach thinking about how one can never know what the future will bring. Munni had all the money she could ever want, but without the love of her family, she couldn't enjoy it.

The next morning, I flew to Chennai, a four-hour flight and a distance of 1,100 miles. Bauji was waiting for me at the airport, and from there we went to Varsha's apartment. Chaeji was still recovering nicely, and Bauji's angioplasty would be in two days. We spent a nice evening together.

I had brought with me two bottles of non-ionic dye for Bauji's angioplasty, as his kidney function had been borderline for the past twelve years, and this dye was safer for his condition.

I accompanied Bauji to the hospital. It was state-of-the-art, even by U.S. standards, and the cardiologist was reputable, the best in India. The doctor was in his fifties, and he presented himself very professionally. He was also personable and told me that he had been to Boston. This experience was completely different than the one we'd had at the private Ahmedabad slum hospital where Chaeji had gotten her EKG.

I stayed with Bauji even when he went into the OR. I held his hand and watched the procedure. Everything went according to plan, and he was to stay overnight for observation. I also stayed and was in his hospital room when suddenly, in the middle of the night, he was doubled over with severe abdominal pain. By the morning, his discomfort had lessened, and the doctors had no explanation for it. Two days later, he was back at Varsha's, recovering alongside Chaeji, and I left for Boston.

One week later, Bauji and Chaeji were back in Ahmedabad. Bauji was keen on getting settled into their new house, but then he started feeling ill again. Being the informed consumer he was, Bauji went to his doctor and requested labs to test his kidney function.

To Bauji's dismay, the results showed that his potassium serum level was very high, a sign of kidney failure. He needed emergency dialysis immediately. Unfortunately, the only hospital his nephrologist (a doctor who specializes in kidney care) offered dialysis at was in the same unhygienic hospital where Chaeji had had her Echocardiagram. This was very disturbing to me, but it was our only option. I could only hope that Bauji's stay would be short, and the nephrologist assured me it would.

Once Bauji was in the hospital, I spoke to the nephrologist frequently. He was a smooth talker, very diplomatic and reassuring. Bauji's angioplasty had caused emboli (blood clots) to migrate into his kidneys. Bauji was not improving, but the doctor did not seem to be concerned about it. My mind was a whirlwind of worry; no matter where I was or what I was doing, I could not stop thinking about Bauji.

In September 1997, Raj and I planned to go to India again. The doctor's latest update was that Bauji was stable but needed to remain in the hospital on dialysis. I saw right through that charade. The ugly truth the doctor was trying to hide was that the dialysis was doing nothing for Bauji, but it was the only thing the doctor could offer us, along with the false hope of improvement. In short, the only thing driving this doctor was his insatiable greed, using dialysis machines that were obsolete.

Unlike in the U.S., it is much more difficult for Indian patients to question their doctors, and the doctors themselves have no fear of malpractice suits.

When Raj and I were in India, we laid out the next plan of action: Bauji would transfer to a better hospital, a hospital specializing in kidney care in Nadiad, a city one hundred miles from Ahmedabad. Bauji was still fully cognizant and ready to fight for the best care possible, no matter how perilous the journey.

After two weeks, it was time to say goodbye and return to my responsibilities in Boston. The evening I was leaving, Bauji asked me who was taking me to the airport. I said, "Jolly," Chachaji's daughter. Bauji immediately replied that I had better get going and remind Jolly to be on time, as Jolly was notoriously late for everything. Even in his physical state, Bauji was still as sharp as ever.

As predicted, Jolly was late picking me up, and when we got to the airport, my gate was closed. If I couldn't get on another flight soon, I'd miss my connection from Bombay to Boston. After an hour of apprehension, I managed to get on the last flight that night and make it back to the States. Bauji had been right, and Jolly and I often recapture this memory to remember him.

Life at this time was very demanding for me. To be needed in two countries across the globe was exhausting. At MetroWest, I had to work odd hours, many weekends, and all the holidays to make up for my trips to India. I also had to keep up with the regular updates on the situation in India. So, after a full day at the hospital, I would call Varsha at 10 p.m. my time (8:30 a.m. her time) and get the daily update on Bauji's condition based on the doctors' rounds. Most of the news was frustrating. Then I'd go to bed, get a restless night's sleep, and wake up at 5:30 a.m. to talk to Varsha again before leaving for work at 6:30 a.m. While at work, a part of me was always in India. Varsha had my work number and my beeper if she needed to contact me for an emergency consult (since cell phones were not an option back then).

I could feel my mental and emotional resources depleting, but I willed myself to remain strong and optimistic. During this time, a human-resources employee, a very nice lady, lost her nineteen-year-old son to viral meningitis after a sudden and acute twenty-four-hour illness. He was at home, on break from college, and never returned. My heart went out to her. Her suffering was far beyond my own; nothing is worse than a parent losing a child. Somehow, though, this lady still had a smile on her face when I saw her at the hospital. Another doctor on staff lost her teenage son to a brain tumor. Her grief will last for a lifetime, yet she still smiles.

As planned, Bauji was transferred to the hospital in Nadiad, and Chachaji and Auntyji were doing everything possible to support him, turning the hotel next door to the hospital into their second home. Luckily, Chaeji was still recovering nicely, and my siblings from the U.S. were taking turns flying to India to be with them.

In October 1997, I visited Bauji in Nadiad for the first time. The hospital was much better than the one in Ahmedabad, but it was not the best. There was no progress on Bauji's health. In fact, he was getting weaker and had developed other physical problems. I felt so helpless, but the doctor was still hopeful. We were doing everything within our power to manage the catastrophe. After a short visit, I had to return to Boston.

By now, I had flown between the U.S. and India so frequently and in such a short timeframe that customs at the Bombay Airport had started giving me spot checks to make sure I didn't have some hidden agenda in my all-too-familiar blue suitcase.

Back in Boston, my nights became punctuated with nightmares, and I woke up frequently. When daylight finally came, I would get up and instantly feel the weight of stress and worry pressing down on me. These were turbulent times. Every once in a while, a ray of hope would break through the dark clouds, but more often than not, the turmoil was never-ending. Family was my pillar of strength throughout this critical situation. Even though we were continents apart, we leaned on each other for courage and resilience, which we had learned from Bapaji. Ultimately, it was his teachings that carried us forward and held us together, even as hope became more and more distant.

In November 1997, Raj had hernia surgery. With Bauji's sudden problems, Raj's surgery had been put on the back burner for a while, but it needed to be done. My friend and mentor, Dr. Capobianco, performed the surgery at LMH, and everything went well.

Bauji, though, was still not improving, and the hospital in Nadiad had nothing more to offer him. Bauji, though, had a strong desire to live and told Varsha not to give up. Our last option was to transfer him back to the state-of-the-art hospital in Chennai. Chaeji was in agreement.

The transfer was done, but nothing was gained by it. As more complications arose with Bauji's health, I continued consulting with as many doctors as I could in different specialties to discuss the options. Bauji now had blood in his stools, but due to his poor health, the doctors did not want to risk surgery. My mentor, Dr. Capobianco, was shocked by this and offered to pay his own way to Chennai to operate on Bauji. His offer was serious, and I was smitten and deeply grateful for it, but I told him it was too late. I have never forgotten his kindness.

In December 1997, Raj had recovered from his surgery, and I was again juggling my work schedule to plan another trip to Chennai at the end of the month. Then I got a call on December 21: Bauji was going downhill. I was on a sixteen-hour call schedule at work, but still, no stone was left unturned in our attempts to help Bauji recover. The hospital at Chennai could do nothing more for him, so the plan was to bring him back to Ahmedabad. I planned an emergency trip to Ahmedabad for myself; it would be my fifth trip in nine months.

I wanted to leave on December 23 from Boston's Logan Airport, but snow was delaying flights. I booked a seat with whatever airline was still flying and had seats available (and with the holiday season and inclement weather, this was not an easy task.)

My flight took off three hours late, and I barely reached Amsterdam in time to make my connecting flight. My luggage, however, did not make it onto the plane, and I could not stop and wait for it. Time was crucial; I needed to get to India in time to say goodbye to Bauji.

When Varsha flew with Bauji from Chennai to Ahmedabad, she decided to give him one last chance to recover, and she drove him straight to the hospital in Nadiad, where the doctors had been so hopeful before. Now, however, their attitudes were the complete opposite. They could see Bauji did not have long, which meant that the money coming to them would dry up soon. To Varsha's hurt bewilderment, the hospital neglected Bauji. Varsha called me and asked if she should put Bauji on life support so I could see him one last time. My answer was not to hurt him anymore. "Keep him comfortable, and I will take the chance," I said.

I landed in Delhi at 3 a.m. on December 25. I immediately called Varsha from a pay phone. She told me that Bauji had passed away in Nadiad the previous morning, just as they were getting ready to bring him home.

I was shaken and alone at the airport, with nobody to embrace. A few hours later, I made it into Ahmedabad, where Varsha was waiting for me. She expressed how much my presence meant to her; we both had peace of mind knowing we had done everything we could under the circumstances. Hindsight, though, is twenty-twenty, and we still wonder what we could have done differently: maybe Bauji could have tolerated his heart condition and we should not have run the risk of surgery; maybe we should have caught on earlier to the greed of the doctors in Ahmedabad and Nadiad; maybe we should have taken him to Chennai right away. There had been so much fraud and malpractice, and no accountability.

I did not make it for Bauji's cremation, but I was able to attend *chautha*, the fourth day of mourning. The service was held in the Punjabi Samaj community, in a function hall packed to full capacity. Bauji had helped this hall get built and expanded on. Eulogies and tributes poured out; people cried. Bauji was described as a one-person, multi-dimensional, mega-institution with endless energy. A bus full of Hindu children from his school came, each of them holding a rose for Bauji. Bauji had started their Hindi school and had labored ceaselessly over the years to expand and improve on the curriculm and staff.

The entire service was very touching. My brother Vijay was surprised by the outpouring of love and gratitude; he said he would be lucky to have 10 percent of this at his funeral. Chaeji stayed calm throughout it, but inside I knew she was suffering.

After the service, Vijay went to Haridwar for Bauji's final rights. I offered to accompany him, but he wanted to do it alone. When you lose one of your two parents, you don't lose just half; your loss and mourning is much more. Even doctors like myself who confront mortality every day have no better ability to let a parent go. Bauji would have been eighty-one on January 8, 1998. His new house, which he had been so passionate about, had been lived in for only less than a month. Bauji lost the battle of time, but he remains timeless in my memory.

Reflecting on Bauji's life, his ambitions and accomplishments were unmatched, especially his focus on education. He was a man of self-respect and pride, always wanting the best for his family. He had class, was never cheap, and enjoyed luxuries within his means. He gave me the best he could afford and indulged me with gifts; the one I cherish the most is the saree he bought me before my wedding because he liked it so much. He had excellent taste in every way.

Even now, I cry at the poignant memories from that year leading up to Bauji's passing. There is no yardstick to measure the indelible impact his life had on everyone around him.

On January 9, I had a flight back to Boston. My first flight was in the evening from Ahmedabad to Delhi, and then I had a 12 p.m. connection from Delhi to Boston. Halfway to Delhi, the pilot announced that we were returning to Ahmedabad due to heavy fog in Delhi. I was already beyond stressed and ready to cry. As any traveler knows, missing a connecting flight has a domino effect on the rest of your trip.

At 10 p.m., I was back in Ahmedabad. First I called Vijay and asked him to pick me up, and then I called Raj to notify him of the change.

The next morning, I was once again on a plane to Delhi, full of apprehension, worried I would be delayed again. Luckily, my flight out of Delhi had also been delayed due to the fog, and I made it back to Boston, exhausted.

Raj and I had a small gathering at our house to remember and celebrate Bauji's life. All our friends had come to know Bauji over the years and shared fond memories of him.

Then I threw myself back into my work, both at home and at the hospital. I didn't want to return to India for some time.

# Chapter Twenty-Three

*In March, my sister Nirmal* traveled to Ahmedabad to bring Chaeji to the U.S. With Bauji gone, the new house felt disconnected from the hustle and bustle of their old place at Chhabil Villa. Chaeji was self-sufficient, independent, and in good health, so she flew around visiting all her children in rotation. I was the oldest, but due to my limitations with work responsibilities, I had to share caring for Chaeji with my sisters. Meanwhile, Varsha's work was winding up in Chennai, and she was planning her return to New York.

When Chaeji was with us in Weston, she and Shayru were good buddies, enjoying each other's company throughout the day in the kitchen, the family room, her bedroom, and the sun room. Chaeji spoiled him, but still, she struggled with loneliness. She missed Bauji.

Chaeji also complained frequently about minor health issues. I wish I could have done more for her, but I reminded her how lucky she was to have such good quality of life. I told her about a nurse, PG, I used to work with who was now in an Alzheimer's facility;

it was tragic to remember how accomplished she had once been. Chaeji suggested visiting her, and I thought it was a good idea.

When we met with PG, her health had declined since I had last seen her. Chaeji was shocked and overwhelmed; she had never seen so many compromised human beings in her life. They were disoriented, and many of them were bound to wheelchairs. It was a wake-up call for her.

After returning home, Chaeji said to me, "I will never complain again." This vow had a short life of two days. I empathized with Chaeji's struggles, but there was nothing I could do for her. At the end of the summer, Varsha flew with Chaeji back to Ahmedabad.

During this time, Mohit was applying to law schools. He was waitlisted for his first choice, Columbia, and he was accepted to Georgetown. Raj and I were happy; Mohit was not. Still, though, Mohit decided to go to Georgetown.

Raj and I traveled with him to DC and surveyed the campus. It was excellent. Mohit's dorm, which he shared with a roommate, felt like a five-star hotel. We got Mohit settled and then returned to Boston and returned to work. Then suddenly, my world was turned upside down. While at work, I received a subpoena. I was shocked. After opening it and reading the contents, I was even more shocked: I was being sued for malpractice, under the claim that I had provided improper care for a newborn.

I immediately got in touch with my lawyer and dug into the history of the case. In a nutshell, at 8 p.m. one evening while at LMH, I had given anesthesia to a patient in preparation for her C-section. The pediatrician was not present, so I had to assume the role of attending to not only the mother but also the newborn.

Even before birth, the baby was compromised in utero. She aspirated meconium into her lungs and should have been born earlier, but the ob-gyn was busy with another delivery. I was an expert in neonatal resuscitation and was able to improve the newborn's APGAR score from a one at birth to an eight within five minutes of his birth. Even though my primary responsibility was to the mother, I would have felt terribly guilty if I hadn't stepped in and given the baby appropriate care as well. But now, here I was being punished for it. There was no pediatrician despite hospital policy, which dictated a pediatrician be present for every caesarian section to care for the newborn.

After reviewing the situation, my lawyer agreed that I had given appropriate care. Two independent experts also agreed and were ready to testify if the case went to trial.

The whole thing was a can of worms. The ob-gyn was unethical beyond imagination, lying through her teeth, and the process went on forever, deposition after deposition. I was mentally and emotionally drained. Every minute of the day, my mind was consumed by the case. I knew I was innocent, but I felt guilty. Doctors are not gods, and many of them go through similar devastating stress during malpractice claims, even when they, too, have met the standard of care.

Finally, after five grueling years, the case was settled, and for ten years afterward, this was documented on my medical-license-renewal application every two years. Because of this experience, I have a great deal of empathy for any medical care provider who has to defend him or herself against a malpractice suit. Even after the situation is resolved, your subconscious never truly lets it go, because it knows that another suit could hit you again at any moment.

I often asked myself during those five torturous years, *If a similar situation were to happen again, would I risk making the same call?* My answer was, *Yes.* Because of Bapaji's DNA. I could not stand by with a clear conscience and watch a newborn suffer. And for that reason, I cannot forget or forgive the ob-gyn who put me in such a precarious position and, furthermore, put a newborn in jeopardy. I still do see the ob-gyn occasionally, and I give a forced smile. It is what it is.

Of course, life still moved on throughout the malpractice suit. In December, on Bauji's death anniversary, we visited Chaeji in Ahmedabad. We had an intimate *puja* (prayer) with the priest in her new home, surrounded by family.

Chaeji was in good spirits during our visit, but after we left, I knew she'd return to her lonely life in her big, empty house. She was not happy there, but neither was she happy with us. It was a vexing problem with no solution. When the New Year rolled in and winter came to an end, Chaeji wanted to come to the U.S. again.

Meanwhile, Mohit was not happy at Georgetown. He was working extremely hard—dedicated and goal-oriented as usual— and he had set the bar high for himself: he wanted to attend an Ivy League school. His grades were perfect, so he applied for a transfer. Parents never stop worrying about their children, but we had always encouraged Mohit to be an independent thinker, and although we were ready to help him if he asked for guidance, we supported him 100 percent.

While Mohit waited to hear back from the schools, he landed a sought-after associateship at Ropes & Gray in Boston for the summer. They had been impressed by his grades. Then, in August 1999, we heard the good news: Mohit had been accepted into the University of Pennsylvania, an Ivy League school. We were happy for him, and he immediately sent in his deposit. But then, he also got word that he had been accepted into New York University and Columbia. Mohit couldn't decide between NYU and Columbia. Eventually, he settled on Columbia, another Ivy League school.

The next step was challenging—finding housing in New York. Since Mohit was transferring, it was too late to get on campus, and it was no easy task to find an available, decent apartment.

Mohit was knee-deep in work, so Raj and I did our parenting duty and went to New York for an apartment-hunting trip. After looking at a few places, we put down a mighty large deposit on one of them only minutes before another party wanted it. It seemed the landlords were doing us a big favor, almost like this was a bidding war.

Mohit got settled at Columbia and was happy to be there, and Raj and I had peace of mind. We were also happy that Mohit could come home by train, bus, or plane to visit us, and we made frequent trips to New York ourselves, as the drive was easy. It's always fun to see the Big Apple, but I prefer living in Boston.

One weekend in October, Mohit was home visiting when he discovered that Shayru had a small cyst and needed to see the vet. As usual, this task fell under Raj's job description. So, in mid-November, Raj dutifully brought Shayru to a new clinic close by in Weston, and the vet prescribed some antibiotics.

Meanwhile, Raj and I were planning a trip to Delhi in December. I visited a new luxury kennel near Weston and made a reservation for Shayru. It was indoors and climate-controlled; it felt like a four-star hotel for dogs.

Mohit came home for Thanksgiving, and, as always, Shayru was beside himself with excitement. We were celebrating Thanksgiving over at some friends', and I had made a dish to bring. When it was time to go, however, Shayru was not himself; it seemed he had some sort of GI upset. Mohit decided to stay home, as he did not want to leave Shayru alone, but I still had to deliver my food contribution, so Raj and I decided to go for a short visit and then return home.

While at our friends' house, we got a panicked call from Mohit. Shayru was very sick. Raj and I left immediately. Some of our friends who did not have pets could not understand the seriousness of the situation, but we didn't hold it against them.

When we arrived home, we knew that Shayru needed to get to the Angell Memorial Hospital immediately. Before we left, I quickly gave Shayru a tiny piece of pecan pie (without the pecans), just enough for a lick, to keep with the Thanksgiving tradition of sharing our pie with him.

By the time we arrived at the hospital, Shayru was passive, a complete one-eighty from his usual personality. Mohit wanted the vet to use whatever means and interventions necessary to save Shayru. The vet was very attentive and said that Shayru needed gallbladder surgery. We agreed and left Shayru at Angell in preparation for his surgery the next day. We returned home in sad spirits.

The day after Thanksgiving, Shayru had survived the surgery and was recovering in his ICU cage, wrapped up in a Bair Hugger blanket to keep him warm. His condition, though, was still deteriorating: he was in liver failure. The vet put a feeding tube into Shayru, and we all hoped he would bounce back.

On November 28, we visited Shayru again. Thanksgiving break was over, and Mohit needed to go back to Columbia. He said goodbye to Shayru with a heavy heart. He had wanted to take Shayru back with him to New York, as we were planning to go to India, but Shayru was in no condition.

On November 29, Shayru developed Disseminated Intravascular Coagulation, or in other words, internal bleeding. Nothing else could be done; he needed to be put to sleep. I finished my day at work, and then Raj and I called Mohit. He was devastated. Shayru was like a brother to him. Before any decision was made, Mohit first wanted to talk to the vet himself, to make sure all other options had been exhausted.

Finally, we knew we could not put it off any longer. Raj and I went to Angell to say our last goodbye to Shayru. His final look was so endearing. Raj and I were both at his side when he was injected, and within seconds, he was asleep forever.

Shayru's death reminded me of the time when my colleague Toni, a nurse, was crying on the phone and telling me about the death of her son's dog. I could not identify with her then, but after losing Shayru, I had much greater empathy and understanding.

Raj, Mohit, and I were all at a loss. Shayru was not just a dog. He was Shayru. He was such an important member of our family that I would often mix up his name and Mohit's.

But Raj and I also knew that Mohit's loss was greater than ours. Shayru was everything to him, and he was having to mourn Shayru's death all by himself at Columbia. Mohit was so distressed by it that he wanted to postpone his exams. It took a lot of persuading to keep him on schedule. Mohit wanted Shayru cremated according to our Hindu religion, and we requested that his ashes be returned to us.

Like Mohit, Chaeji also had to mourn Shayru's death alone. She was in Ahmedabad by herself, crying on the phone. Shayru was an exceptional personality. You could not ignore him; he forced you to give him attention. He was like a child who never grew up, and like a child, he gave us all unconditional love.

I need to confess that I feel guilty about Shayru's death. After Shayru got sick, I looked at his prescription of antibiotic pills and was shocked to see that they were for a dog ten times his weight, and he had been taking them for ten days! Those pills were the cause of his suffering and death, and I felt guilty for not checking the prescription myself, for trusting the vet.

After Shayru passed away, Raj and I brought the bottle of pills to the vet who had prescribed them. He apologized for the accident. Now, more than ever, we were distraught and disturbed by Shayru's death. He had not died of natural causes; it could have been prevented.

The vet had been negligent. There was nothing we could do about that. Now the question was, *Do we tell Mohit?* We still have not told him, and I am living with the guilt of not only the cause of Shayru's death but also not sharing it with Mohit. I wish I could ask Shayru for advice on how to handle this. The family still talks about him all the time, and we admire his photographs, remembering his handsome looks and big heart.

Even in his death, Shayru planned his life for our convenience. He passed away on November 29, and Raj and I were not leaving for Delhi until December 14. He had made it easy on us, but it was sad when I had to cancel his reservation at the new luxury kennel.

Our trip to India was uneventful, and when we got back to Boston, Shayru's ashes had arrived in the mail. Mohit came home at Christmas break and said a prayer as he sprinkled the ashes under the trees in our backyard, Shayru's favorite spot.

As always, life marched ever onward. With some worrying and fuss, the world welcomed in a new millennium in the year 2000. We joined family and friends for a special celebration, and then Mohit returned to Columbia and slowly started the healing process after losing Shayru. He agreed that postponing his exams would not have been a good idea. Together we kept Shayru's memory alive, reminiscing about his       games, tricks, and funny ways.

My work was still going smoothly after the merger. It was tough driving through the snow at six in the morning—not my favorite pastime—but, over the years, I had gotten used to it. I was still on the executive committee, with some administrative responsibilities, but many fewer than before. I enjoyed having more time for myself, my family, and my friends.

In the summer of 2000, Mohit decided to take a summer associate job in New York. He was still debating whether to take a permanent job in either New York or Boston after graduation. He was excelling at school, his grades were excellent, and he was lucky to have options. No matter his decision, Raj and I simply wanted him to be happy.

Mohit still had no girlfriend, though. Raj had offered his assistance to come and review eligible students at Columbia. The offer was denied. Again, just like Mohit's professional choices, we had no expectations or conditions on his life partner, so long as he was happy.

Some of our friends' kids were starting to get married, and the summer went by quickly with social engagements. Chaeji was visiting for quite a while, too, and she was keen on seeing Mohit married; it was one of her dreams. She was a practical and modern-thinking woman, and she frequently spoke to Mohit about marriage, giving him carte blanche support for whichever girl he chose.

In December 2000, a daughter of one of our Indian friends in our neighborhood whom Mohit had known since childhood was getting married in Delhi. The wedding was going to be huge, and fifty of us from Boston would be attending.

We all had a great time. The wedding was held outdoors, complete with marquees, fireplaces, and gourmet food; the weather was excellent. Our American friends were infatuated with all the singing, dancing, and camel and elephant rides.

After a fun, memorable vacation, we returned to Boston in January at the start of the New Year, 2001. Mohit went back to Columbia, and he had decided that, after finishing up his associate job in New York, he'd take a full-time position at Ropes & Gray in Boston after graduating in May. Raj and I were thrilled. It was a dream come true for all of us.

Graduation finally came, and we went to Columbia to participate in the two-day celebration. The weather was in our favor, and the campus was very impressive. The two days were full of smiling, picture-taking, and meeting classmates and their families.

This time around, after some persuasion, Raj and I convinced Mohit to celebrate with his own graduation party on May 22. We suggested the venue be at a nice hotel, but Mohit said, "No"— only in my own backyard, and no tent." So be it.

Since he wanted it outside, we had to limit the guest list in case of inclement weather, but luckily, the weather held up, and it didn't start drizzling until after the party.

The atmosphere was fun and festive, with a group of neighbors, who had watched Mohit grow up and were important to him, as well as colleagues and friends from work, and family members. Most important of all, Chaeji was there. Her presence was special to all of us. She had flown in from India accompanied by Ujwala (the niece she and Bauji had adopted) and Ujwala's son. Chaeji had always enjoyed social gatherings and being in the company of friends, and we all knew that Bauji was looking down from heaven, too, smiling and showering us with blessings.

Next for Mohit was the Bar Exam. He had to take the New York Bar Exam in Albany and then, the very next day, the Massachusetts Bar Exam in Boston. Always the dutiful father, Raj drove Mohit. It was a tense two days, but Mohit passed them both.

We attended Mohit's swearing-in ceremony at the majestic Faneuil Hall, appropriately nicknamed "the Cradle of Liberty." With all the other lawyers' grandparents in attendance, Raj and I couldn't help but think how proud Bauji would have been and how much it would have meant to him to be there. He would have happily flown across the world, especially since education had been a bedrock foundation for him.

During the ceremony, I got an indescribably special feeling that Bauji truly was in our presence within that great Hall, soaking in the grandeur of it all. I got very emotional and thought back on all the times during my growing-up years that Bauji had played a pivotal role in my life. I was lucky to have had him as a father.

# Chapter Twenty-Four

*The rest of the summer* went by quickly. Mohit rented a luxury apartment in the Back Bay neighborhood and was ready to start his job. His first day of work was September 10, 2001. The office was a familiar setting, since he had done his associateship there in 1999, but now he had a higher status.

On September 11, 2001, I gave anesthesia to two patients for their C-sections and finished up around 9:30 a.m. As I was returning to the OR, I walked past the doctors' lounge and saw everyone's eyes glued to the TV. The Twin Towers had been hit. The horror was unfolding right in front of us. I can only hope I will never witness anything like that ever again.

Like everyone else in that moment, I wanted to contact loved ones. I tried calling Raj, no luck. Then I tried calling Mohit, again nothing. It was only Mohit's second day at his job, and I was worried about him. I wished I could gather up my little family and be together for moral support, but my patients still needed me. I went back to work, trying to focus my distracted mind. The rest of the day went by in mental turmoil, not knowing where Raj and Mohit were and whether or not they were safe.

Finally at the end of the day, I was able to get in touch with Mohit. His entire office had been ordered to evacuate immediately. There was utter confusion as people rushed down the steps, afraid to use the elevator. Mohit rode the subway and was sandwiched between hundreds of other people who were evacuating, too. He had never experienced such panicked horror before, and he was relieved to safely arrive at his apartment.

We all did the only thing we could do, which was console everyone around us, at home and at work. No words were sufficient to convey our sorrow to the innocent people and their loved ones who were simply at the wrong place at the wrong time. The tragedy was made all the more unbearable by the fact that the hijacked plane which flew into the South Tower originated from Boston's Logan Airport.

Every year on September 11, in commemoration of the tragic events, three thousand American flags—one for each life lost—are placed on the Weston Town Green. When I drive by it, the sad memories wash over me. For all of us in the U.S., we could never forget; September 11 left permanent scars.

Life moved on, though, as Americans found ways to help and heal the nation. Mohit was busy at work but still had no girlfriend. Raj and I were waiting to hear any news on that front.

We were enjoying our house in Falmouth, sharing it with friends from all over the world, including Rick and Veena, my classmate from medical school and her husband. They had come to visit us from the UK, and Rick gave Raj some boating lessons. Surprisingly, Chaeji enjoyed boating, too, and whenever relatives were in town, she'd insist on bringing them to the Falmouth house. She also liked visiting Provincetown, which is at the northern tip of Cape Cod.

We welcomed in the New Year, 2002, and with it came more hospital politics. I tried to excuse myself from them as much as possible, as I was enjoying my work and my social life. Around this time, the malpractice suit was settled. I can usually compartmentalize the frustrating, sad experience, but the shadow of it never completely leaves me. I could never have dreamt that I would be sued for saving a newborn's life after providing critical, appropriate care. Still, though, I continued practicing medicine with the same intensity and attention, even though I knew it could happen to me again due to someone else's negligence. As an anesthesiologist, I worked on teams with surgeons, ob-gyns, and other specialty doctors, and if they fell short, I could be at risk as well. After going through a malpractice suit, you never get over that fear.

In the summer of 2002, Raj and I took a short trip to Barcelona with my sister Varsha. We enjoyed learning more about Barcelona's rich Roman history, and we also visited the Roman Catholic's Sagrada Basilica, which was started in 1882 but is still not completed today. It is estimated it will be completed in the year 2030.

The rest of the year flew by, and we cruised into 2003. Chaeji was still alternating between Ahmedabad and the U.S., but her health was declining, and she was unhappy. Fortunately, when she stayed with us, she had a traveling companion with her, Arg, whom Varsha had hired to help Chaeji from Ahmedabad. Chaeji had a sweet tooth, but she also had diabetes, so Arg's challenge was to keep Chaeji's desserts in check. When Chaeji demanded more, Arg refused, saying she was only following Varsha's orders. Chaeji replied, "I am paying your salary, not Varsha." Arg had a silent chuckle over this (in fact, we all did).

I tried my best to keep Chaeji happy. Inviting my friends to tea was one of her favorite pastimes. She also did a lot of reading, especially religious books, and she started to do some writing on Hindu verses. She gave them to Raj to print, with the hope of distributing them among the family.

In 2004, I was still working hard at MetroWest. My hours were long and taxing, but the appreciation I got in return for being an excellent anesthesiologist made up for them.

Then in 2005, we added some new staff to the department, a couple of nice, young male and female anesthesiologists. They were a fun bunch who enjoyed a little gossip and entertainment, and I had a wonderful time working with them.

In September of 2005, I turned sixty-five and decided I'd like to ease back a bit on my demanding schedule. Night calls in particular were exhausting, so I reduced my hours to part-time with no night calls. I was still enjoying my work, but now I also got to spend my evenings at home.

The following year, in December 2006, Chaeji said she wanted to return to Ahmedabad for good; it was difficult for her to go back and forth between India and the U.S., and she wanted to be in her own house. We all understood the difficulty of her situation and had empathy for her.

Varsha accompanied Chaeji to Ahmedabad. We arranged staff to be at her house for alternating night and day shifts, and my siblings and I worked out a schedule to visit her in rotation. It wasn't the best solution to have Chaeji so far away, but it was what she wanted, and we were glad we could fulfill her wishes.

On January 11, 2007, we celebrated Mohit's birthday, and it turned out to be an extra-special celebration. After dinner, he broke the news that he was dating a nice girl. Raj and I were overjoyed and, of course, wanted to meet her as soon as possible. Our excitement was uncontainable, and Mohit knew it.

A few days later, Mohit brought Payal around. She was as excited to meet us as we were to meet her. The introduction was warm, and we immediately had a mutual fondness.

Raj and I were so happy for Mohit. Our only regret was that Chaeji had not had a chance to meet Payal before flying to Ahmedabad for the last time. Chaeji had been waiting impatiently for this wonderful news.

In February, my sister Nirmal and her husband, VK, visited Chaeji. Then in March, I visited Chaeji for two weeks, and my sister Veena was scheduled to come after me. Chaeji and I had a nice time, and we visited her favorite temple together. Chaeji had also started reading *TIME* magazine and kept me updated on all the news. Chachaji's family, including his daughters, frequently stopped by, and Ujwala, Chaeji's niece, came every day and ran errands for her, as she lived one mile away.

We were lucky that Chaeji was ambulatory and independent enough to live on her own with a 24-hour attendant, but I still worried about her, especially since she refused staff help at night. I left Ahmedabad with a heavy heart, not knowing how she would fare or what the future would bring. Back in Boston, my thoughts were constantly divided between my life here and Chaeji in India. I spoke frequently with Chaeji over the phone, and she seemed to be doing fine.

Then on June 1, I received some disturbing news: Chaeji had suffered a heart attack and was in the hospital. I immediately flew to Ahmedabad and visited her in the ICU of an expensive private hospital. She was in critical condition and sedated, with assisted breathing.

I was spending most of my time next to her bed. When I reviewed her medical records, I was disturbed to see multiple specialty consultations that were completely unnecessary for her situation. There was only one reason for them: greed. All the specialists simply showed up and signed their names in the register so they could be billed. Many unnecessary invasive tests had also been ordered. More greed. They were trying to squeeze as much money out of Chaeji as possible before she died. It was gross malpractice. They had no conscience; their only goal was money, with no thought whatsoever for the care of the patient. They were violating the Hippocratic Oath: *First do no harm.* I was distraught.

Even though I was a doctor myself, I was at the mercy of these doctors to keep Chaeji comfortable. She had now developed pneumonia, and her cardiac status had been compromised. She was on a course that would be very difficult, if not impossible, to reverse.

On June 8 at 10 a.m., Chachaji, Varsha, Auntyji, and I considered all sides of the situation and, in the end, unanimously agreed to take Chaeji home for her final few hours. As soon as we informed the doctors of our decision, the nurses abandoned their care of Chaeji.

Even though our hospital account already had a surplus, all bills still had to paid before discharge, so Varsha had to wait in line for clearance. With the nurses now gone, I monitored Chaeji's vital signs, increased the medicine in her IV drip, maintained her blood pressure, and adjusted her oxygen saturation. I was doing everything I could to extend what little time we had left together. The whole time I talked to Chaeji, hoping she could hear me, and reassured her that she was going home. I knew that she was facing death, and I prayed to God that He grant her peace in these last few moments by allowing her to die in her own bed.

Dying in her own home had been Chaeji's wish, and we desperately wanted to see it through, but the hospital's politics and greed were delaying the arrival of the ambulance and oxygen tank. We didn't know if Chaeji could hold on much longer. I felt so helpless, and as a doctor, I was glad I was not part of this underhanded hospital.

Finally, we surmounted all the obstacles, and Chaeji was in the ambulance, monitored and with an oxygen tank. Her home was only three miles away, but the drive felt like an eternity. On our arrival, Auntyji and the rest of the family at home were ready for us.

We transported Chaeji into her own bed, and we all had a sweet but ephemeral moment of satisfaction. Only a few minutes later, Chaeji passed away peacefully, surrounded by family, and we even had enough time to move her onto the floor, according to Hindu ritual. All her wishes had been fulfilled.

My only regret was that Raj could not make it in time; he was on his way. Earlier I had thought Chaeji would improve, so he had waited to leave. Raj and Chaeji had a strong connection, son-in-law to mother-in-law, and Raj has many wonderful memories of her.

The funeral was the next day. For her final journey, Chaeji was dressed in a beautiful saree, covered in red roses, with garlands draped around her neck. She had made it clear to us that she wanted a traditional cremation with wood, not an electric crematorium. Bauji had not planned his final days, and when those days did come, he did not have time to express his last wishes, so we were glad we could at least honor Chaeji's. Varsha and I, along with family and friends, attended the cremation, giving us one final chance to say our goodbyes to Chaeji.

Raj arrived in time for *chautha*, the important fourth-day ceremony, and then Chachaji, Varsha, Nirmal, Raj, and I went to Haridwar for the final ritual of submerging Chaeji's ashes in the Ganges River. We hoped she and Bauji had found each other and were together again. Our sadness was deep, and yet, fueled by our faith and the support of family and friends, we were able to move on.

We returned to Chaeji's house; the place felt bare without her, but at the same time, it was also full of happy memories. Looking into her now-empty bedroom brought tears to my eyes.

A few days later, Raj and I left for Boston. Being able to travel together made it a little easier to cope with our grief. At home, we spent a day having friends stop by and sharing fond memories of Chaeji. She was loved by my friends, and she treated many of them like her own daughters, always kidding that she had adopted new daughters as time went by.

Chaeji was different from Bauji in that she was humble and practical rather than diplomatic. Their personalities complemented each other. Chaeji was also a true erudite scholar of Hindi and the sacred Hindu books of Ramayana and Gita. I was privileged to be Bauji and Chaeji's child and am grateful for all the wonderful things in my life that I owe to them.

With Chaeji and Bauji both gone, I felt empty. All my siblings and I had been clinging to Chaeji as our last and only pillar holding up the family. She gave us a purpose every day to connect with each other. Losing her made me think of everyone else I had lost who had brought meaning into my life and helped me navigate troubled waters: Baji, Bapaji, Mataji, Pitaji, and Bauji. They were lost to time, but thankfully, they were still alive in my memory. I was lucky to have had them guiding me, molding me into who I am today. Their teachings and values were unparalleled in enriching my life.

By the time we arrived in Boston, I was exhausted by loss and grief. My mind felt like it had been shattered into a thousand

pieces. Sometimes the best treatment for grief is throwing yourself back into work, which I did with fervor. Luckily, I found my
work fulfilling and rewarding.

By July 2007, Mohit and his girlfriend, Payal, had become
quite serious, and their relationship brought great happiness to
all of us. We were all looking forward to the exciting events on
the horizon. Every get-together with Payal was full of joy. Like
Bauji and Chaeji, Payal complemented Mohit. She was easygoing
and fun, while Mohit was serious and an obsessive-compulsive
perfectionist. Raj's and my only desire was for them to be happy
together, and so far, it seemed like our wish would come true.
We hoped and prayed for their future.

In the fall, we celebrated Diwali at home; it was a low-key
celebration with Mohit and Payal. Chaeji was still constantly in
my thoughts.

Around this time, we finally met Payal's parents at their home.
They were nice people and as excited as us about the progression
of Mohit and Payal's relationship. Raj and I kept asking Mohit
when he was going to propose, but he wouldn't give an answer.
He didn't want to rush anything. We knew Payal was anxiously
waiting to say "Yes," but as parents, we had our limitations and
kept quiet.

Finally in December 2007, Mohit announced he was ready to
propose. Raj, Mohit, and I went ring-hunting together; we were
so excited. I insisted that Mohit indulge Payal with a beautiful
ring, perfectly balanced in size and sparkle. She deserved to have
wonderful, lifelong memories of her engagement.

After some searching, we found the perfect one. To safeguard
the ring, I deposited it in our safe-deposit box at the bank; Mohit
would have to give two days' notice to retrieve it. We were ready
and awaiting the perfect moment.

All the while, I was dreaming of how I could be the best mother-in-law to Payal. I did not want to be like Alka—greedily hunting for her son's bride with the sole requirement being money. Mohit was our only son—our heart of hearts, the light of our universe. Raj and I had no constraints on whom he chose. We were excited for his future, and it was extremely important to us that we support him in this next chapter and that we show our unconditional love for the girl he loved. I wanted Payal to create only happy memories with her new family; I did not want her to ever have to face what I had to.

The New Year, 2008, brought Raj and I even more excitement and happiness as we awaited Mohit's proposal. On January 11, we celebrated Mohit's birthday, and on January 19, Raj and I had a nice evening celebrating our wedding anniversary. Then finally, Mohit was ready to propose. On the evening of Saturday, January 26, Mohit surprised Payal with the ring while standing on the bridge of the Boston Public Garden. She was thrilled.

The next day Mohit and Payal came over to the house, and we all, including her parents, celebrated with champagne. Mohit and Payal replayed the details of the evening, and we were so happy for them. Payal said she had been running out of patience: Diwali went by, then New Year's, then Mohit's birthday, and still no ring. At last her wish came true, and she had a beautiful diamond on her finger.

Raj and I were also glad that Payal had a sister and brother, so Mohit would have an extended family. For us, family unity and strength were paramount.

Immediately after the celebration, I called Bhen in India, now the eldest in the family, to share the happy news. I could hear the excitement in her voice from thousands of miles away. Next I called Chachaji and Auntyji, followed by the rest of the family in the U.S., and then then I sent out an e-mail to all our friends, and finally, I shared the good news with everyone at work. The next couple of days were overwhelming with the deluge of excited, happy responses.

Now it was time for my ultimate project: helping Mohit and Payal plan their dream Indian wedding. The date was set for July 18, 2009. It needed to be an event of the highest magnitude, worth remembering for a lifetime, and I had a million ideas bouncing around in my head. I invested every spare second into planning; I was a part-time anesthesiologist and a part-time wedding planner. During this time, I often recalled my own wedding and all the exhaustive work Bauji put into it.

Throughout the planning, summer was in full bloom, and now that I was working part-time at the hospital, I could actually stop and enjoy nature's beauty. The weeping cherry in the backyard was bursting with red buds, and the kousa dogwoods had their beautiful white flowers; surrounding them were evergreens and different varieties of azaleas and rhododendrons. It was like we had our own miniature botanical garden.

We also enjoyed the wildlife, especially all the beautiful birds—robins, bluejays, highly intelligent and loud, and many other varieties. Raj had even installed a couple of birdfeeders, but he was frustrated with the conniving squirrels that were storming the feeders and devouring all the food. He tried several innovative solutions, but every time the squirrels outmaneuvered him.

Raj, Mohit, Payal, and I planned a two-week trip to Delhi for wedding shopping. We all arrived together but returned separately. Raj and I felt like we were on a wild roller coaster, trying to complete everything on our list.

One of our biggest priorities was designing and ordering the wedding invitations. Every detail needed our complete attention. We decided on the sacred symbols of Om (god of good luck) and

Ganesha (god of beginnings and remover of obstacles) combined in white and gold with Swarovski crystals. It was absolutely beautiful—very classy without being gaudy—and everybody approved. Mission accomplished.

We also needed festive clothes for all the different wedding functions. I was planning on buying some new sarees but also wearing some I already owned that had deep meaning. Also, Raj and Mohit needed custom-made suits, *achkans* (long, festive jackets), *churidars* (tight, pajama-like pants), and *dupattas* (scarves).

Lastly, we shopped for wedding favors and decided on Ganesha sterling silver ring holders. In the end, we were all happy with the results.

Once back in Boston, our next priority was deciding on the venue. By Indian standards, we were having a small wedding with only two hundred fifty guests. Raj and I had our preferences on location, and we hoped Mohit and Payal would agree. After exploring different hotels in the greater Boston area, we all decided on the Seaport Hotel. It perfectly fit our vision for the wedding.

Our out-of-town guests would stay at the Hyatt Regency Hotel, and a shuttle would bring them to our house. We also chose the Westin Hotel for the site of *sangeet*, a celebration hosted by the groom's family before a Hindu wedding.

With the locations and timetable set for the wedding, Raj now had a full-time job (even though he had retired from his actual job) following up on the invitation details and keeping track of all the guests' replies.

Next was menu planning. Mohit and Payal along with her parents taste-tested different caterers. There were many shared decisions to be made, and we were lucky to be working with such agreeable, cooperative people. It was so nice not to have the additional stress of conflicts of interest.

Time flew by. In April, Mohit and Payal's wedding invitations were mailed out, and in June, we tallied up the final count of out-of-town guests. We were delighted to hear that Chachaji and Auntyji were attending. Auntyji's presence meant a lot to Mohit, as she was a great believer in rituals, mantras, and traditions, unlike Chaeji, who had been more practical. Mohit respected Auntyji and shared her deep faith. She was one of Mohit's greatest guiding forces and moral supports. Also attending were three of my classmates from medical school as well as friends from Atlanta and New York, and family from all over the U.S. and the UK, including Raj's cousin Lataa and her husband.

But I still had a lot on my plate. With the wedding date closing in, I was fueled by inexhaustible energy. I reviewed and revised every tiny wedding detail, even after coming home from a taxing day at the hospital. Part of my energy I owed to the sweet, poignant memories of my own wedding and all the hard work Bauji had put into it. He had overseen every minutiae with unsurpassable passion, and I missed him.

Before long, it was July, and the wedding was upon us. We were all praying for good weather, and our prayers were answered. The start of the festivities was at noon on July 16 with the Ganesha *puja* (prayer) service, followed by a vegetarian lunch. The service was held at our house with close family and friends, and the prayer was performed by a knowledgeable part-time priest. That evening, about fifty family members came over to the house for music and song; my cousin from Dallas got the rhythm going. Payal and her friends joined us, and this was the first time many of them would get to meet Payal.

The next day at noon, Payal's parents and family arrived for the *sagan* ceremony (the engagement ceremony), offering gifts and blessing Mohit. Afterward, we enjoyed a nice Thai lunch.

At 2 p.m., Raj's cousin Lataa as well as my siblings and I went to Payal's house for a ceremony of gift-giving to her family. We needed to fit many important ceremonies into a short amount of time.

That evening, starting at 7 p.m., we had our big *sangeet* bash at the Westin Hotel, with one hundred eighty guests, many of whom were adorned in henna and bangles. Payal was a good painter, and she had one of her paintings on display. The wedding planner had decorated the reception hall beautifully. It was a night full of gourmet good, festive music, and a lot of dancing. Payal was an excellent dancer and had nonstop energy the whole night; Mohit was no match for her, but still, everyone had fun. Chachaji and Auntyji were good sports and joined in the dancing, and we even managed to hire a group of local college students to surprise everyone by performing the Bhangra, the most popular Punjabi folk dance.

We ended the party at 10 p.m. so that everyone would be ready for the wedding the next day. Before leaving, all the guests received a beautifully decorated red-and-gold gift box of *laddoos* (Indian sweets) catered from New York.

Finally the big day came, July 18. Luxury buses transported the guests from the Hyatt to the Seaport Hotel. Raj, Mohit, and I had arrived early to make sure everything was ready. The plan was to gather all the guests at the convention center, four hundred yards from the hotel, and come in a procession to the wedding venue. Golf carts for transport were provided for the elderly.

Mohit and our immediate family members were wearing *pagris* (turbans), which we had bought in India on our shopping trip. Mohit's *pagri* was a majestic red and gold, and the family members' *pagris* were adorned with long *dupattas* (scarves).

To start the procession, Auntyji performed a blessing *puja*, then my brother helped Mohit mount a horse decorated in festive accessories. The *baraat* (groom's party) made its way to the Seaport Hotel, accompanied by drums and music and everyone singing and dancing. The short walk was beautiful with a view of the Boston Harbor over a pedestrian-only bridge with the magnificent backdrop of the Boston skyline. This route was what had convinced us that the Seaport was the perfect venue for the wedding. Everyone was filled with joy, and all our friends from the U.S. were mesmerized by the scene and its ambience.

There was, however, one moment of anxiety that nearly put me into cardiac arrest. Under the beautiful dome, during the procession, the echo of the drums disturbed Mohit's horse, and it bolted, completely out of control. The crowd fell silent and I was dumbstruck. Fortunately, Mohit held on tight, kept his wits about him, and was able to rein the horse in. The image still sends shivers down my spine. God was protecting Mohit with all the divine blessings from his grandparents and Shayru. We resumed our singing and dancing, and we reached the hotel without further incident. Nothing is ever perfect, but this was close to a perfect celebration as we could ever hope to get.

We were greeted at the hotel by Payal's family and friends, and then Mohit and Payal exchanged garlands, and he said to her, "You don't know what I went through to get here." It was a very touching moment. Payal looked beautiful in her *lehnga* (wedding gown).

We proceeded to Seaport's grand ballroom, which had been beautifully decorated, complete with rose petals all along the path leading to the *mandap* (a pillared, covered altar), which was all white.

The forty-five minute wedding ceremony was in Sanskrit with English translation, and then everyone indulged in gourmet appetizers and bottomless drinks. After that came dinner, served on *thalis* (stainless steel plates) with four bowls on them, per Indian tradition. Music filled the air, people danced, there were intermittent, short speeches as well as a video on a big screen of old memories Payal and Mohit had selected; also, within twenty minutes, the video included footage from the wedding itself. All the guests were amazed by the quick turnaround and watched in amusement their participation in the ceremony.

Everything was perfect, but the most remarkable and memorable part for me was Mohit's short speech. He thanked everybody and gave a wonderful, warm tribute to his parents. He expressed the values he had absorbed from Raj and me, and he told us we didn't need to worry anymore; because of us, he could now navigate life on his own. His speech touched everyone's hearts, and for days afterward, family and friends called to express their appreciation for his words.

The wonderful evening came to an end with the cutting of the cake, and then the luxury bus brought the guests back to the Hyatt. Raj and I stayed at the Seaport Hotel overnight and left the next day for home. Then later that morning, we hosted a brunch with family to welcome Payal into our fold. Under Auntyji's guidance, we received the married couple into the family with the *aarti* (a Hindu prayer). The perfect weather added to the festive atmosphere.

Following lunch, the relatives left, and Raj, Mohit, Payal, and I were alone after four days of nonstop festivities. Together we recollected the wedding day, and Mohit said, "All the planning for months was over in one evening. And never mind all the tasting we did; we don't even know what we ate." So true. But it had been a grand celebration, appreciated by everyone and awe-inspiring to our non-Indian friends. In the days following, we received an overwhelming number of phone calls from guests expressing gratitude and endless compliments.

Then Raj and I said goodbye to Payal and Mohit, as, the next day, they were leaving for their honeymoon to Greece and Paris. We couldn't have been happier for them. Our dream had materialized: Mohit was married, we had stepped into a new chapter in our lives, and I was determined to be the best mother-in-law in the world.

Now with the wedding over, Raj and I settled back into regular life. On September 16, Raj had surgery for total knee replacement, just another part of getting old. All went well, and Mohit and Payal, who were back in town, were a big moral support.

Then, in October 2009, we got a surprise call from Darshan—the sleeping giant had awoken. The court had ordered him to sell the house in the suburbs as well as the business at 182 Tilak Bazaar as no amicable division was practical. He had already tried unsuccessfully to sell them on his own with fake documents (which was how he had managed to illegally sell eight other properties in the past). Darshan was not interested in negotiating with us on the deal, because he had found some buyers offering him a giant illegal share under the table. Darshan had tried to keep this fact hidden, but Raj and I were fully aware of the ugly situation. On the other hand, Raj and I did not want to entangle ourselves again in a bitter, caustic relationship with Darshan, so we agreed to move forward with the deal.

Throughout the winter, Raj and I made several trips to India to complete paperwork for selling the properties. This was an ordeal as Darshan tired to prolong the process so that we might get frustrated and quit. Raj and I always traveled together now, as I didn't trust Raj to be as cautious as he needed to be while negotiating the crazy and overcrowded streets of Delhi; he had the reputation of taking unnecessary risks.

Between our trips, we were enjoying the beautiful snow in our backyard and all the winter wildlife. The deer population in particular had multiplied, and they were now bringing all their extended-family members to party at our place. While they made for a lovely greeting card, they had also developed an attitude problem and had become more and more aggressive, destroying all our mature shrubs. Even when we tried to chase them off, they always returned.

In January 2010, the closing documents for the properties were ready to sign, so Raj and I flew to Delhi one last time, finally ending a difficult seventeen-year chapter in our lives since Pitaji's death. We could never have dreamt that this ordeal would have been drawn out for so long.

Raj and I decided to plan a vacation into the trip by visiting Goa on the western coast of India for four days. It was a two-hour flight from Delhi, and we stayed at a seaside resort with beautiful sandy beaches. We had always wanted to visit this area, and it was beautiful.

Even though Goa is part of India, it felt like we were in a different world. It is full of ancient history, including a great deal of Portuguese influence, as it was a Portuguese colony until 1961. It also has many different places of worship, including a Jewish synagogue and the UNESCO World Heritage Site the Basilica of Bom Jesus ("good/holy Jesus"), which is a big tourist draw.

Raj and I learned a great deal while touring Goa's spice gardens, and we went for a drive on the hilltop made famous by the romantic legends of Dona Paula.

The Goa area had also become very fashionable and affluent, and chartered flights from all across the Middle East, Europe, and even Afghanistan brought patients who wanted to combine cosmetic surgery with a luxury vacation. Doctors from Bombay and Delhi flew over regularly to operate. I guess the world of the rich has no constraints.

After our brief vacation, Raj and I returned to Boston, and I got back into my regular work schedule, waking up at 5 a.m. in the pitch dark and commuting through snow and black ice to the hospital. Every year I became more and more leery of driving in Boston's winters; whenever I heard about bad car accidents, I worried that I'd be next. Raj and Mohit continually brought up the idea of retirement, urging me to enjoy a little leisure.

Even though I loved my work, I understood their reasoning. If I'd had my own office practice, I could have dictated my own schedule and patient load; I would have been in control, and I would have kept working for as long as my health would allow. As it was, though, my specialty was dependent on working with others, and moreover, it was high risk and demanding.

I began weighing the pros and cons of retiring versus continuing to practice. It was like I was trying to solve a difficult puzzle in my mind. I thought about my achievements at work, the many rewarding experiences I'd had saving lives, the joy it had brought me, and the personal growth I'd gone through as a result.

After a lot of soul searching, I decided it was time to retire. I had a long list of unfinished projects as well as many broken New Year's resolutions that I would finally be able to work on. I often hear stories of people who retire too late and don't have enough time to enjoy their health and life after work. I did not want to be one of those people. So, in April 2010, I spoke with Raj, and then I went to work and filled out the official papers (even though I was retiring, I'd keep my staff privileges, in case the hospital needed me in the future).

It was a difficult decision, but it was the right one. I'd had a wonderfully rewarding career that required many big decisions, and I was lucky to have gotten the most important ones right. I also knew I was very lucky to find my way to the U.S., truly the land of opportunity. I had worked hard and pushed myself to the limits. A few times, I'd had to change course in order to avoid volatile situations, but, each time, I did so with optimism and persistence, and only after exhaustively vetting the options.

For forty-six years, I had devoted myself to work. Other than a three-month maternity leave, I had never taken more than three weeks off for vacation. In short, as difficult as the decision was, I was ready to retire.

My last day of work was scheduled for June 30, so I had the rest of the summer to do with as I pleased. I immediately started writing a To Do List, which got longer and longer. A hospital colleague and good friend of mine at LMH, Dr. Sabin from Pulmonology, introduced me to the Massachusetts Medical Society's Committee on Senior Volunteer Physicians, and I was voted to serve on it. I also decided to volunteer at MetroWest's free medical clinic on Tuesday evenings.

The free clinic was staffed by volunteers from many different medical backgrounds, including interpreters and social workers, all working in unity for a noble cause. I enjoyed giving of my time and expertise. It was also an eye-opener for me to see both young and old patients whose health was suffering because they had lost their medical insurance in the 2008 economic crash. These people weren't from some remote rural area; they were living right in my backyard, in affluent residential suburbs of Boston. It made me realize how quickly life can turn on you, and I was grateful for the opportunity to help them in whatever way I could.

Soon enough it was June 30, my last day at work. I went to both MetroWest hospitals to say goodbye to my colleagues and friends; it was a bittersweet day. Even though I was not leaving town and we would still see each other at conferences and social occasions, we all knew it would be different. I felt empty, emotionally drained.

When I got home, Raj was waiting for me, and we celebrated that evening with a bottle of champagne. As we enjoyed our drink together, my feeling of emptiness was replaced by an epiphany that the future would be wonderful, a chance for me to dance to the beat of a new drum.

So, the first thing I did was ditch my alarm clock. No more waking up at five in the morning. Even today, the joy of sleeping in has not diminished at all.

# Chapter Twenty-Five

As always, I leaned on Bapaji's teachings and values to guide me in retirement. There were, though, still some growing pains at the beginning, especially for a workaholic like me. For one, it was difficult for me to slow down, and I felt guilty for enjoying too much, but eventually I adjusted. My goal was to age with a positive attitude, and I drew up future plans that would give me vitality and purpose. I had many dreams, including writing; I had always wanted to share my life experiences and was hoping to find the right person to give me direction in getting them down. My first immediate plan, though, was to go on a Mediterranean cruise with Raj.

We left in September and vacationed on a ship of the utmost luxury. We started in Istanbul, the only city in the world on two continents, then we went to Ephesus, where we learned more about ancient Turkey; from there we stopped at different Greek islands, including Santorini, which was by far the most mesmerizingly beautiful; and our last stop was Athens, a city Raj and I had always wanted to see.

We loved our vacation, but we also loved coming home to Boston with its beautiful fall in full swing. Raj and I were enjoying every day of our retirement, doing the little things we had always wanted to do but had never had the time to before. We went to Cape Cod and then visited Martha's Vineyard, walked its cobblestone streets, and admired the well-known "Gingerbread Houses," where people actually lived and are available to rent; they started as a collection of old Methodist camp-meeting houses. And, of course, we enjoyed plenty of time in our own home in Falmouth, which itself felt like a miniature private resort. We loved sitting outside and watching the seagulls and ducks and swans float by.

I was also doing volunteer work, regularly helping at MetroWest's free clinics, where I had the opportunity to attend to people with many different needs.

We rang in the New Year, 2012, and my resolution this year was to go on a pilgrimage in India. I wanted to express appreciation and gratitude for all my dreams that had come true.

Raj and I went together, and our first stop was the Holy Shrine of Shri Mata Vaishnov Devi Ji, located at the Trikuta Mountains near Jammu in the state of Kashmir. It is the second-most-visited Hindu temple, after the Venkateswara Temple in Tirupati. Raj had been to this shrine several times before, but this would be my first.

Mohit was supposed to join us as well, but his flight had been canceled due to four inches of snow at London's Heathrow Airport. For us Bostonians, four inches of snow is nothing. Mohit tried his utmost best to join us, but he remained stranded and miserable in Boston. I promised him that I would return to the shrine with him whenever his schedule permitted, as I was now retired.

To get to the temple, Raj and I first flew into Jammu from Delhi, and then we took a two-hour cab ride to the hilly region of Katra. We stayed overnight in Katra and soaked in the beautiful mountain scenery and the funny antics of the red-faced monkeys. The next day, we took a helicopter ride to the top of the mountain where the temple was located. Back when Raj was younger, in the old days, he used to make the trek by foot. Out of the helicopter window we saw many people on ponies, winding their way up the switchbacks.

From the helicopter's drop-off point, it was another one mile to the shrine. We shared the rough path with ponies and men carrying people in chariots called *palkis*. We had to be constantly alert, making sure we didn't rub against the sweaty ponies or step in their pee or poop; plus we had to keep a sharp eye on the conniving monkeys that were waiting for the perfect moment to grab our belongings. But despite all this chaos, Raj said it was still an improvement from the past.

We finally made it to the shrine, but we had to wait in line to get thirty seconds in front of it. Luckily, it was a sunny day with a beautiful view of the valley, and we watched as people down the mountain made the several-hour hike dodging the falling rocks. Some say it's more rewarding if you do something the hard way, but Raj and I weren't young anymore, and our way *was* the hard way. In fact, we were lucky that Raj didn't have any complications from his recent knee surgery.

It was very satisfying to see the shrine in person, although we were sad that Mohit could not be with us. We returned to Katra by helicopter and rewarded ourselves with a nice Ayurvedic massage as a reward for completing the journey. The next day, we took a cab to the airport, flew back to Delhi, and flew from there to Boston.

Back home, winter was in full force. I was thoroughly enjoying my mornings without an alarm clock and not having to drive in dangerous weather. I was starting to get into the swing of retired life: I reached out to old friends and reminisced, and I spoke to my siblings over the phone more often. In the past, Raj had been the one with the social life; mine had consisted of "Hello" and "Goodnight," but now we were able to share in each other's daily activities.

Raj and I also joined a sports club. Mohit had been asking us to join one for a long time, but, before, I simply could not spare the time in my schedule between running around at work and running around at home. Back then, going to the gym on the weekends was sufficient; now, though, Raj and I were regulars. We enjoyed the challenge, both physically and mentally, and it was so motivating to be around such determined people, pushing themselves.

Then, in March, Mohit surprised me by suggesting we visit the Vaishnu Devi shrine that month, as he had some time off. Our original plan had been to go in October, and I wasn't sure if I was ready for another rustic adventure so soon, but I had promised Mohit I would go with him, and I wanted to keep my commitment. After a lot of brainwashing, I agreed to go for one week at the end of March.

On the upside, our trip coincided with Bhen's granddaughter's wedding in Delhi. Seeing Bhen was always a pilgrimage for me. She was warm and loving and full of spirit, even though she suffered from declining health. Her presence brought me joy and rekindled many sweet memories. She was Wonder Woman, with a smiling face and a sharp intellect.

When Mohit and I arrived in Delhi, the spring weather was perfect, and all across the city flowers were blooming. We stayed at the Mauyra Hotel, a beautiful five-star hotel with excellent service. The grounds were perfectly manicured and even had waterfalls. With so many amenities, we could have just stayed at the hotel and called it our vacation.

I had stayed at the Maurya before, but this was Mohit's first time, and he was very impressed. He indulged in the delicious breakfast, and, being a dedicated exerciser, he also enjoyed its workout facilities. He wore his Patriots shirt at the gym and met some tourists at the hotel who were from Boston—small world!

After a day in Delhi, we flew to Jammu, and from there we took a cab to Katra. Mohit had never seen so many monkeys in his life! We stayed in the same hotel in Katra, and then we left the next morning for a five-minute helicopter ride to the top of the mountain; from there, we walked the remaining one mile.

Since I had already been to the shrine, this was familiar territory for me, but Mohit needed my guidance to keep from stepping in the puddles of liquid and piles of solids. Luckily, we both made it to the shrine uneventfully.

Mohit and I did *darshan* (viewing the deity) and got the *prasad* (blessed food after worshipping), and then we turned back around for the one-mile trek to the helicopter. We were doing well navigating the rocky path and avoiding accidents when suddenly a red-faced monkey attacked Mohit's bag of *prasad*. Luckily, Mohit managed to save it by swinging the bag to me. What a relief! I did not want to think about the repercussions if the monkey had succeeded. Mohit probably would have said, "Let's go back for the *darshan* and get another *prasad*." For the rest of the hike, we both were on high alert, protecting our treasured cargo. Then it was a quick helicopter ride, another night at the hotel in Katra, and a drive back to Delhi. The trip had been a grand slam home run. I had passed the test and successfully completed the pilgrimage, twice.

The following evening in Delhi, we attended Bhen's grand-daughter's wedding. Chachaji and Auntyji had also come up from Ahmedabad. Bhen was absolutely thrilled to finally meet Mohit. He had a special place in her heart, and she never missed his birthday. Bhen's quiet strength and endurance mystified me, always caring for others and seeing to their comfort. She had wanted to meet Payal, too, but sadly, that never happened due to the distances and the circumstances.

For me, the wedding was a wonderful reunion with Bhen's in-laws and her family, some of whom I had not seen in years. Then it was time to say goodbye, and Mohit and I flew back to Boston. The trip had been short but successful, a time for mother and son to bond and create wonderful memories to reflect on for for years to come. I was so glad I had followed through on my commitment, especially while still in good health, and I was even glad we had gone in March instead of October, as it would have meant missing out on family.

It was spring in Boston, a season I look forward to every year with its beautiful buds blooming and birds chirping. Raj was still trying to keep the squirrels out of the birdfeeders, and still failing. He was also fighting a losing battle trying to protect our plants and shrubs from the deer.

We were staying busy outside of the house as well with some philanthropy. We visited a homeless shelter, which was educational for both of us, especially Raj. I was also attending the biweekly medical conferences at the hospital to stay connected with my colleagues and updated on the latest research. The conferences featured many accomplished speakers from the greater Boston area, who shared the latest innovations in medicine. The speakers all looked very young to me, but maybe that was because I was getting older. They reminded me of my early years as a doctor.

The short summer season rolled around. Raj and I wanted to make the best of it, so we drove up to Boothbay Harbor, Maine. Its botanical gardens were beautiful. Then we went to Acadia National Park for the second time after many years. Our two-day stay was refreshing and relaxing. We loved the breathtaking views along the winding road leading up to the 1,500-foot summit of Cadillac Mountain. It is the most beautiful place to watch the sunrise—the earliest place to watch the sunrise in the U.S. If it weren't so far of a drive, we'd visit much more often.

Back at home, I was juggling many projects, including developing my computer skills. Before I had retired, my secretary at the hospital typed up my minutes, but now I was on my own, and Raj was my teacher. While I practiced typing, I kept mental notes on my writing ideas, mulling over which ones would be best, and I continued looking for the right person to guide me.

In December 2012, the daughter of a very close college friend of Raj's was getting married in Delhi. This would be my third trip to India within a year, but I knew it would be a great time. Plus, I wanted to go on another pilgrimage, this time to the towns of my childhood, and I wanted Raj at my side.

The multi-day wedding affair was vibrant and full of joy. Most importantly, Raj got to spend time with his dear friend, Vinod, and his family. Despite not having seen each other for years, they reconnected instantly. Like all strong friendships, seeing Vinod both re-energized and soothed Raj. It was as good as therapy, bringing freshness and vitality back into his life. Although they had stayed in touch via e-mail, nothing beats seeing a friend in person.

Together, Raj and Vinod reminisced on the good old days. Their memories of college were full of humor and teenage indulgence. Now we were all older and aging gracefully.

Our next stop was Ahmedabad, where we rang in the New Year, 2013, and started our pilgrimage. The weather was perfect, sunny with temperatures from 50 to 75 degrees. Our first pilgrimage was to the seventeenth-century Hindu temple Shrinathji, twenty-five miles outside of Udaipur.

It was a six-hour drive from Ahmedabad to Udaipur. Udaipur is known as "the city of lakes." It is a very popular holiday destination and has a long history of royalty and palaces, including the Lake Palace, which sits on a four-acre island and looks like it's floating on water.

After spending the evening in Udaipur, we set out for Shrinathji, a one-hour drive. I had visited the temple as a kid, and I wanted to see it again with Raj. We did *darshan* and said our prayers, and then returned to Udaipur, where we enjoyed strolling around the colorful bazaars full of shops. We saw many *pichwai* paintings, which are intricate paintings of Lord Krishna, usually done on cloth; the paintings can be as large as two feet by four feet, or even larger. We were lucky to already own a beautifully framed, two feet by four feet *pichwai*. Dr. Ashraf and his lovely wife, Dr. Mary Ann, had given it to us. The Ashrafs had been gifted the painting from a dear Hindu friend, and they had hung it in their hallway. Imagine a religious Hindu painting in the entryway of a Muslim home. True friendship is about affection and respect, not religion.

From Udaipur we went to Mount Abu. My favorite childhood summer resort was here—an old palace that had been converted into a hotel. Raj and I revisited the famous Dilwara Jain Temples, known the world over for their intricate carved marble.

After that, our next pilgrimage was to the Ambaji Temple. Here again Raj and I offered our prayers and thank-yous, and then we drove the four hours back to Ahmedabad.

After resting for two days, we drove an hour to our final pilgrimage destination: the Lord Krishna temple Ranchhodraiji in Dakor. Raj and I said our prayers and then walked around the grounds, reminiscing about my childhood. According to Hindu mythology, I tried finding a herd of turtles in the water, but I didn't see anything; perhaps they had migrated to a faraway land. All Hindu temples have a mind-boggling number of tales intertwining religion with mythology.

Raj and I returned to Ahmedabad. We had completed our pilgrimage of gratitude, and I was euphoric. I no longer felt guilty; I had honored my commitment. Above all, I was filled with appreciation for the Divine and His intervention in helping us achieve our dreams.

Raj and I returned to Boston safely. The pilgrimage had been very rewarding, but I knew I would not be going on another one. It had been taxing physically, and I was only getting older.

By now, I had adapted to retired life and was an expert in the art of relaxation. I absolutely did not miss my alarm clock, and I enjoyed reading the newspaper as well as medical journals (although, like most people, I had a growing pile of unread ones). I was still hoping to start a writing project soon.

Spring came and went. Summer was short, as always, and then we were into the fall. In November 2013, I was at MetroWest attending my grand rounds, when the CMO (chief medical officer) pulled me aside and asked if I would return to work for two months, as they were short-staffed. I went home and discussed the proposition with Raj. It was only a two-month commitment, and we had no plans anyway, but it would mean driving in winter conditions at six in the morning.

After much deliberation, Raj and I decided that I would accept. One of the things on my life bucket list had been to travel to third-world countries and help children, but I had never had a chance to, and now it was not possible to leave Raj. So, we found a compromise: I would work these two months and donate my earnings to a charitable foundation for children. This would be very gratifying for me. Of course, Mohit was not thrilled by my driving in the winter, but at least I had a good reason for doing it.

When I went back to work, it was like I had never left. For me, nothing had changed; I still enjoyed my job and my colleagues. However, when I was driving to work early in the morning, I was still nervous about the icy roads. I'd be asking myself, *Why am I doing this to myself and my family?* But at least it was a calculated risk. I had made a commitment, and I was going to see it through.

My two months ended up turning into seven months due to hospital politics and a department changeover. I agreed to the extended schedule. This meant once again putting everything else in my life on the back burner, but I had no regrets.

My "second" retirement was scheduled for the same day as my first—June 30—but this time, I'd be leaving alongside many of my old colleagues, because a new department was being put into place. There was lots of anxiety and sadness among them, but I had been through this before. So when June 30 came, I happily bowed out. Unlike everyone else, I'd already had a taste of retired life, and it was addicting.

The second, and final, phase of my retirement began in July 2012. My growing pains were in the past; I had graduated with a Fine Arts Degree in Retirement and I was enjoying summer to the fullest. My life was focused, balanced, and full of happiness.

I was still working on my computer skills and had since become a fan of Google. But even now, my shelves are still packed with books that I haven't opened in a long time: the *World Books* set, *Encyclopedia Britannica, Webster's' Dictionary*, and my *Physicians' Desk Reference*. I could get rid of all my cookbooks and not miss them, because I have Google at my fingertips.

Mohit, always extraordinarily practical, suggested I give away my books because I don't use them anymore. I'm not a hoarder, but I still cling to them. My excuse is that they're part of my decorating scheme. A friend has offered to take my *World Books* whenever I'm ready to let them go, so at least I know they'll end up in a good home.

I used to stop by the hospital's library on the days I went for grand rounds after retiring. I had known the librarian for years, and it was a nice place to catch up on the *Wall Street Journal* and the *New York Times*. But then the librarian retired, and the library was shut down. I suppose with technology and the ability to read the news on your phone, the library had become a relic of the past. Who could have dreamt of this twenty years ago?

In September 2013, my next big retiree adventure was going on a cruise with Raj around Northern Europe. We visited Amsterdam, Copenhagen, St. Petersburg, Gdańsk, Stockholm, and Oslo. Ten days of wining and dining in the magic of a new world. Raj and I had a lot of fun spending time together and learning about the different cultures and histories. By now, I was able to enjoy R&R without guilt.

Back in Boston, I returned to my regular, balanced schedule. I still carried around my appointment book like it was my life support, even though Raj had tried to convince me that it was a thing of the past with the arrival of smartphones. I prefer, though, to hang on to it as a backup and second opinion. I'm not against new technology, but I am slow to adapt to it; every day I take another small step into its constantly evolving world. Meanwhile, I continued thinking about possible writing projects, hoping to find direction and someone to guide me.

Looking back on my life so far, I've grown a lot, but I know I still have a long ways to go. There is still so much to learn. I will never be a true erudite scholar, but as Aristotle said, "Well begun is half done." My goal is to continue growing in Bapaji's teachings of integrity and discipline. I could never completely emulate him, but I can at least follow in his footsteps.

I've been blessed with a good life, and I've been especially lucky to custom-tailor my retirement to continue pursuing my dreams. Looking to tomorrow, I hope to enjoy grandchildren, good health, and quality time with friends and family.

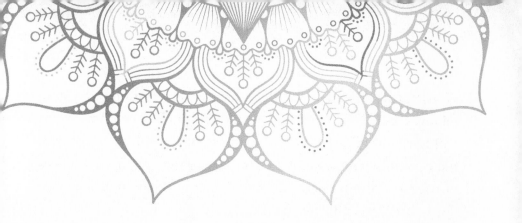

# Acknowledgments

*I have been privileged from birth* to receive the endless love and caring of my grandparents, my parents, and my uncle and auntie in an extended family under one roof. We were not rich but we were comfortable and I enjoyed my childhood in simple ways.

At the age of three, my grandfather, Bapaji, started giving me his inspiring teachings at bedtime. He emphasized the strength of willpower to triumph over both the minor and major issues in one's life. His own existence proved a fruitful example: from the outside he appeared quite tranquil, but on the inside he had a resolve of iron. Bapaji ingrained in me that to become a doctor was a noble profession. He was a hundred years ahead of his time with his thoughts and teachings, including the fact that being a female made one in no way inferior; I never experienced discrimination on the basis of my gender. In fact, I was granted the gift of self-confidence as he illuminated my path. Bapaji passed away shortly before my high school graduation, when I was just 15 years old. Yet, in that space of time, he had laid the foundation of my future. Bapaji also helped mentor and train many young relatives and friends that later would create successful lives.Their children and grandchildren today are well-established all over the world. By doing small deeds, this one man changed the lives of over a thousand people. I and so many others had the good karma to receive his blessings.

I am eternally thankful to both my parents, Bauji and Chaeji, for giving me motivation, discipline and encouragement at every step. They had very different personalities: Bauji was a strong-minded perfectionist who accomplished a great deal in business, yet he still always found time to guide me. Chaeji was easygoing, and performed her enormous responsibilities as wife, mother, and daughter-in-law with grace and courage. Both instilled lasting values into me and my siblings. I could not be more lucky to be their daughter.

I would like to thank the OR staff and the hospital staff at Leonard Morse Hospital. After a period of adjustment, I earned their respect and we learned from each other with patience and determination. Working as a team in stressful situations bonds you together like a second family; having done so over a period of so many years (35!) brings back many happy memories.

Finally, I would like to thank members of my book team, including my editor, Stuart Horwitz, whose direction I appreciated at every step. Thank you also to all of the talented and professionals behind the scenes at 1106 Design who had a hand in producing the book you now hold.

More than anyone, though, I would like to convey greatest appreciation for my late husband, Raj, for our wonderful life together and for his help in writing this memoir. I could not have accomplished this endeavor without his inspiration and support from start to completion. Unfortunately, Raj passed away suddenly on November 18, 2020 and was not able to see this book be published. His departure shook the foundation of my world, but Mohit and I remember him as the most loving father and husband possible. We take solace in knowing that he lived his 86 years to the fullest, and recognize that having him in our lives was our greatest blessing ever. As Mohit wrote in his eulogy, "I am absolutely blessed to have had the best father possible. With his passing almost three weeks ago, I lost not only my father, but also my best friend, my #1 wingman, my protector, and my ever willing

companion. He was always completely unselfish with the most precious of commodities: his time and love. It is unlikely that I will ever be able to live up to his legacy as a father, but I will always cherish it: I will love you and miss you forever, Dad."

I wish to express my endless gratitude for all life has given me and apologize if I have offended anybody unintentionally. As Abraham Lincoln, said: "And in the end, it's not the years in your life that count. It's the life in your years." I have had a wonderful life.

Made in the USA
Monee, IL
15 July 2021